IMAGES
of America

CHIPPEWA LAKE

ON THE COVER: Businesses and companies from Cleveland, Akron, Barberton, Wooster, Medina, and surrounding areas welcomed their employees and their families to Chippewa Lake Park for annual summer outings. The picnics were a mainstay of the park, drawing thousands on any given weekend. In the early days, families arrived by train; later, they came by car, picnic baskets in hand, for a day of fun and games. Pictured here is the Builder's Exchange Company outing that took place on August 5, 1920. (Cyndy Naragon.)

IMAGES
of America

CHIPPEWA LAKE

Amber Dalakas, Gayle Foster,
and Sharon Karhan

ARCADIA
PUBLISHING

ISBN 978-1-4671-2666-3

Published by Arcadia Publishing
Charleston, South Carolina

Printed in the United States of America

Library of Congress Control Number: 2017932660

For all general information, please contact Arcadia Publishing:
Telephone 843-853-2070
Fax 843-853-0044
E-mail sales@arcadiapublishing.com
For customer service and orders:
Toll-Free 1-888-313-2665

Visit us on the Internet at www.arcadiapublishing.com

Dedicated to the memory of Chad H. Grubb—
"This is Where the Journey Began."

Contents

ACKNOWLEDGMENTS

This work would not have been possible without the cooperation of members of the community, past and present, who shared their photographic and historical treasures and memories. Special thanks to Kathy Schmitz for her support and research.

Introduction

Glacier-formed and originally covering approximately 700 acres, Chippewa Lake—Ohio's largest natural inland lake—straddles Lafayette and Westfield Townships in Medina County. Native Americans—the Ojibwa (or Chippewa)—hunted and fished the fertile area until European settlers began arriving after the War of 1812. Today, the lake has slightly more than 300 surface acres of water and 2.8 miles of shoreline and is 25 feet deep at its deepest point. The first private owner of the lake was James Fowler, who purchased it from the Connecticut Land Company, and, objecting to the large amount of water, was compensated an equivalent acreage of land.

In 1870, a "pleasure resort" was begun on the area called the Upper Grounds overlooking the lake on the east side in what eventually came to be known as Chippewa-on-the-Lake. The resort drew visitors with its cooling waters, shady picnic grounds, rental boats, dance hall, skating rink, merry-go-round, swings hanging on tall trees, and a crude roller coaster that took passengers over the side of the hill to the lakefront only to be pulled back up the hill by young boys seeking to make some money. A few years later, a hotel was built to the south on what was called the Lower Grounds, an area owned by the Townsend family. They built a summer home at Chippewa Lake in 1914 and called it Five Oaks. Though the last of the original oak trees was recently lost, the estate still stands and is now the popular upscale dining spot The Oaks Lakeside, which offers diners spectacular sunset views.

The Lower Grounds soon contained cottages, a pier, boats, refreshment stands, and a dance hall. Excursion trains brought in large picnic crowds from all parts of the state. The Cleveland and Southwestern Railway, or Interurban, transported visitors to the area from 1903 until it ceased operation in 1931. A 2.11-mile rail spur ran from the nearby Baltimore & Ohio rail line to the lake along the southern border of the park cottages. That spur also carried thousands of tons of ice cut from the frozen lake to towns and cities as far away as Philadelphia. The three-story Knickerbocker Ice Company building that stored the ice was destroyed by fire on July 4, 1902, and never rebuilt.

The Lower Grounds continued to grow and draw large crowds, and in 1878, it became what would be known as Chippewa Lake Park, a popular amusement park, for the next 100 years. The park served as a venue for company picnics, drawing thousands of picnic-toting families throughout the summer months. The lake offered a large sandy swimming beach staffed with lifeguards, many of whom—in the 1940s and 1950s, at least—were young college athletes. The owner of the park, a man aptly named Parker Beach, was well respected and ran a tight ship; he was also a deputy with the Medina County Sheriff's Department.

Ace Brigode, a former band leader, served as Beach's right-hand-man when it came to booking picnics and entertainment. Brigode had connections to bring the big bands of the era to the ballroom at Chippewa—acts like Tommy and Jimmy Dorsey (with the young crooner Frank Sinatra), Benny Goodman, Lawrence Welk, Les Elgart, Vaughn Monroe, Les Brown, Glenn Miller, Guy Lombardo and, later, entertainers like Pat Boone, Jerry Lee Lewis, The Diamonds, Neil Diamond, Gary Lewis and the Playboys, Michael Stanley Band, the Animals, and the Kinks, to name but a few.

Free concerts and vaudeville-type performers could be seen at the outdoor theater on the lakefront every Sunday evening. It was not unusual for politicians to find their way to Chippewa. James Garfield, future president of the United States, made an appearance in 1875. In the early 1900s, Henry Ford, Harvey Firestone, and Thomas Edison all visited the park. Silent screen actresses and sisters Lillian and Dorothy Gish rented a cottage in the park in 1926. Later, Bob Dole, Tricia Nixon, and George McGovern stopped by to "press the flesh."

Local teens assumed summer jobs at the park, serving in roles from ride and game operators to refreshment and souvenir stand employees, with a handful of very lucky young men entrusted with operating speedboats from the park pier.

Following a stay at Chippewa, many families chose to rent a cottage and extend their visit or purchase a cottage in Gloria Glens, Briarwood Beach, or Chippewa-on-the-Lake, as these areas within walking distance of the lake were developed in the 1930s and 1940s.

Having more time at Chippewa helped families to escape the heat of the city while providing children with a safe place to live and play. Eventually, the commute became less tiresome, and many cottages were converted to year-round residences.

After 32 years in the business, Parker Beach and his wife, Janet, sold Chippewa Lake Park in 1969 and retired to a horse farm in Medina before eventually moving to Naples, Florida. Nine years later, without fanfare, the gates of Chippewa Lake Park were closed forever, and it fell into disrepair, succumbing to the elements and arsonists. All that remains today is a crumbling pier, the rusted skeleton of a Ferris wheel, and the equally rusted rail of "The Bug," a ride that once brought squeals of delight from its passengers.

The brick-making business, the bank, the grain elevator, the meat market, the latex factory, the car dealership, the service stations, and the amusement park of yore are gone. What remains are a beautiful lake and the supporting services of a post office, churches, a fire department, and convenience stores, as well as a thriving community of people who care about their surroundings and participate in activities involving the lake—boating, fishing, waterskiing, sailing, swimming, and tennis—not unlike those early picnic-toting families seeking a bit of fun and relaxation.

One

The Park Years

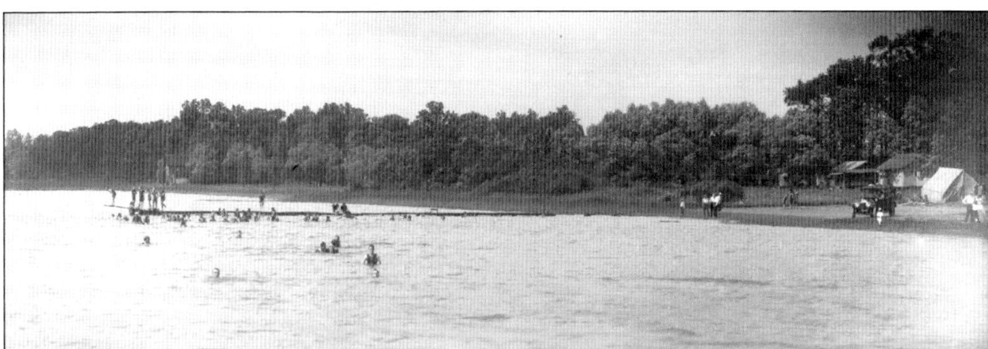

Chippewa Lake had been popular for many years as a destination for fishing, swimming, and picnics when, in 1875, Edward E. Andrews, a druggist from Seville, purchased 10 acres on the east side of the lake from Joseph Robb. This began his development of a picnic grove and pleasure grounds. That first year, it is reported that 3,000 to 5,000 people attended the Fourth of July festivities. Attendance continued to increase, and by the mid-1880s, the east side contained a two-story dance hall, roller-skating rink, roller coaster (crude and dangerous, by many reports), flying horse ride, dining hall, and bowling alley. The Chippewa Fishing and Hunting Club of Cleveland built a clubhouse in 1886 on land leased from J. Fretz near the lake. By the end of the 1880s, tents were pitched for extended stays at the lake. Popularity was growing at the Lower Grounds farther south under the direction of the owners, partners Oscar Townsend and W.H. Hawley. When Andrews retired in 1895, it marked the decline of the Upper Grounds until the 1920s, when the property was formally developed as a residential area. (Beach family.)

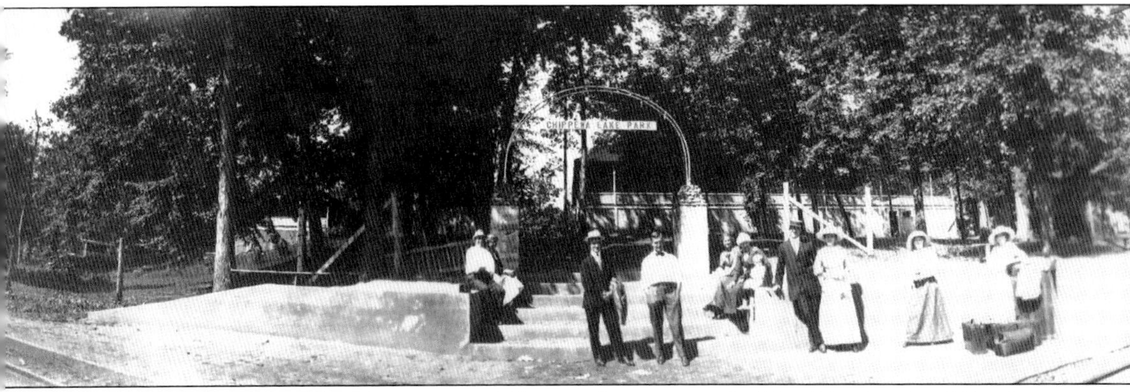

Around the start of the 20th century, folks wait for the arrival of the Cleveland and Southwestern Interurban electric train at the entrance of Chippewa Lake Park. Ohio's Interurban rail system had approximately 2,800 miles of track—more than any other state—and was the predecessor of intercity busing. Not only did the Interurban bring thousands of visitors to Chippewa Lake Park, it was instrumental in Medina County's expansion of farming, allowing farmers to deliver their goods to Cleveland and other cities. In 1903, the Interurban line arrived in Chippewa Lake, bringing as many as 40,000 people to the park for Sunday excursions and company picnic charters. Families from the city would come to spend their summers in cottages at the lake, while the man of the house could travel back and forth to work each day via the Green Line. (Beach family.)

Many company picnics were held at Chippewa Lake Park over the years. Employees of Cleveland Southwestern pose during their picnic on August 8, 1937. (Medina County Historical Society.)

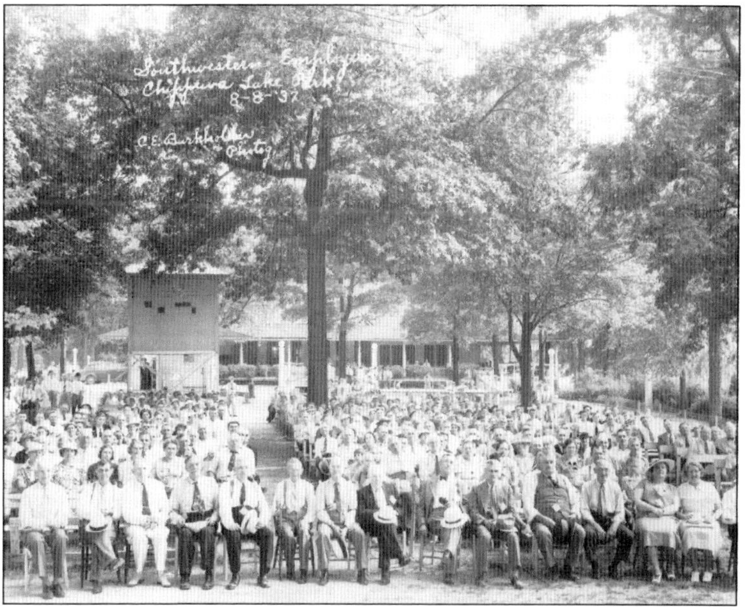

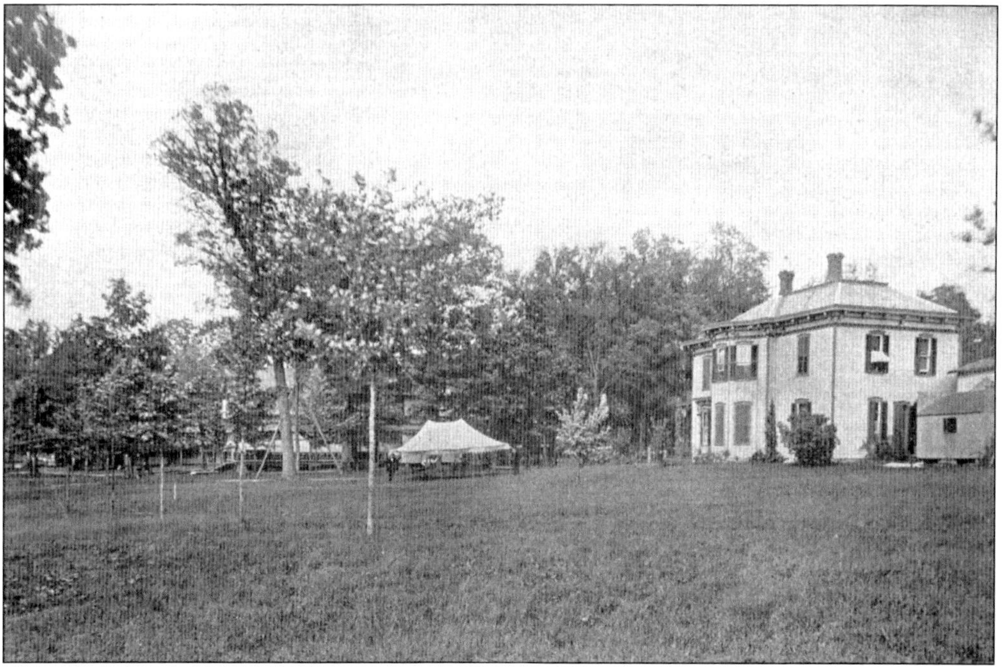

The house known as the Rombach House and the Hunt Club was part of the original Upper Grounds and is located on Shadywood Drive. As the summer activities transitioned to the Lower Grounds, the house was sold to a businessman from Cleveland who made major renovations, which included expanding the living room to a length of 37 feet, adding two fireplaces and three bathrooms, and moving the porch from the west side to the north side of the home. Known as the Estabrook, it was owned by Mr. and Mrs. Arthur Stiegelmeier. During the 1940s, a couple named Schultz owned it and rented out rooms. Theodore Rombach bought it in 1950 and remodeled the interior and built the garage. Rombach was the secretary-treasurer of the Civic League, the group that led the charge to abolish alcohol in the village. (Keith Riedel.)

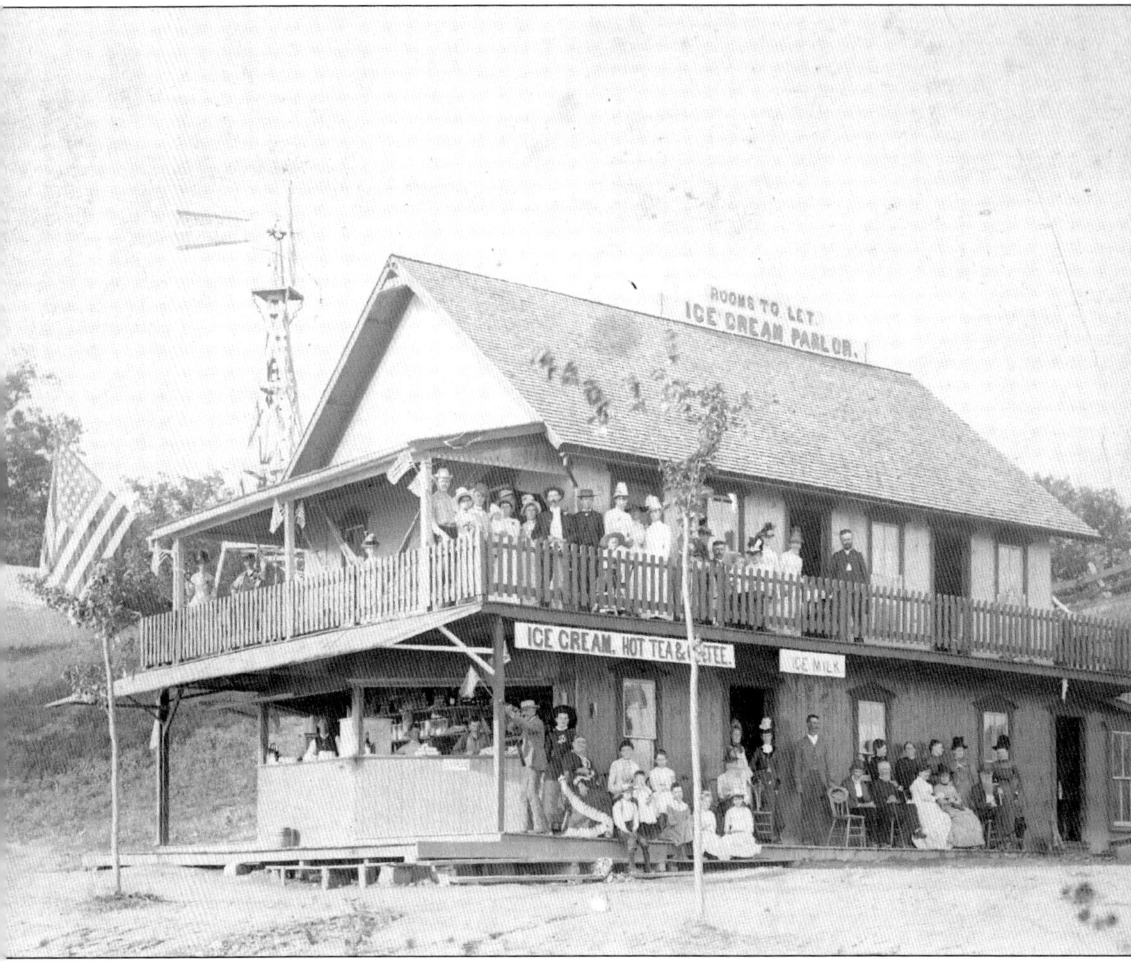

As the country ushered in the 20th century, the pleasure grounds of Chippewa Lake were expanding rapidly. With the arrival of the Interurban electric train, more people began traveling to the area. The Star Windmill sits on the brow of the hill of the Upper Grounds. These windmills, used to pump water from the ground, were manufactured by Flint and Walling of Kendalville, Indiana, and used throughout rural areas of the country by farmers, schools, and other enterprises, most commonly in the Midwest and Great Plains. They were quite attractive with their white wooden blades and red tips; Star Mill is stenciled on the white and red vane sheet. Newton Reese and his family are relaxing on the first-floor porch of the refreshment stand and enjoying the day. In 1887, Reese constructed a building that offered refreshments on the way to the Lower Grounds. (Lorinda Laughlin.)

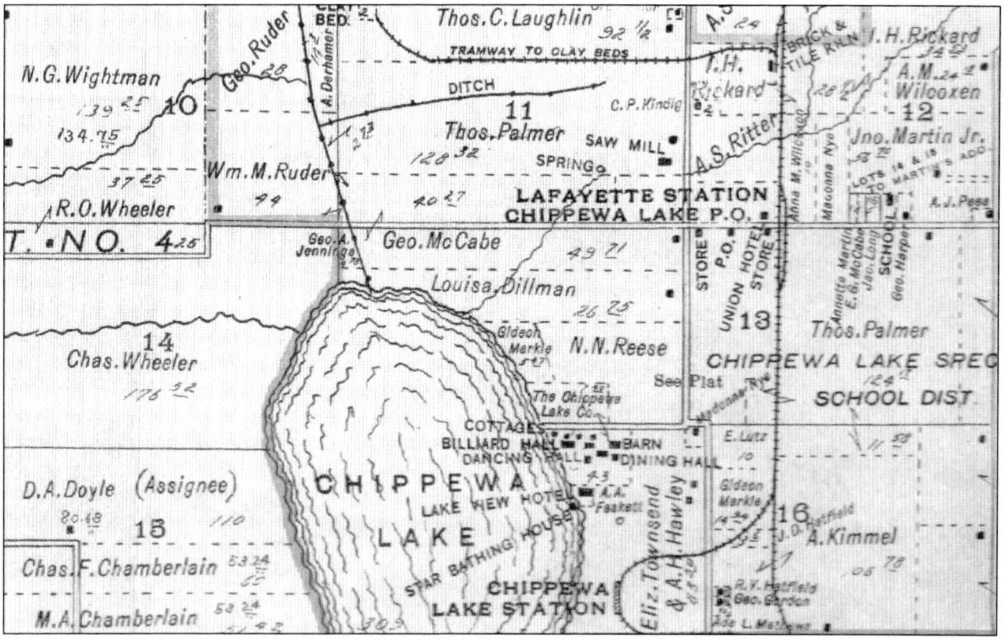

This 1897 Medina County Atlas map shows what was present in Chippewa Lake during this time. The Upper Grounds, or Edward E. Andrews Pleasure Grounds, were well established, having experienced nearly 25 years of development. Oscar Townsend and W.H. Hawley had begun development of their property, known as the Lower Grounds, which would eventually become Chippewa Lake Park. Townsend passed away in May 1894, and the property passed onto his wife, Elizabeth Martin Townsend. Their son J. Fred was prominent in the railroad industry in his own right, as were his father and grandfather Hiram before him. Fred was traffic manager at National Tube Company in Pittsburgh, and spent his summers in Chippewa Lake. He pursued farming at the Townsend estate, breeding Guernsey cattle and Belgian draft horses. (Medina County Historical Society.)

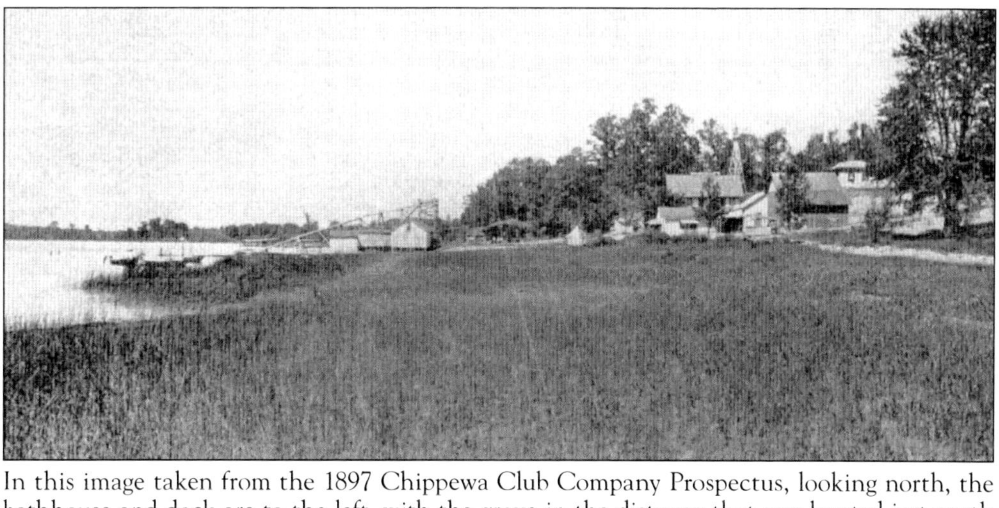

In this image taken from the 1897 Chippewa Club Company Prospectus, looking north, the bathhouse and dock are to the left, with the grove in the distance that was located just north of present-day Longacre Lane. The Chippewa Club Company's clubhouse was located along the northwestern edge of their property facing the lake. The Star Windmill and refreshment building, as well as other barns and structures, are also visible. (Keith Riedel.)

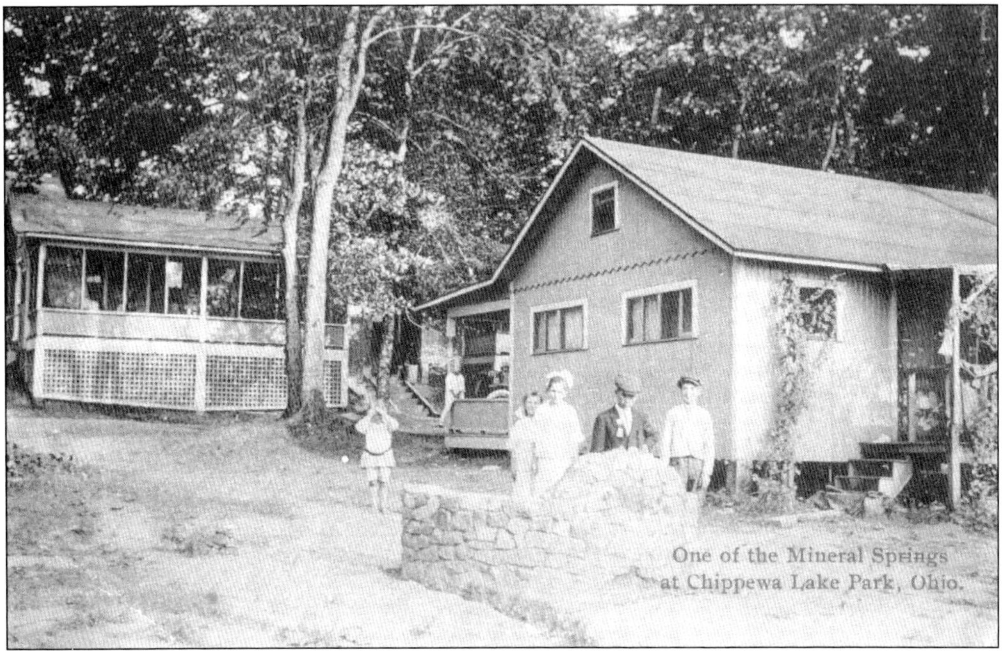

Renting a cottage at Chippewa Lake was a yearlong dream. During the 1950s and 1960s, a cottage could be rented for $60 to $80 per week. Renters brought linens and groceries. Bread, milk, and penny candy could be purchased at Duecker's store located under the ballroom. Cottagers bought a beach pass for the week by announcing their cottage number to pass through the gate, past the dressing rooms and the best-ever candy machines, on the way to a sandy beach with volleyball, ping-pong tables, and a chance to ride the waves when the speedboat *Dynamite* cruised by the shore. Transistor radios played tunes from WIXY 1260, and the smell of baby oil and Coppertone lingered in the air. Parents could return to their cottages for beverages and conversation with no need to worry about their children. Pictured below in 1960 is the Thomas Hoch family (clockwise from front left) Kathy, Tom, Virginia, Eileen, Peggy, Mary and Pat. Both pictures are of 138 Harding's Haven. (Above, Paula Midlak; below, Kathy Hoch Schmitz.)

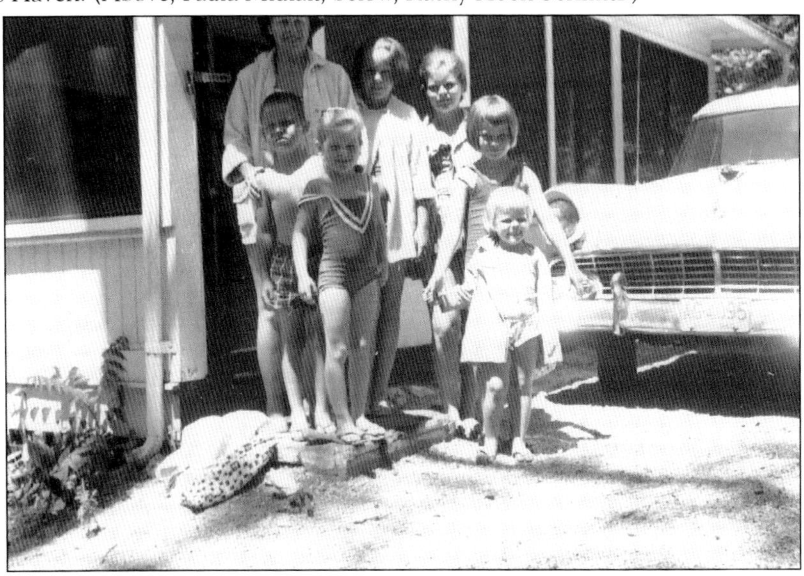

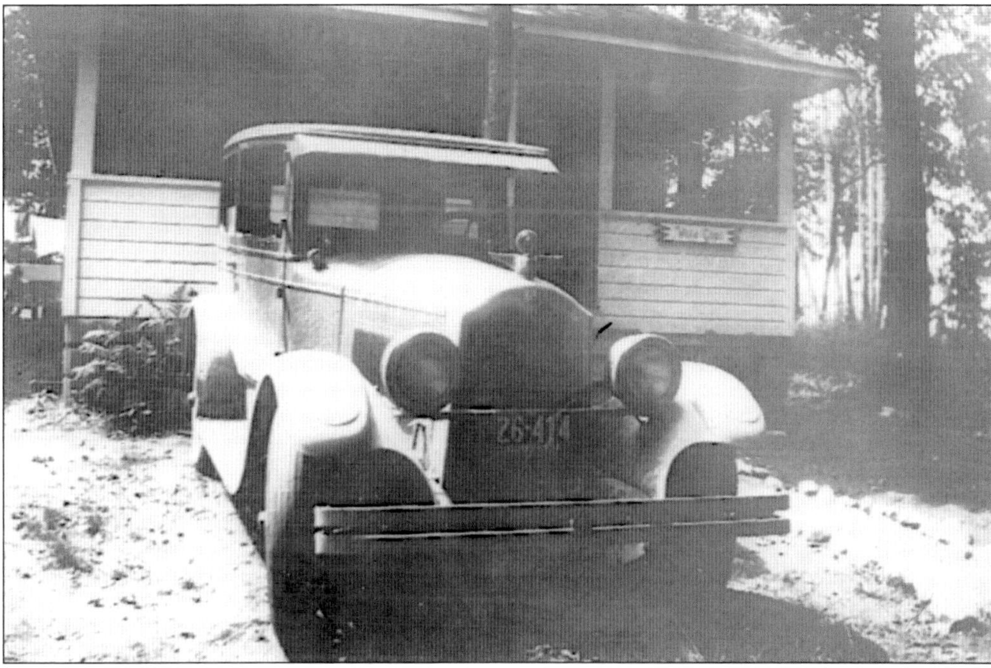

Many of the early cottages in the Chippewa Lake communities of Chippewa-on-the-Lake and Gloria Glens were built during the 1920s. They accommodated families who spent their summers on the largest natural lake in Ohio. They came from Cleveland, Wooster, Loudonville, and other communities in northeast and central Ohio. Joe and Mathilda Dunneback owned the cottage known as White Caps, located at 260 Tanglewood Trail in Gloria Glens, in 1926. (DeeDee Duecker.)

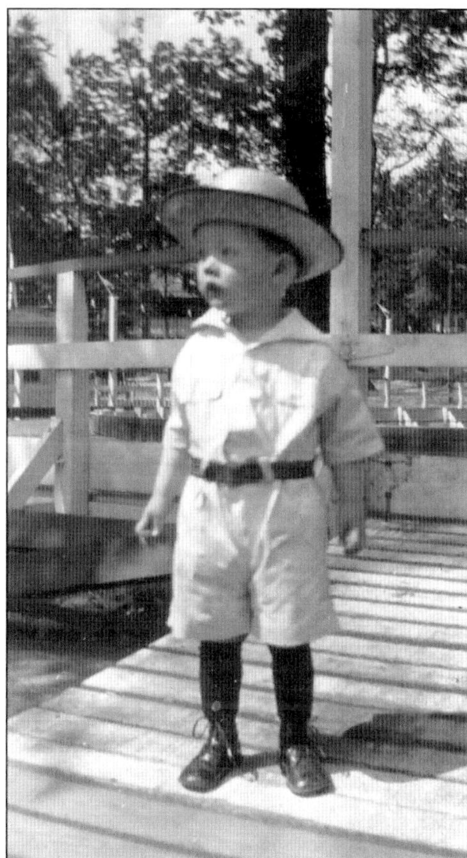

As the lots at Chippewa-on-the-Lake were being laid out, Gerald Melter, age two in 1926, is shown enjoying a day at Chippewa Lake Park. He would eventually marry and bring his young family to Chippewa Lake, building a cottage in the 1950s that the Melter family continues to enjoy today. (Melter family.)

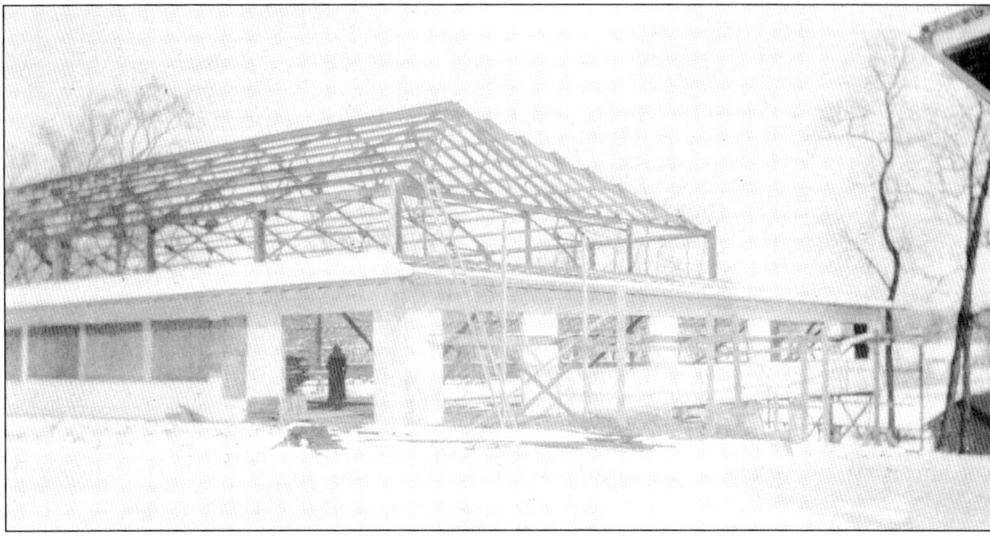

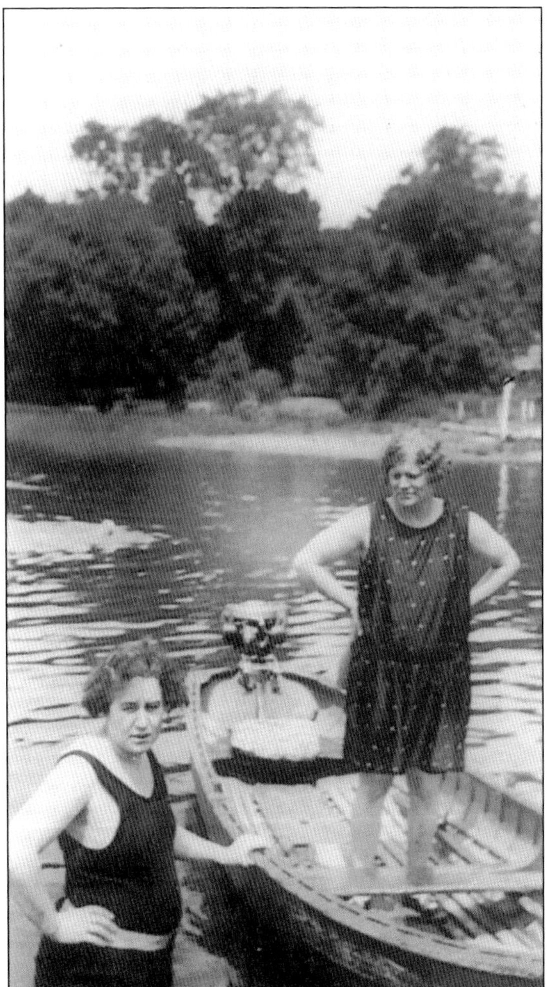

The Starlight Ballroom, built in 1923, came to be known as one of the finest in the state. Generations recounted memories of meeting future mates while dancing to the big bands of the 1940s and 1950s. A light coating of sawdust enabled dancers to glide over the floor, while small lamps flickered from the tables lining the dance floor. (Beach family.)

More fun at the lake! Whether strolling by the north or south end of the lake, one will always spot boats; boating has always been the thing to do at "Chip." These girls at Gloria Glens are getting ready to start the motor, push off, and head out for a great time on the water. (DeeDee Duecker.)

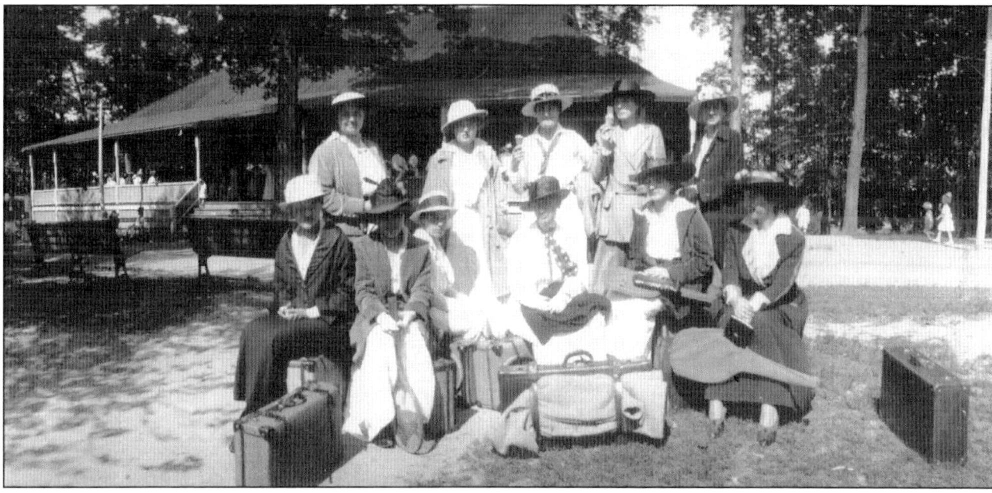

Young ladies, accompanied by a chaperone, often spent a week at a cottage. It was a time to relax, play games, and enjoy water activities, the amusement park, and dancing in the ballroom. Groups ranged from girls' clubs to cousins to school pals seeking fun in the sun. If a handsome lifeguard offered his hand, all the better memory to take home. (Beach family.)

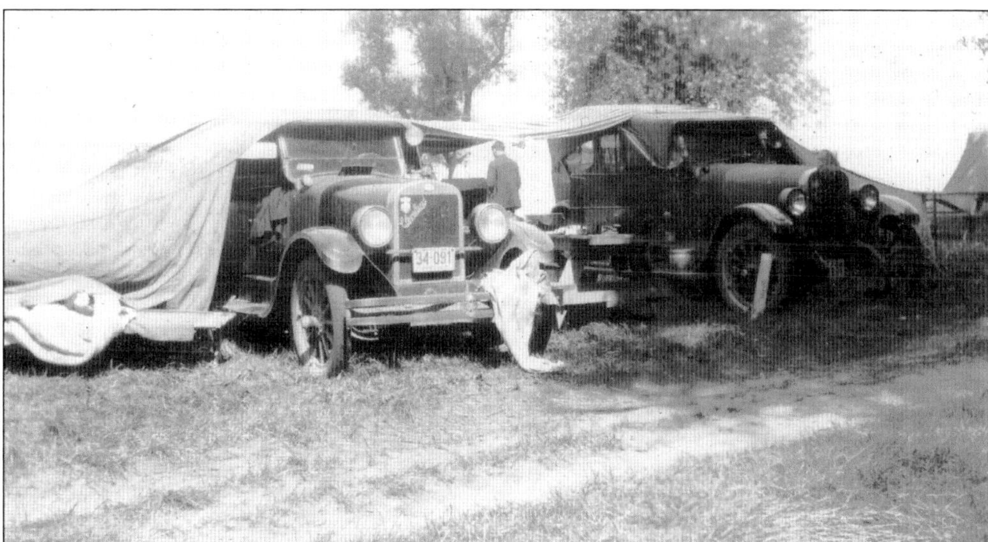

Not everyone was fortunate enough to be able to stay at one of the many hotels at Chippewa Lake. Camping was very popular during the late 1800s and into the 1900s. This makeshift camp at Chippewa Lake Park was made by a group of young men in 1927. (Sandra Bushi.)

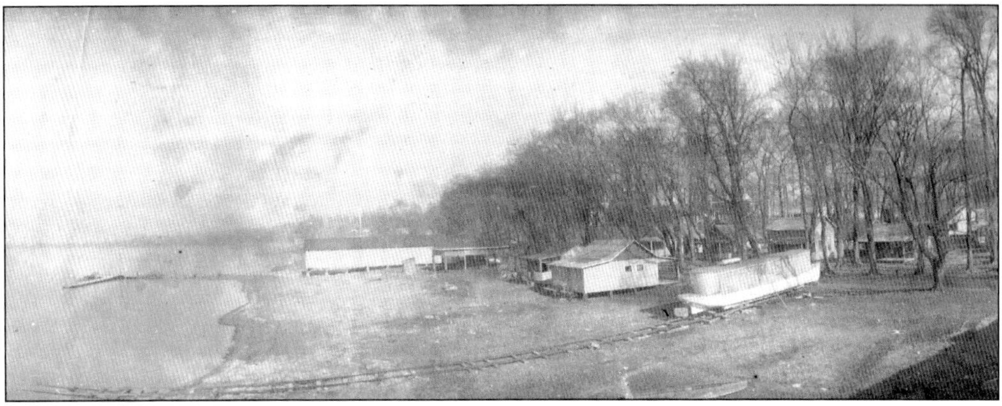

In the early days, the launches were removed from the lake at the end of the season by a tractor pulling them over railroad tracks, and returned at the beginning of the following season in the same way, but via boat power. The bathhouse, built in 1914, is visible in the distance, with early cottages to the right in this view looking at what would eventually become the park's midway. (Beach family.)

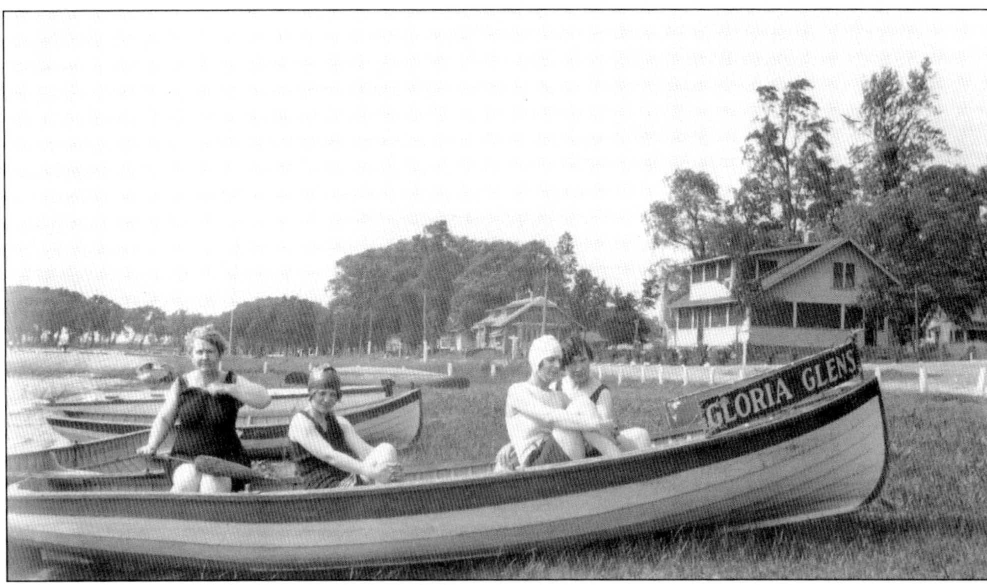

From left to right are Mabel Holly, Mae Grubb, and two unidentified friends on Chippewa Lake in a rowboat. The Village of Gloria Glens, located on the southern shore of Chippewa Lake, rented rowboats. Note the bathing caps women wore to protect their hair when they went into the water. Bathing caps were made of rubber and had a chinstrap to help keep water out of the wearer's ears. The cottage at the corner of Longacre Lane and Beachside Boulevard is visible in the background. (Gayle Baxter Foster.)

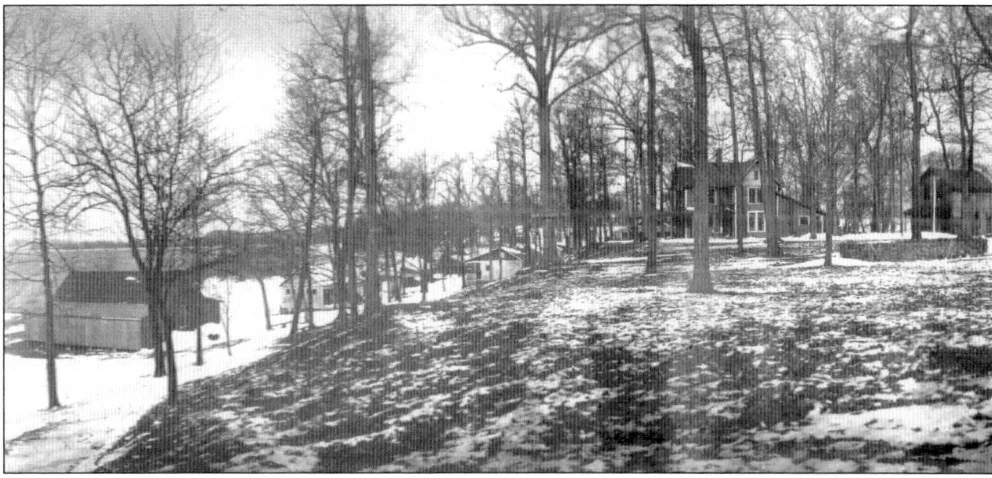

Fred Beach, brother of Parker Beach, had the only house within the boundaries of Chippewa Lake Park proper. It was located steps from the ballroom and the park hotel just to the north of the miniature golf course. Many other homes and cottages were on the outer perimeter of the park and midway. (Beach family.)

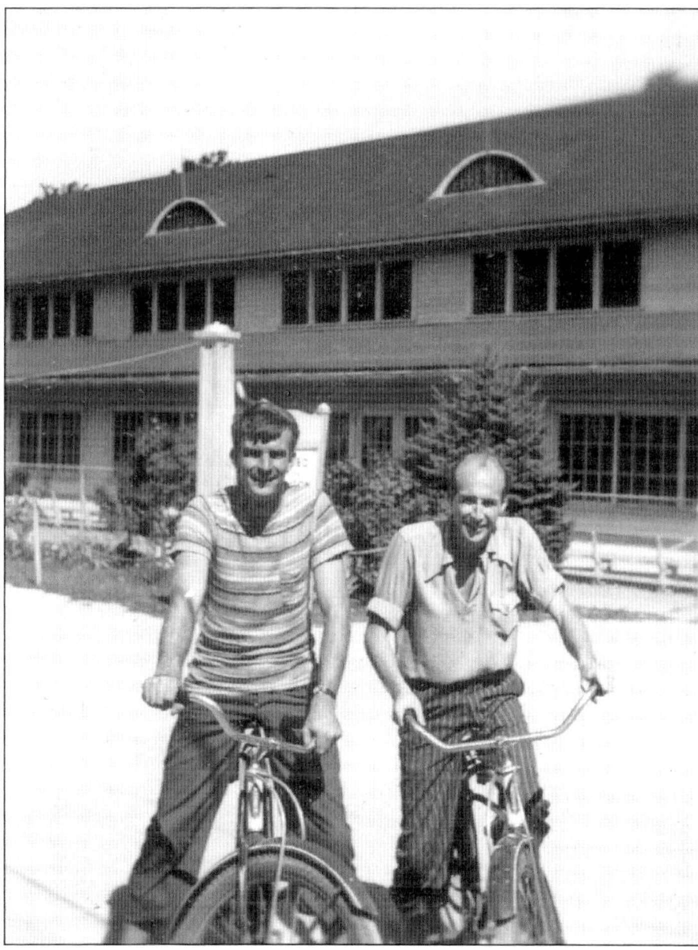

Stopping for a break from their ride around the park in front of the Dance Hall are Williard "Steve" Stephenson (left) and Fred Beach in 1939. Beach was an integral part of the park. He worked in the park office and at the hotel and was in charge of the finances and park personnel. (Stephenson collection.)

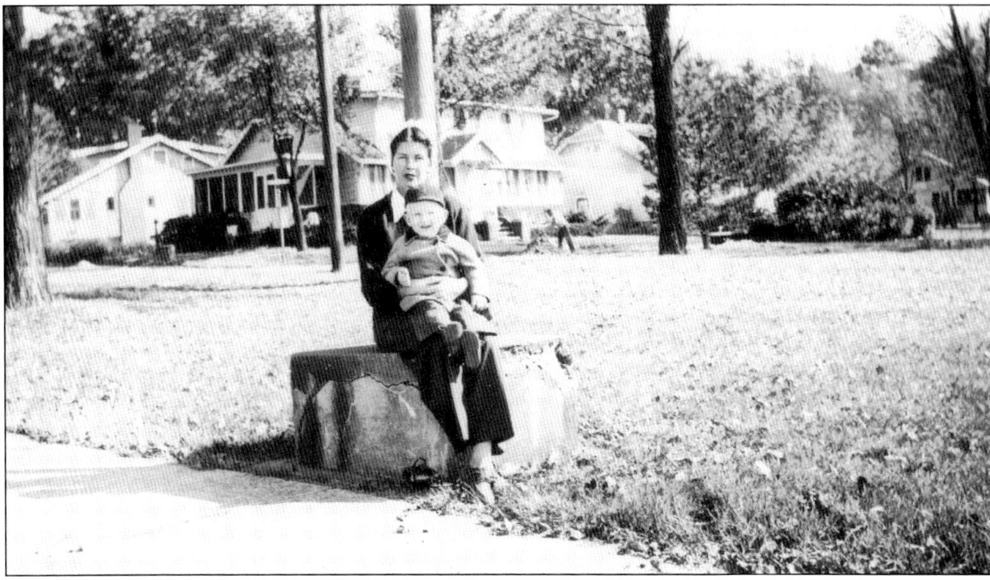

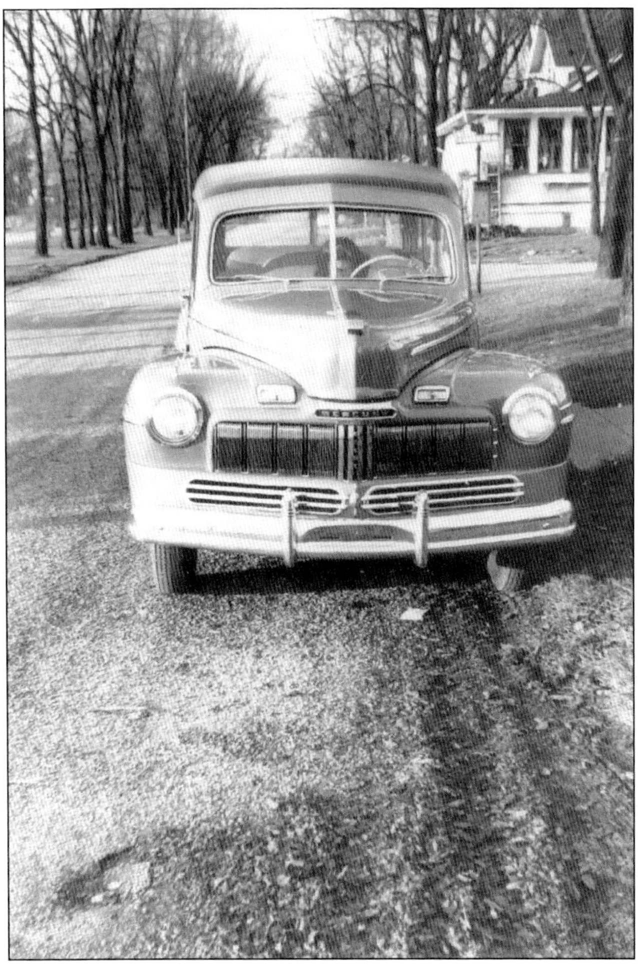

Summer cottages were plentiful, offering families respite from the heat of the cities. In the early days, cottages were rented by the week beginning on Memorial Day and buttoned up for the winter after Labor Day. Many of those cottages have been converted to year-round homes, though many "summer homes" remain, sporting names like Dew Drop Inn and Bide A While. Above, Helen Danforth Stephenson poses with her nephew David on October 22, 1944, as she looks out over the lake with the Stephenson cottage, located at 130 Beachside Boulevard, in the background. This home remains in the Stephenson family. At left is a view looking north along Beachside Boulevard. (Both, Stephenson collection.)

Chippewa Lake Park owned and operated several boats throughout the years for the pleasure of the park's visitors. Parker Beach, center, owner of Chippewa Lake Park, is pictured in 1937 on the park pier with an unidentified young man at left and Joe ? on the right. Note the sign advertising boat rides. A ride in the speedboat *Zephyr* cost 50¢, and rowboats could be rented for 25¢ an hour, while a ride on the launch cost 15¢. (Stephenson collection.)

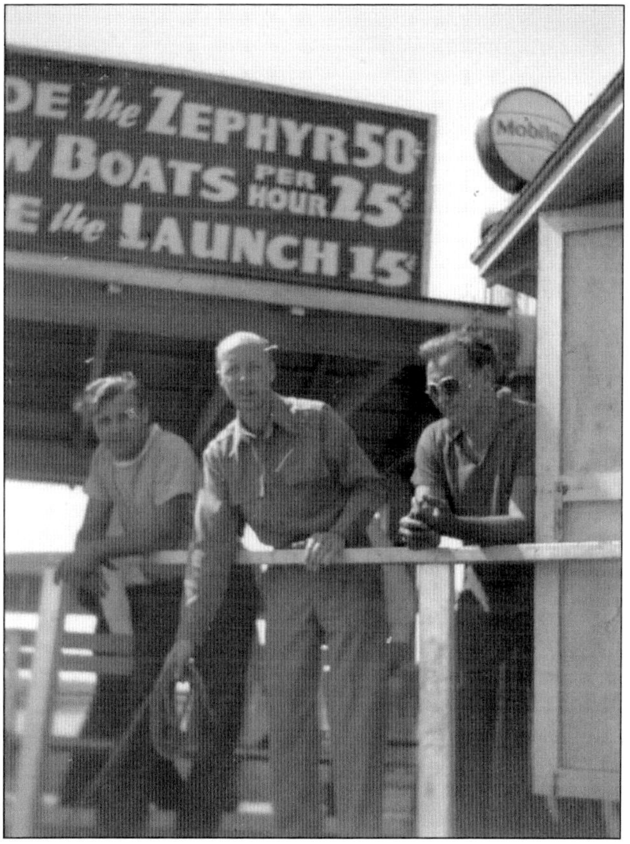

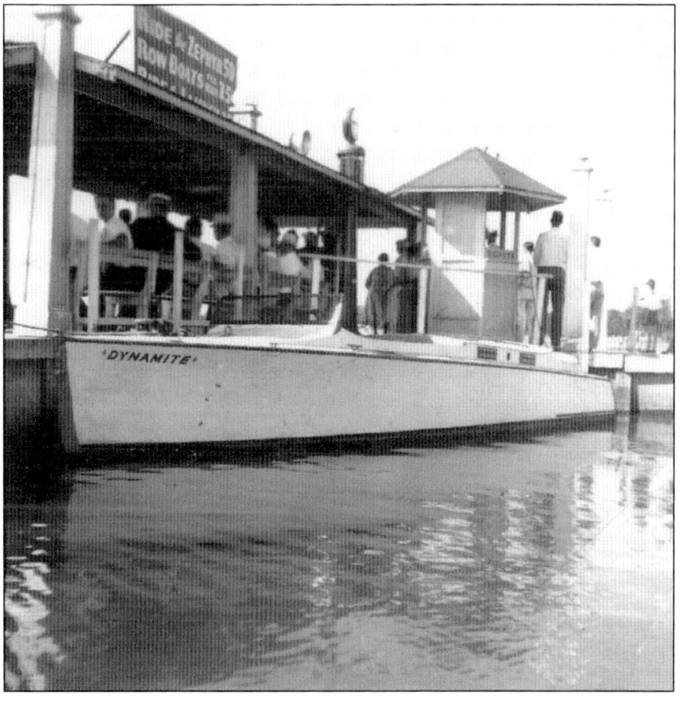

The first of three speedboats, *Dynamite*, a 1929–1930 era Chris Craft, took passengers on a thrilling ride around Chippewa Lake. The second was called *Zephyr*, later renamed *Dynamite II*, and was on the water in the 1940s. The third and final *Dynamite* was a Hacker-Craft that was used from 1950 until the park closed in 1978. A secondary speedboat used on busy days in the late 1950s was called *Firecracker*. (Stephenson collection.)

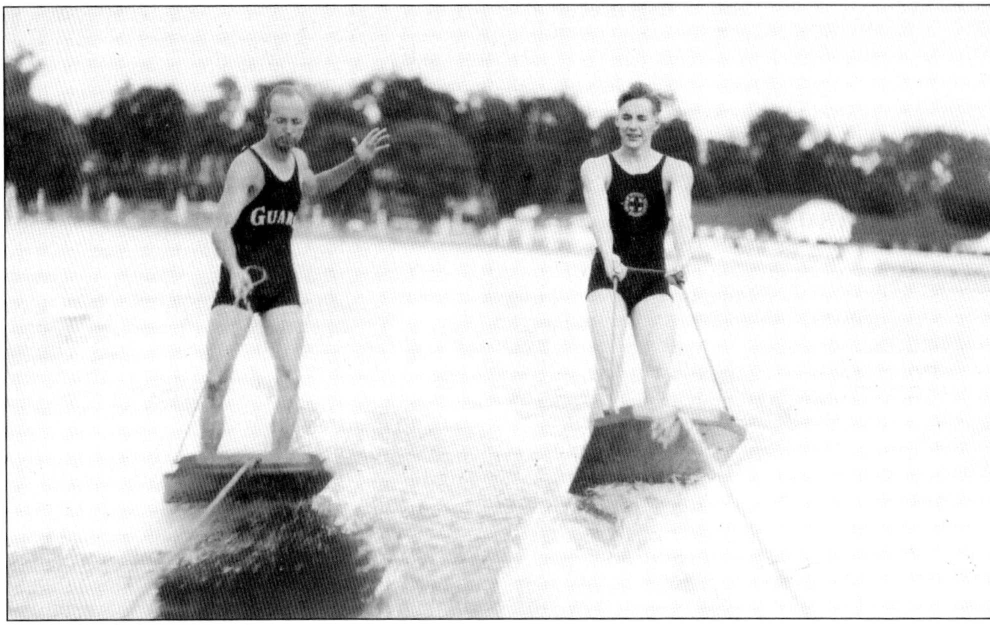

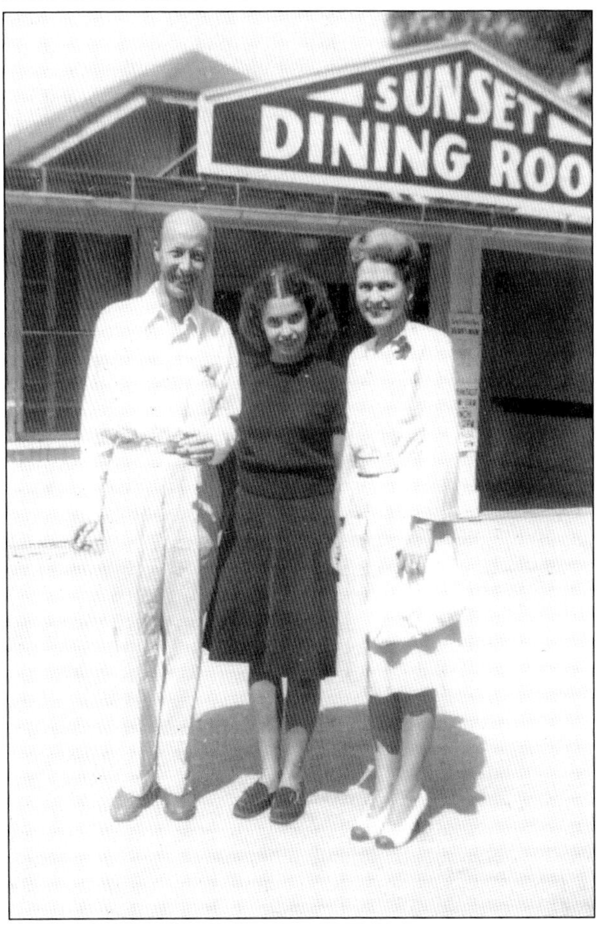

Bert Chatfield was the photographer at Cleveland's Luna Park until it closed in 1929. This is a photographic postcard Chatfield sent to Parker Beach in 1928 of a couple of fellows finding new ways to amuse themselves on the lake. Chatfield came to Chippewa Lake Park following the closing of Luna Park to take on photographic duties. (Beach family.)

The Sunset Dining Room at Chippewa Lake Park offered a cool, comfortable place to relax and enjoy fine dining overlooking beautiful Chippewa Lake slightly apart from the hustle and bustle of the midway. It was located at the base of the pier, and most of the waitstaff were college students on summer break. The girls' dormitory was above the Stand "B" picnic pavilion. Pictured are Parker and Janet Beach with their daughter Lynn on Labor Day, September 1, 1947. (Beach family.)

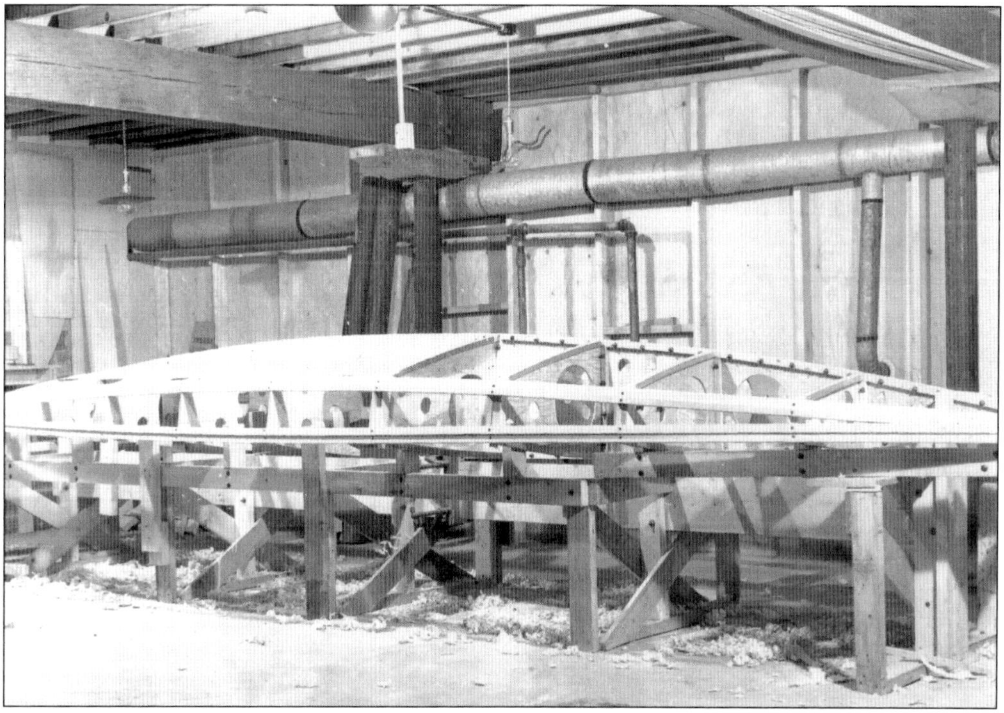

Rev. John Quinton, minister of St. Paul's Episcopal Church in Medina, constructed the first Y-Flyer to sail on Chippewa Lake. The "Y" was designed for the smoother waters of inland lakes. The Snipe class came to Chippewa Lake in the late 1950s. (Keith Riedel.)

Cottages drew summer vacationers, including families and groups of chaperoned teens from northeast Ohio cities, such as Cleveland and Parma, and from as far away as western Pennsylvania. Local boys who worked at Chippewa Lake Park eagerly awaited move-in day each week, and word quickly spread as to how many girls had arrived and what cottages they were occupying. This 1960 photograph shows girls from Magificat High School in Rocky River sitting in *Firecracker*, which was one of the smaller speedboats. (Chad Grubb.)

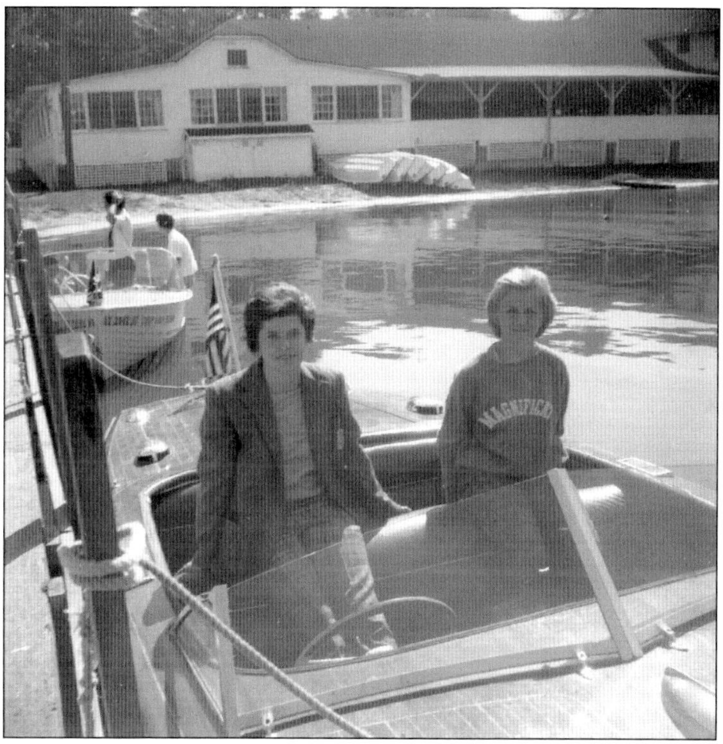

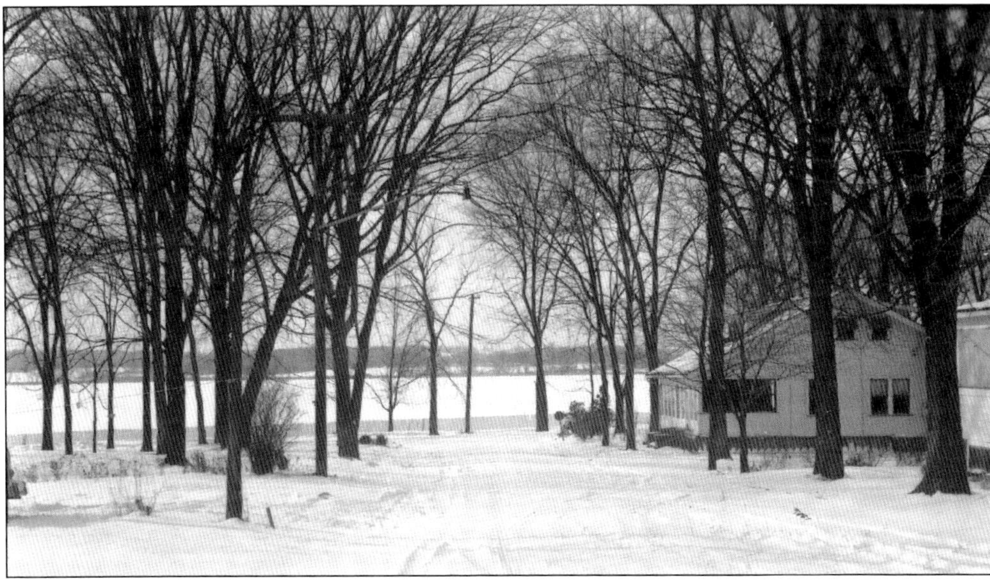

Taken in 1953, when there were still only a handful of cottages in Chippewa-on-the-Lake, this photograph looks west on Cottage Cove Drive toward Beachside Boulevard and a frozen Chippewa Lake. (Melter family.)

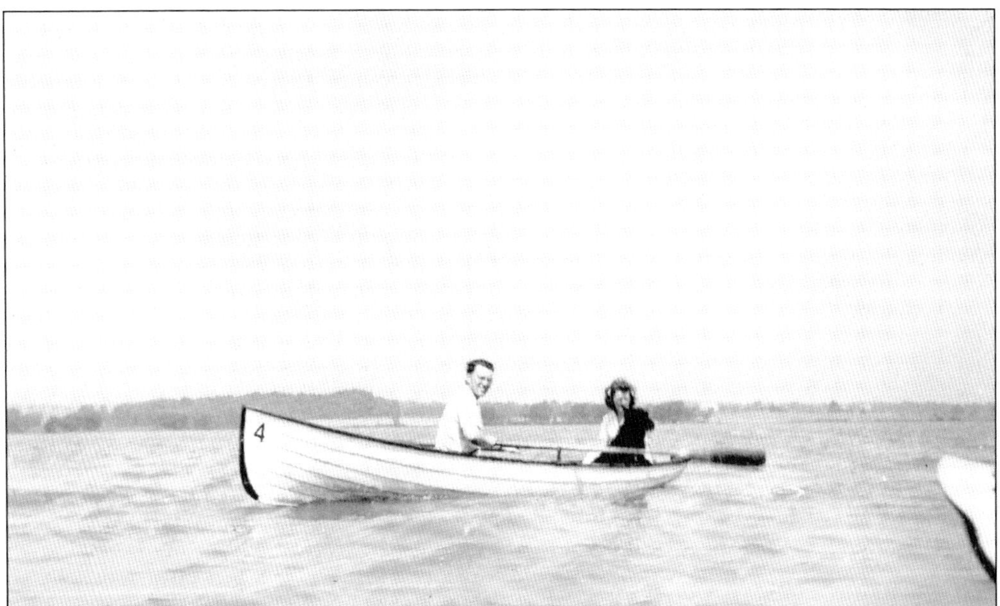

Rowboats could be rented by the hour from Chippewa Lake Park. They were most commonly used for fishing, but also offered a young couple some privacy on the water away from the crowds at the amusement park or beaches at Chippewa. The lake also had many privately owned boats in use during the summer months. (Gayle Baxter Foster.)

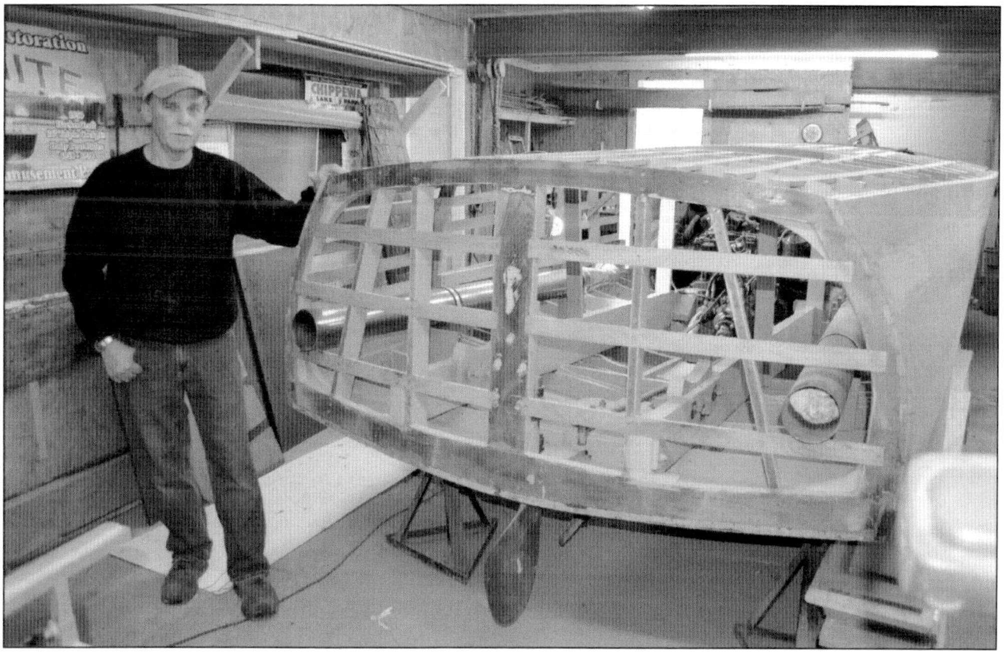

Memories of Chippewa Lake Park come alive with the mention of *Dynamite*, which sped across the waters every summer. The speedboat was a 26-foot Hacker-Craft that weighed 6,000 pounds. Powered by a 534-cubic-inch Ford Seamaster V8 engine, it soared around the lake at an estimated 45 miles per hour and earned the park $15,000 to $18,000 annually. When the park closed in 1978, Bruce Ruessman acquired the boat from Guido DeGeronimo of Continental Business Enterprises, owner of Chippewa Lake Park. Unable to complete any restoration, Ruessman sold *Dynamite* to Larry Prebis (above) in 2010. Prebis is a custom woodworker and has won numerous awards for boat restoration. He is currently working to restore *Dynamite*. Maybe one day, *Dynamite* will return to Chippewa Lake, sounding its siren—as it did many years ago—while it zooms around the lake. (Above, Sharon Sefl Karhan; below, Chad Grubb.)

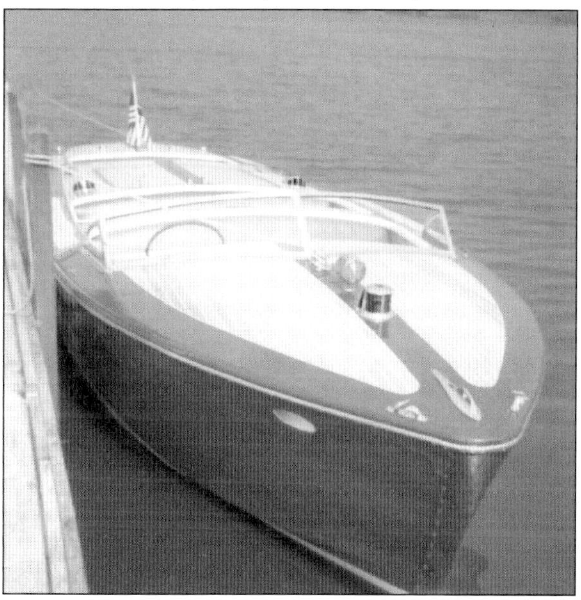

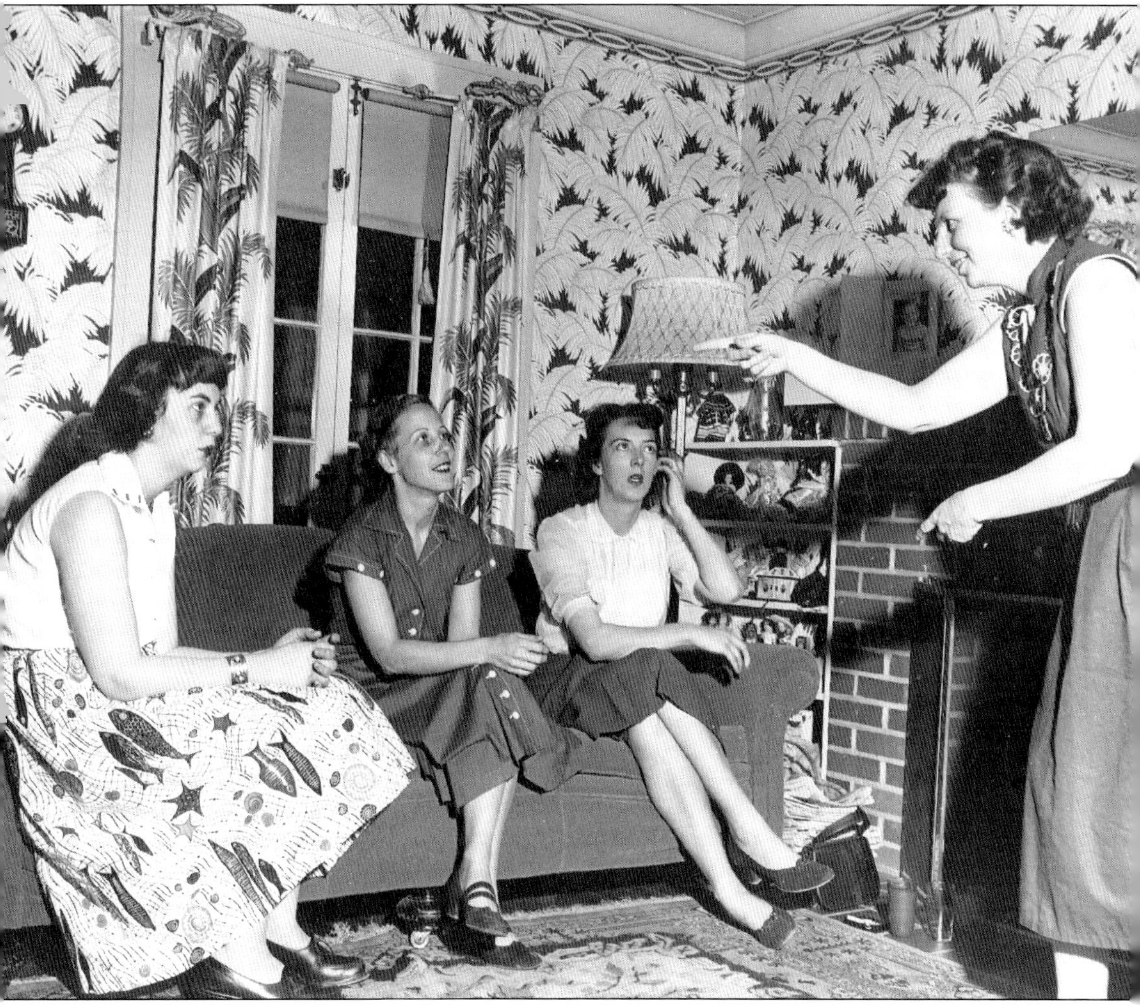

Friends spent many evenings visiting in one another's homes before television became popular. A favorite game, shown here in 1954, was charades, as played by Marian Lietzow (left), Ethel Grubb (center), and Winnie Howe, all neighbors of Vivian Baxter, who is acting out clues for her friends. Card games were another favorite indoor pastime, and it is assumed the husbands were occupied with a game of pinochle in the kitchen while the ladies enjoyed their game in the living room. The evening would typically conclude with coffee and cake and plans for the next get-together; the venue was rotated among friends' homes, which were usually within walking distance of one another. (Gayle Baxter Foster; photograph by Chuck Lietzow.)

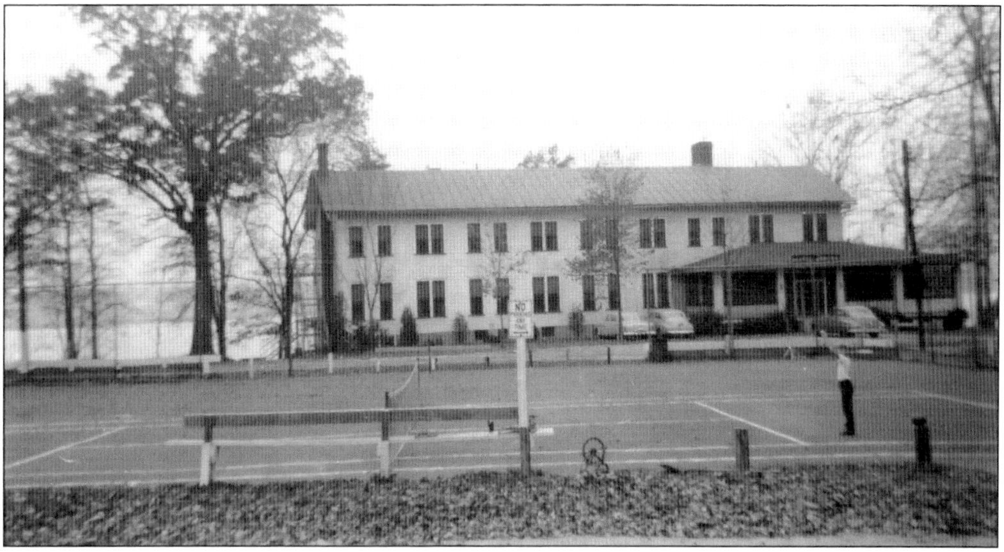

Tarry Tavern was a lively—if questionable—enterprise that sat on Bungalow Bay Boulevard overlooking Chippewa Lake. Rooms were rented as a hotel, while entertainment could be enjoyed in a lower-level bar/restaurant that featured dancing and gambling. In the 1940s and 1950s, vehicles from Cleveland and Youngstown were often found in the parking spaces in front of the building until county law enforcement staged numerous raids and finally padlocked the establishment in the mid-1950s. It later became an "alcoholics' hospital," and finally, a nursing home known as Glenhaven. The building was demolished in 1978 to make room for home construction. (Above, Gayle Baxter Foster; below, Sharon Sefl Karhan.)

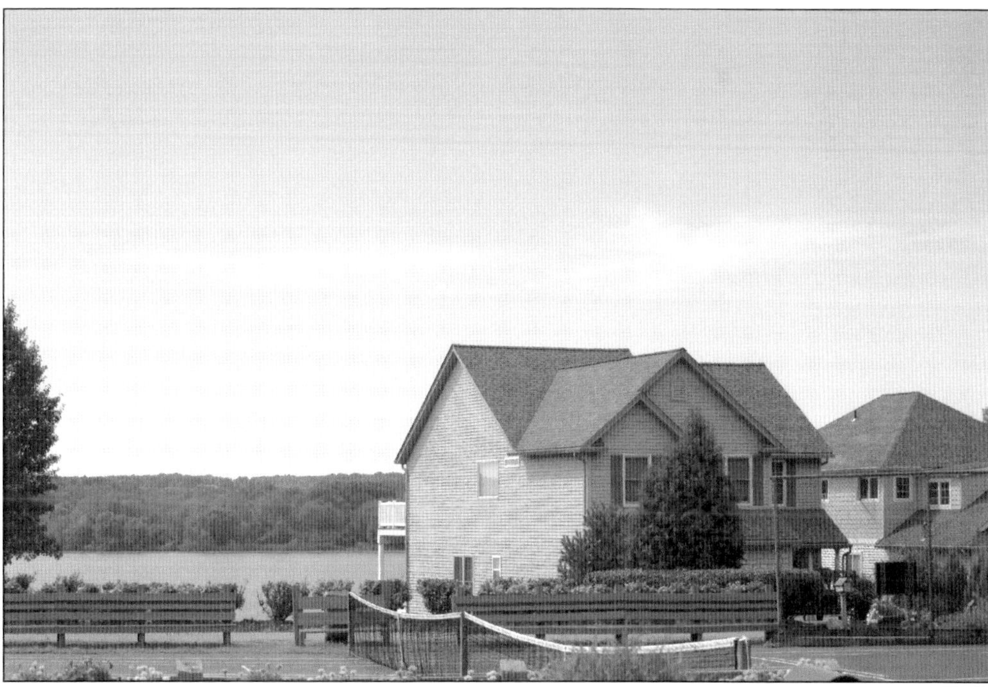

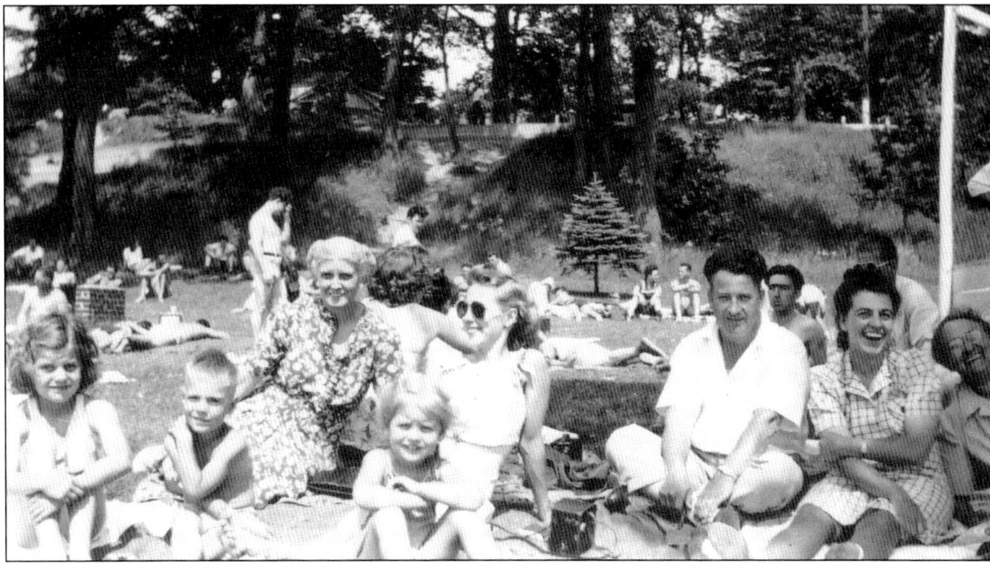

Relatives found Chippewa a logical place to meet for family reunions, as Chippewa Lake Park was nearby and there were always plenty of activities for all ages. Picnics were packed in baskets and carried to a cottage; potato salads and watermelons ruled the day. An after-dinner walk was a common activity. The Peer family from Pennsylvania met at the beach in 1947. (Barbara Grubb Whitlam.)

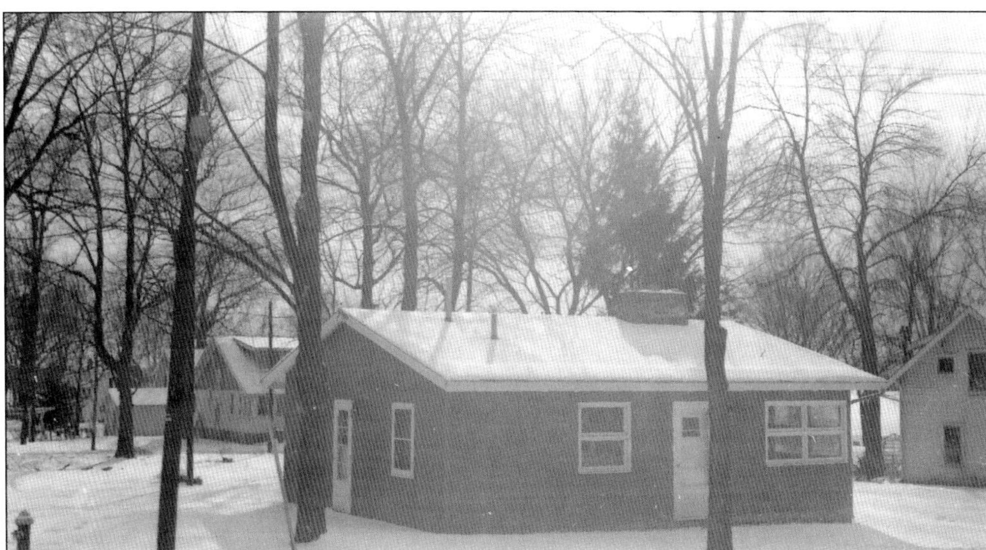

At one time, all the cottages in the village of Chippewa-on-the-Lake were white. Per Ordinance No. 12, passed on July 4, 1930, and amended by Ordinance No. 123, passed on September 24, 1951, "each building shall be painted of same light color." The Melter cottage at 189 Cottage Cove Drive was one of the first that was not white but instead a light brown color. (Melter family.)

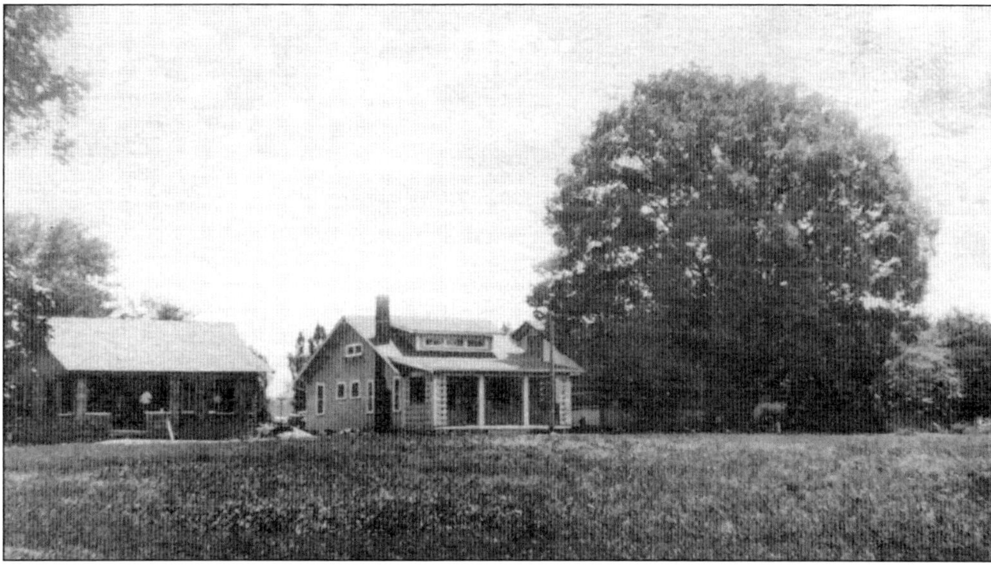

The Bungalow Bay circle area was once home to Native American ceremonial grounds. Over the years, the land changed ownership a number of times and was eventually divided into sublots and sold. A large, beautiful oak tree located on the corner of Bungalow Bay Boulevard and Parkway Path added to the beauty of the Upper Grounds, as it was once known. The junior garden club, the Chippewa Lake Flower Pots, measured the circumference: it was 175 inches around and believed to be over 200 years old. In October 1970, neighbors standing nearby heard a loud crackling noise, and the oak tree suddenly fell to the ground. The cottages pictured are perfect examples of those built in the 1920s. (Above, Cyndy Nargon; right, Barbara Grubb Whitlam.)

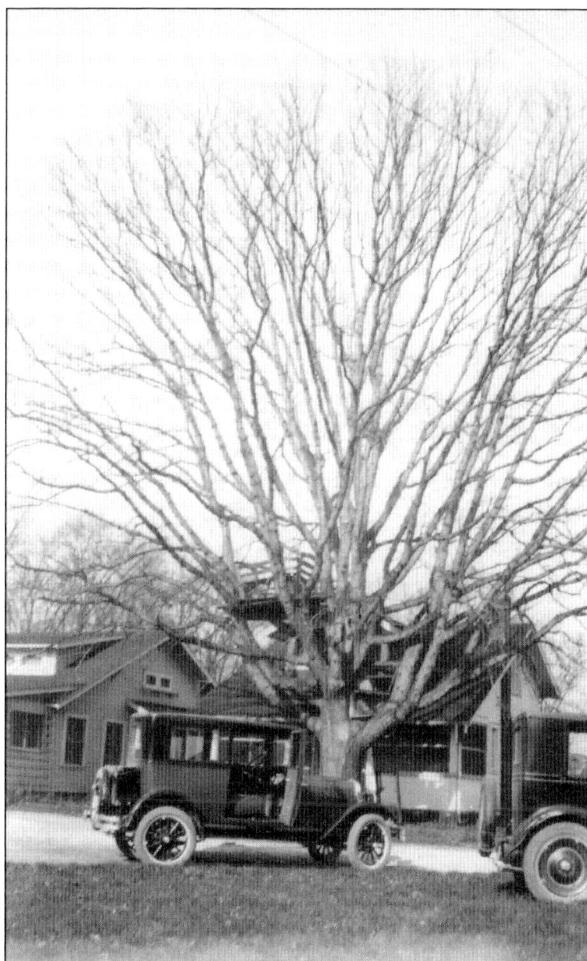

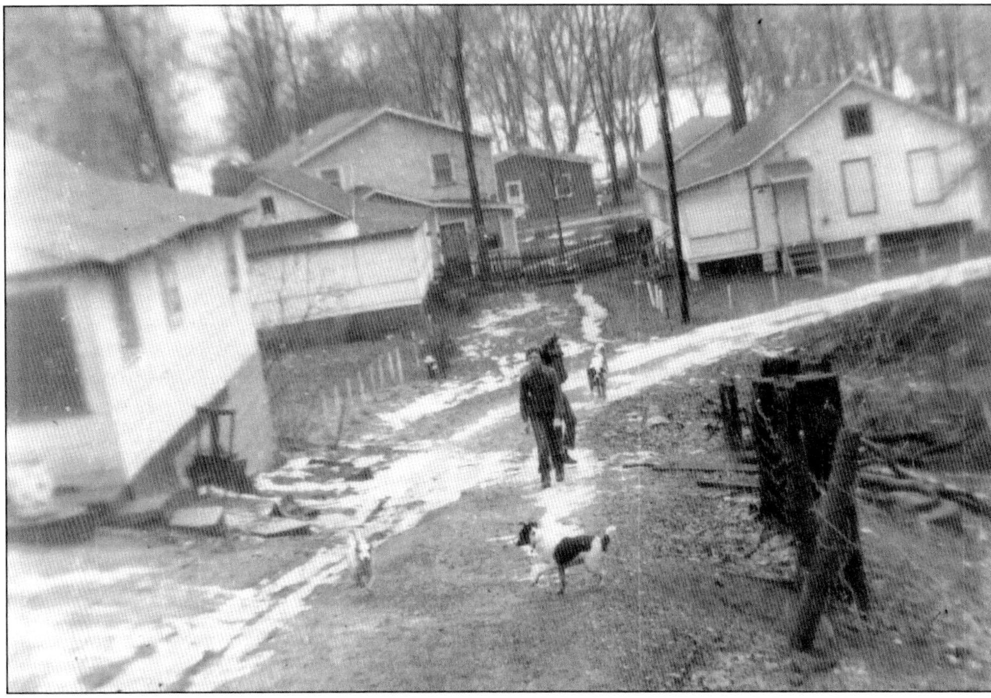

Reese's Grove is a name that dates to the 1800s at Chippewa Lake. It is an area that was originally approximately seven and a half acres north of Longacre Lane along Beachside Boulevard, stretching east to Reese's and Barrett's Plats, which bordered what is now Lake Road (formerly known as Medina Road). These homes, pictured during the winter of 1955, are on First Street looking west toward Chippewa Lake. Pictured below is an early photograph of Reese's Camping Ground. Newton N. Reese advertised in 1904: "Free Grounds at Chippewa Lake—Chestnut Grove free for camping parties and church and society picnics." (Above, Gayle Baxter Foster; below, Jackie Wills family.)

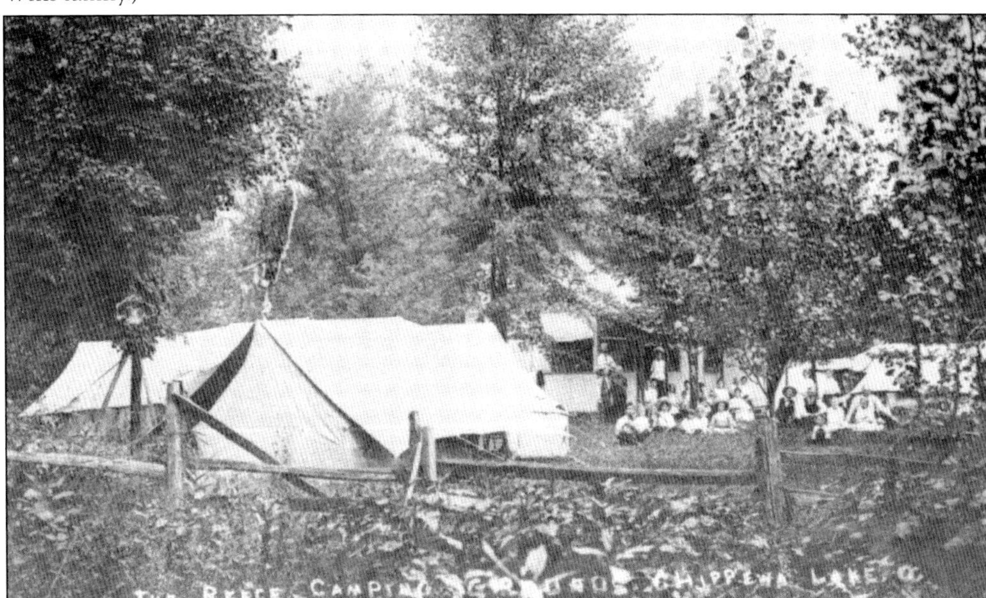

Investors, including W.H. Townsend and A.M. Beach, bought the Chippewa Lake Club Company in 1919. It was known as the Chippewa Club Company (or Chippewa Lake Community Club). The $100,000 purchase included the lake and Upper Grounds. Beach leased the lower section. The Community Club was to allot the shaded sections on the map. A.M. "Mac" Beach bought the property in 1921 and renamed it Chippewa Lake Park Company. The Depression, coupled with the loss of the Interurban railroad, caused the company to fall into bankruptcy. Mac's son Parker bought it at auction in 1937. (Keith Riedel.)

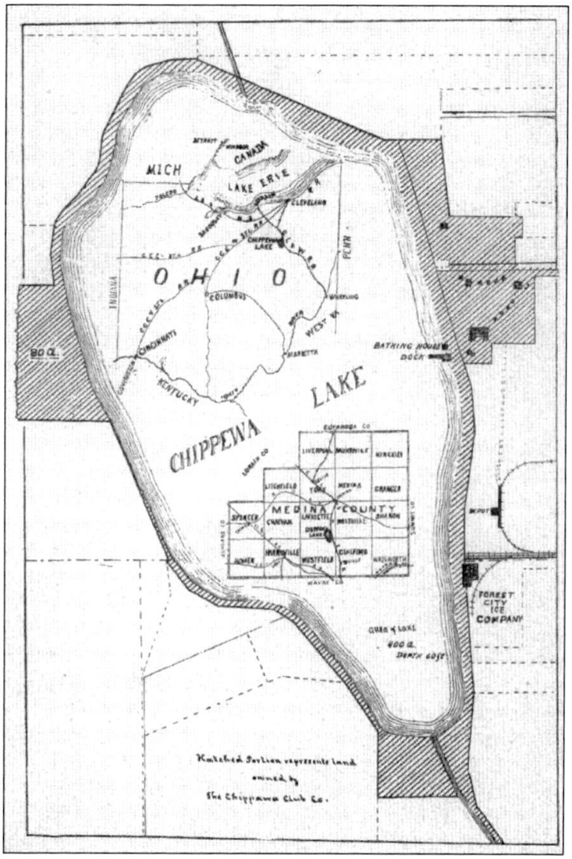

This early photograph taken by the lake shows the fencing left over from the early farming days. The pathway to the Upper Grounds is visible. (Medina County Historical Society.)

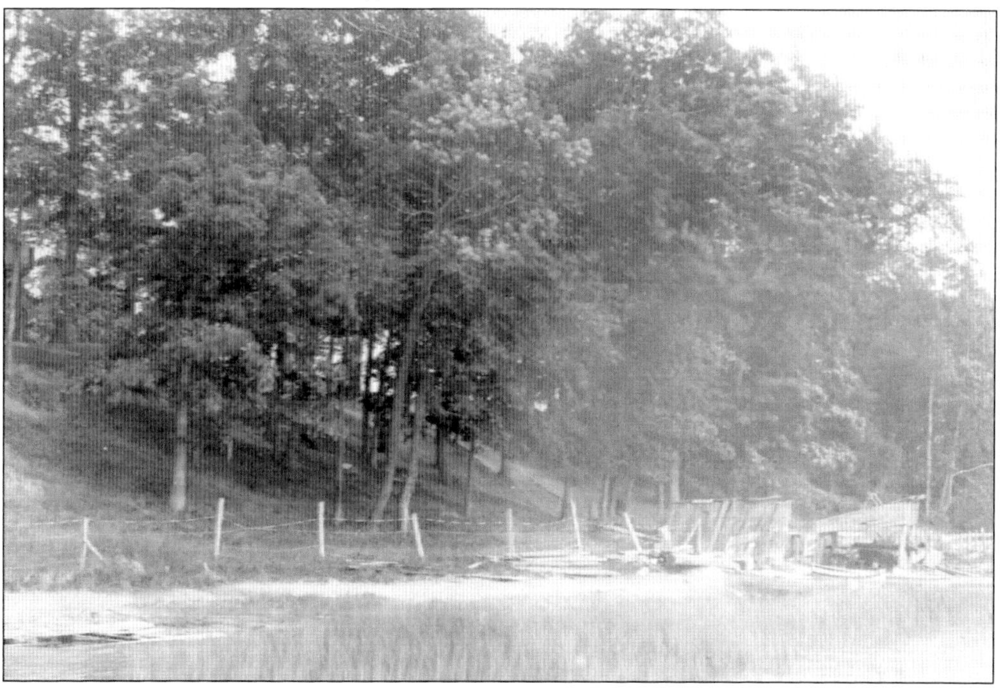

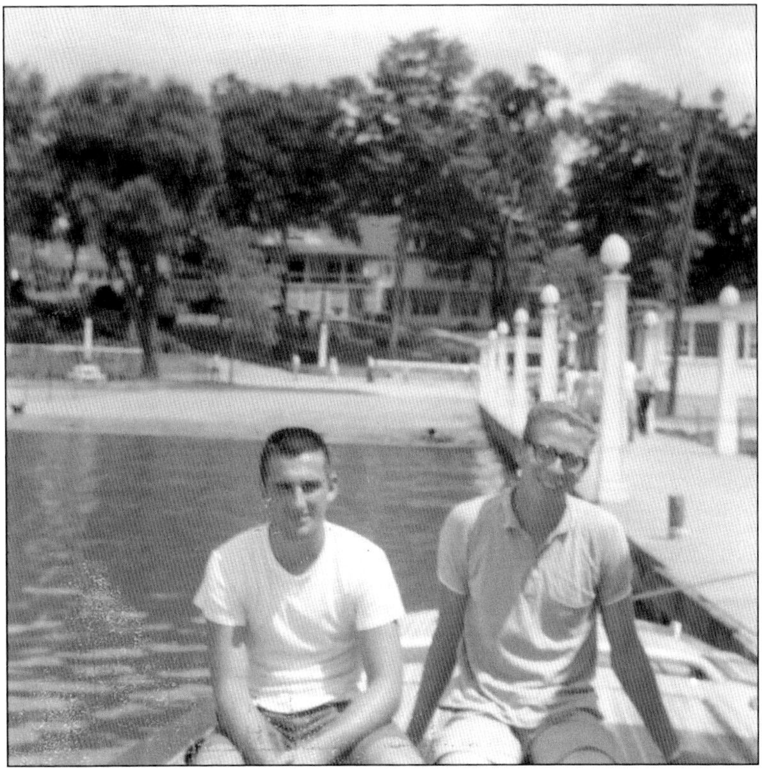

Dynamite is shown with her crew, Tim Emerick (left) and "Buzz" Van Pelt, sitting ready to depart at the Chippewa Lake Park pier in 1961. Parker Beach owned Chippewa Lake Park and the lake. On the park pier, a flagpole was utilized to notify folks of when to stay off the lake and when they could waterski. A red flag meant stay off or clear the lake due to bad weather, while the white flag meant resident boat owners could ski on the lake. (Chad Grubb.)

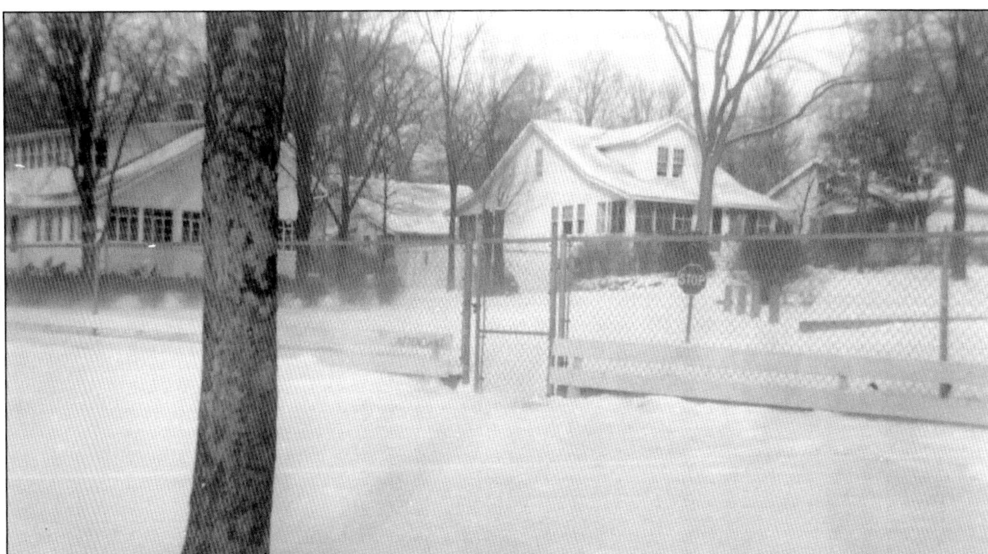

This image is looking north from the beach in February 1958 toward Beachside Boulevard and Longacre Lane. The cottage on the left, located on the corner of Beachside Boulevard and Longacre Lane, was built by 1929 as part of the original Community Club section. (Chad Grubb.)

The communities of Gloria Glens, Chippewa-on-the-Lake, and Briarwood Beach that once surrounded Chippewa Lake Park continue to come together for the Fourth of July parade. In 1958, the wives of mayors from the three communities stood on the bandstand at Chippewa Lake Park. Pictured from left to right are Mrs. Adolph Anderson from Gloria Glens, Dorothy Garman from Briarwood Beach, and Violet Thomas from Chippewa-on-the-Lake. (Carla Thomas.)

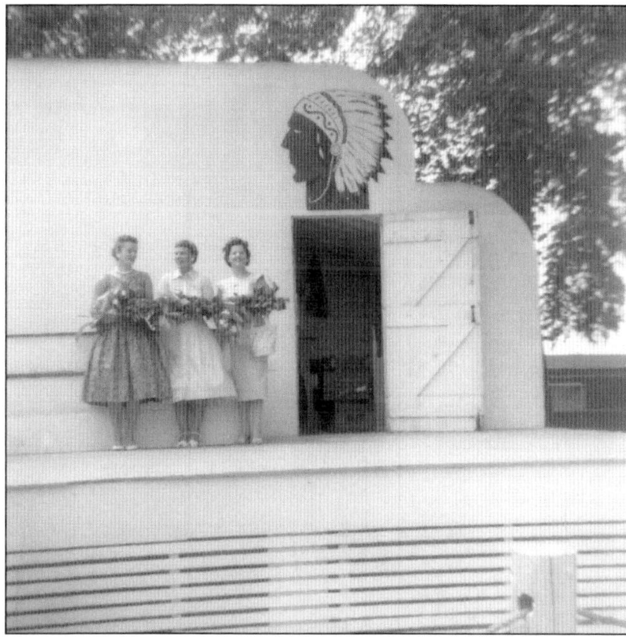

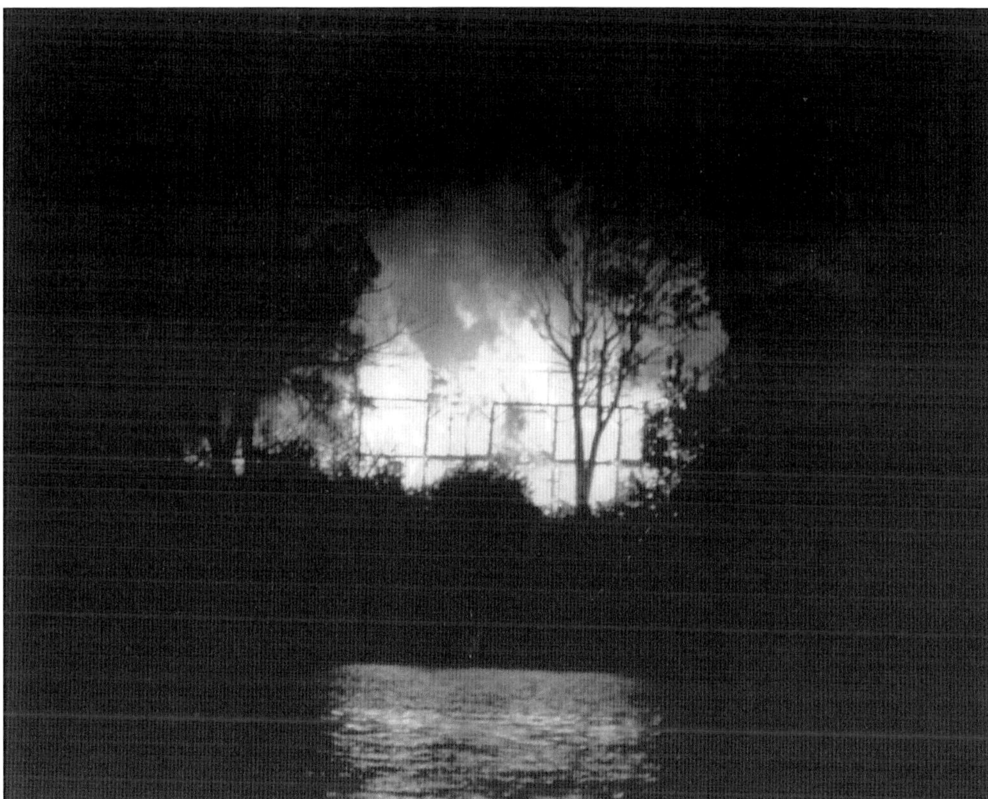

Inside the deteriorating Chippewa Lake Park, adding insult to injury, the old hotel caught fire on the evening of September 29, 1991. After Parker Beach sold the park in 1969, the new owners closed the hotel. (Bill Glasenapp.)

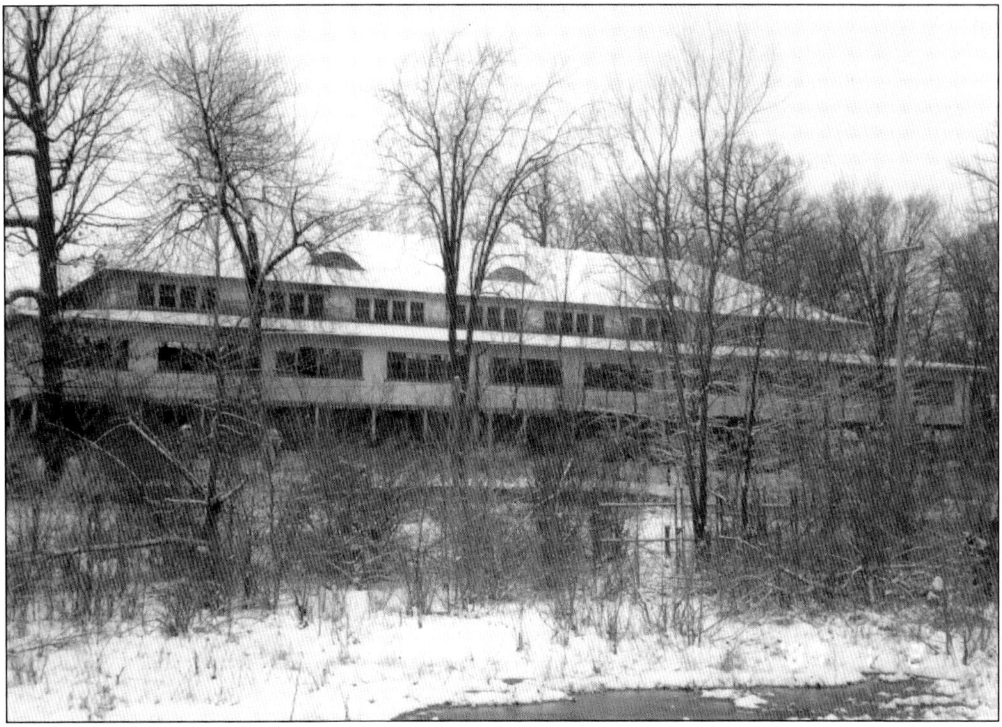

After 100 summers, Chippewa Lake Park quietly locked its gates in 1978, leaving nothing but fading memories and photographs and a handful of keepsakes to attest to its former place in history. Hundreds of thousands of visitors came from throughout northeast Ohio for a day or a week of family fun. Teenagers and college students found summer employment as ride operators or lifeguards, in food service, or on the grounds crew. Fond memories remain of the Starlight Ballroom, roller coaster, train, kiddieland, rockets, and boats. Many marriage proposals were accepted at Chippewa. The property was left to nature and vandals, with the remains finally succumbing to the wrecking ball in 2010, but the memories linger, and old-timers delight in sharing their stories of the special time and place that was Chippewa Lake Park. The ballroom and bathhouse are pictured here in 1987. (Both, Brad and April Winter.)

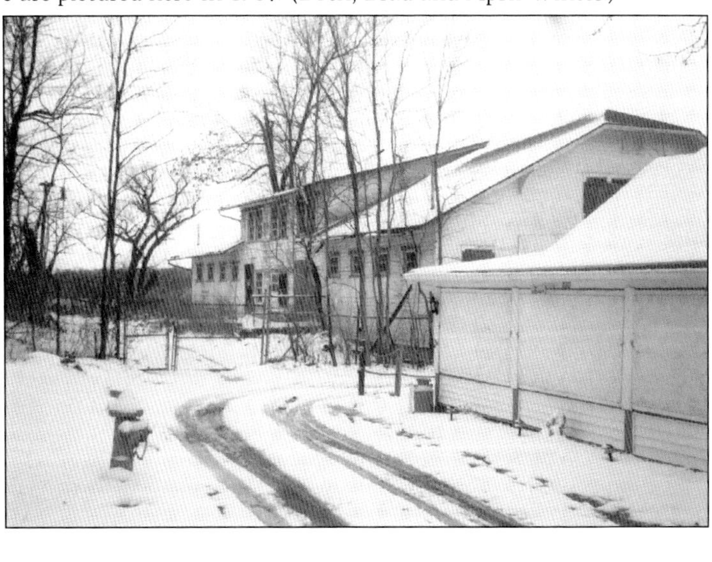

Two

Community Happenings

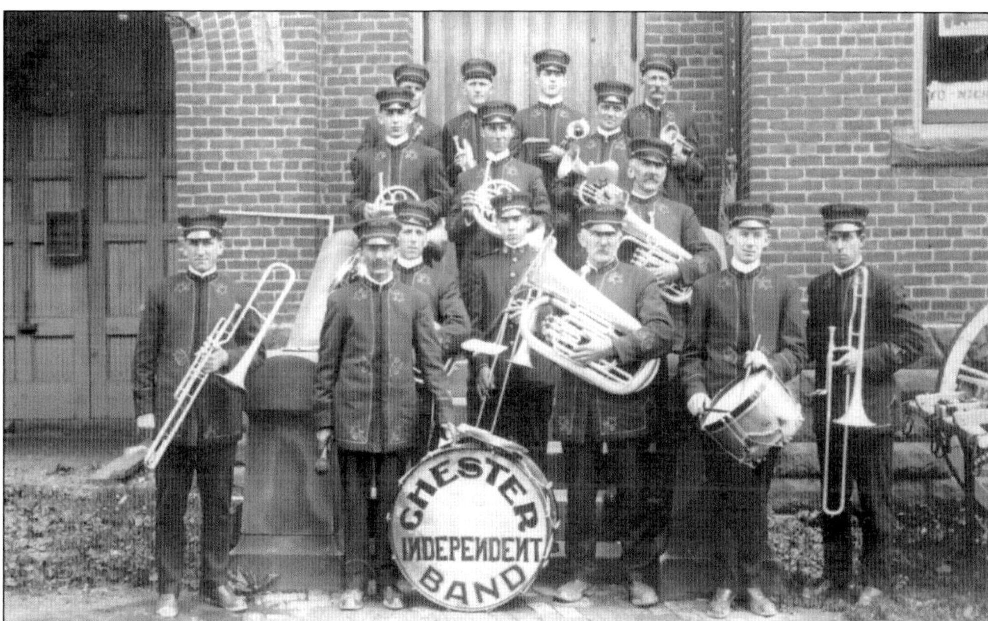

The Chester Independent Band furnished music for the community grange rally held on June 14, 1917, at Chippewa Lake. Several members of the grange were musicians in the band. Music played a big part in the growth and sustenance of the park, especially during and after the Depression. (Cyndy Naragon.)

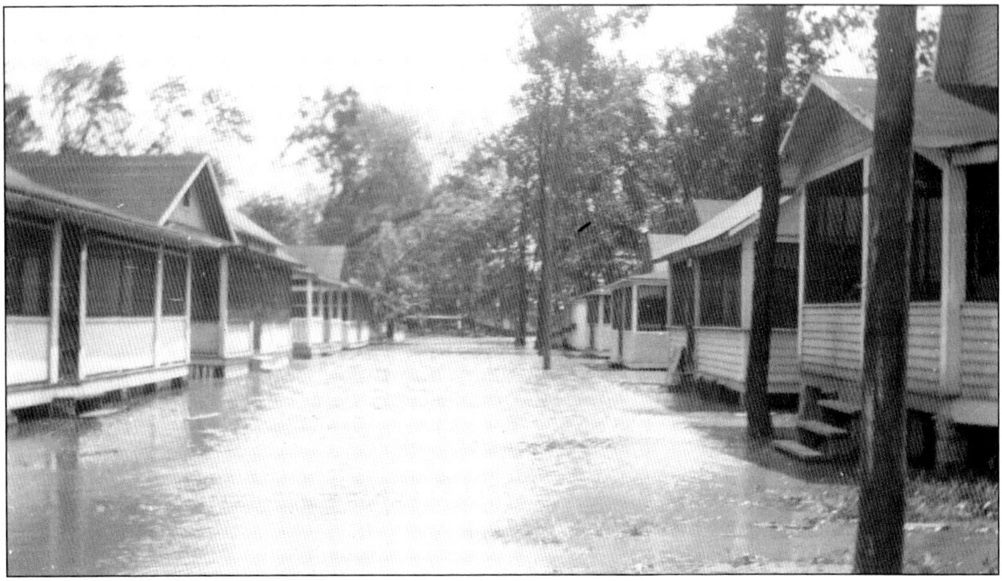

Flooding in the area of Chippewa Lake is nothing new. In search of a solution to the flooding in the late 1930s, Parker Beach worked with Westfield Township and Homer Bricker, county engineer, to find a solution. They settled on placing a dam at the south end of the lake that is removed each fall to lower the water, and reinstalled in the spring. (Beach family.)

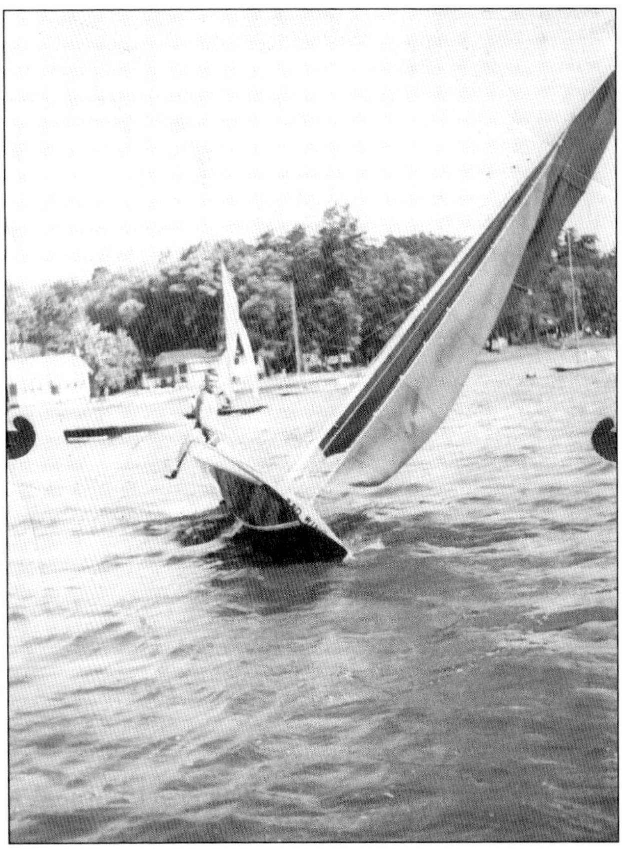

Designed in 1938 by Alvin Youngquist, a naval architect from Toledo, the Y-Flyer is an 18-foot sloop-rigged racing dinghy intended to be sailed by two people. Y-Flyers were constructed in the basement of the Chippewa Lake Park ballroom. Willard "Steve" Stephenson is pictured here in 1935 with his Y-Flyer *Red Wing*. (Keith Riedel.)

Henry Gween, police chief of Chippewa-on-the-Lake, started a boys' club to keep the rambunctious local boys out of trouble. Meetings were held at Chief Gween's house, where he taught the boys about the laws of the village and that they were not to race their bikes on the ramp to and from the circle, as well as the necessity of respecting public property. The boys were also given cool hats to wear. In 1953, the Junior Police held a bike inspection for the children of the village. (Chad Grubb.)

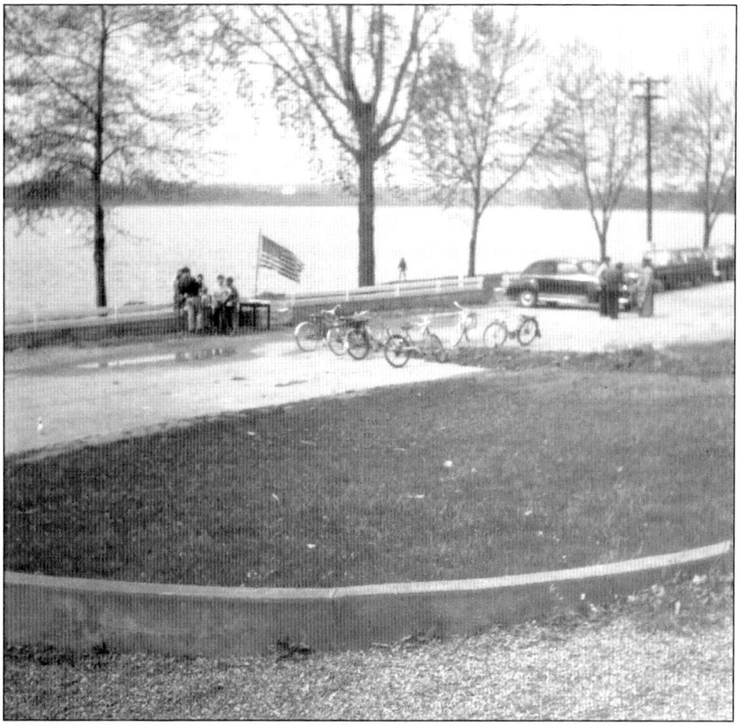

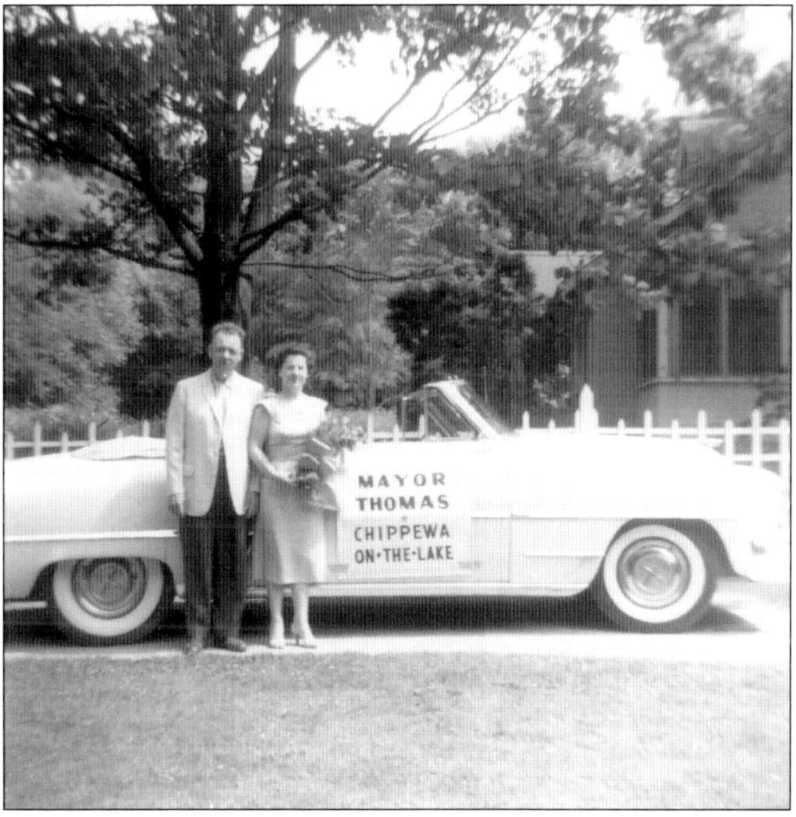

Preparing for the start of the Fourth of July parade in 1958 are mayor Carl Thomas (left) and his wife, Violet. At this time, the parade started on Lake Road north of Chippewa Road and traveled south to Chippewa Lake Park. (Carla Thomas.)

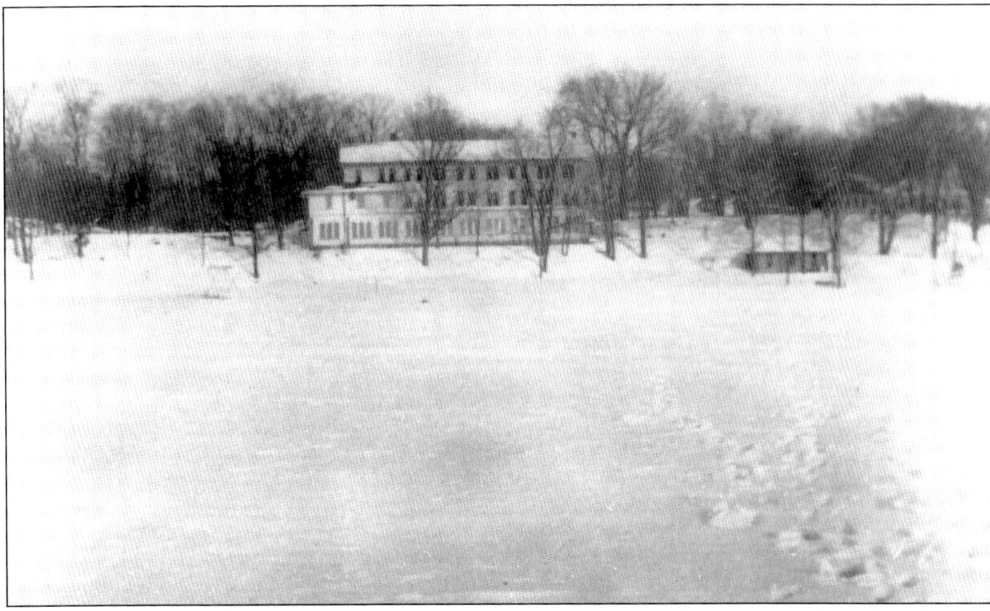

Tarry Tavern was a 34-room hotel and tavern located on Bungalow Bay Boulevard within the Village of Chippewa-on-the-Lake. In 1945, Joe Francek shot and killed James Nolan in the hotel lobby. Francek was given life imprisonment after he pleaded guilty to second-degree murder. For many years, the tavern was a hangout for mobs and gangs, like the Mayfield gang in the 1940s. Over the years, it was known for prostitution, nude swimming, illegal gambling, and bootlegging. A Civic League was formed in 1952 to curb operations of the tavern. Liquor sales were finally banned at the hotel when the village voted in November 1952 to permit only 3.2-percent beer; however, the raids continued. Tarry Tavern was finally shut down shortly after a July 1954 raid. The tavern is pictured above from a frozen Chippewa Lake and below from the tennis court. (Both, Gayle Baxter Foster.)

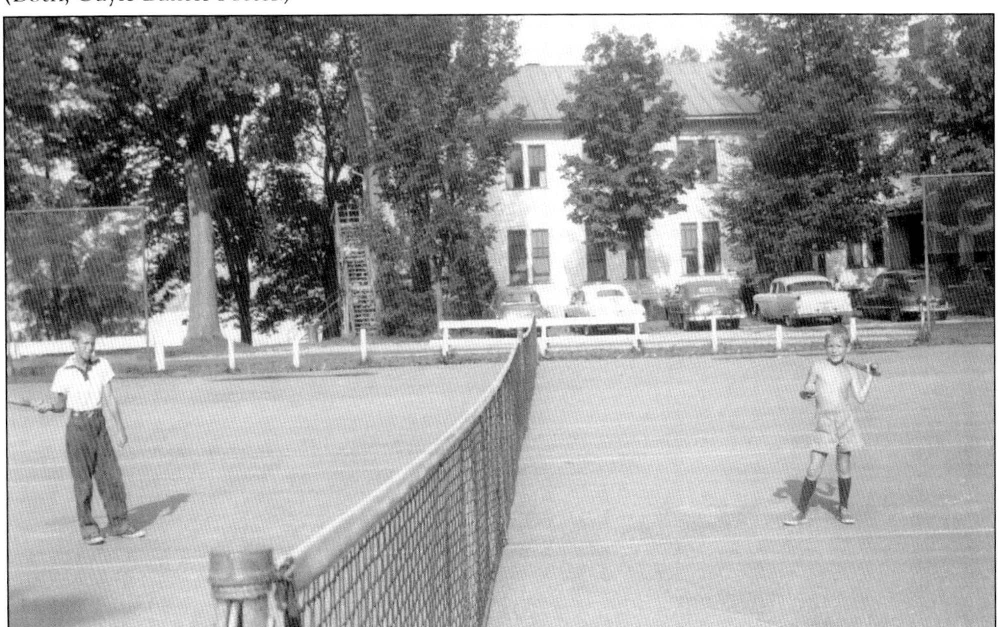

At this Fourth of July parade in 1966, the Gloria Glens Women's Club took first prize, winning $50 and a trophy. Their float was representative of women's suffrage, with signs reading "Equality," "Right to Vote," and "Equal Justice under Law." Pictured are Loretta Kunz (left), Mildred Lawrence (center), and Jane Gleason. (Jan Harmon.)

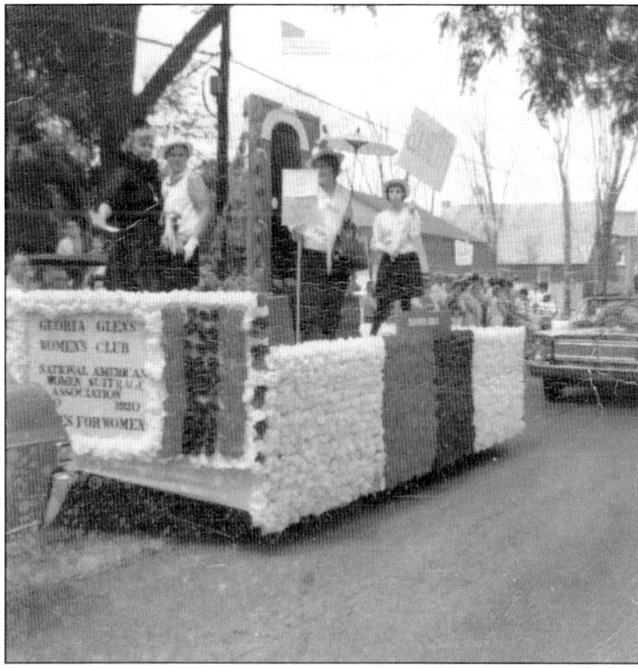

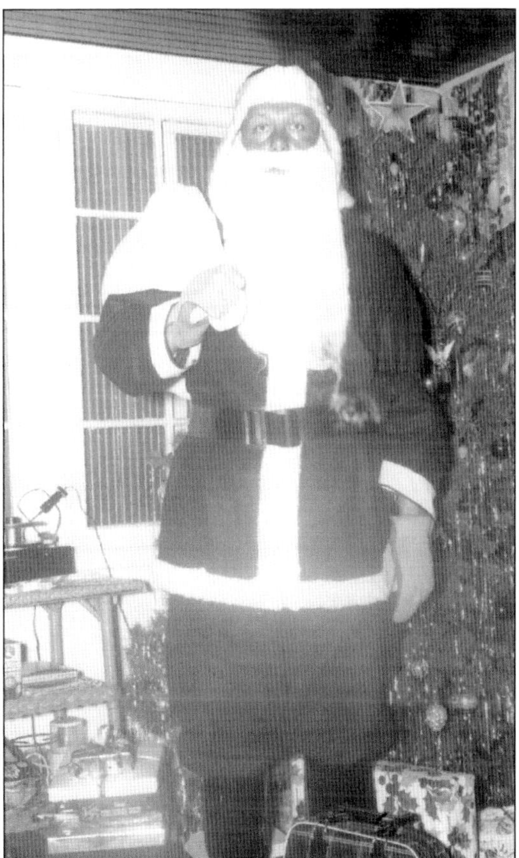

Mayor Carl Thomas is shown dressed as Santa Claus in 1956. One of the Chippewa-on-the-Lake mayoral duties was dressing as Santa each Christmas and being chauffeured around the village by the police chief to distribute stockings to all the children. (Carla Thomas.)

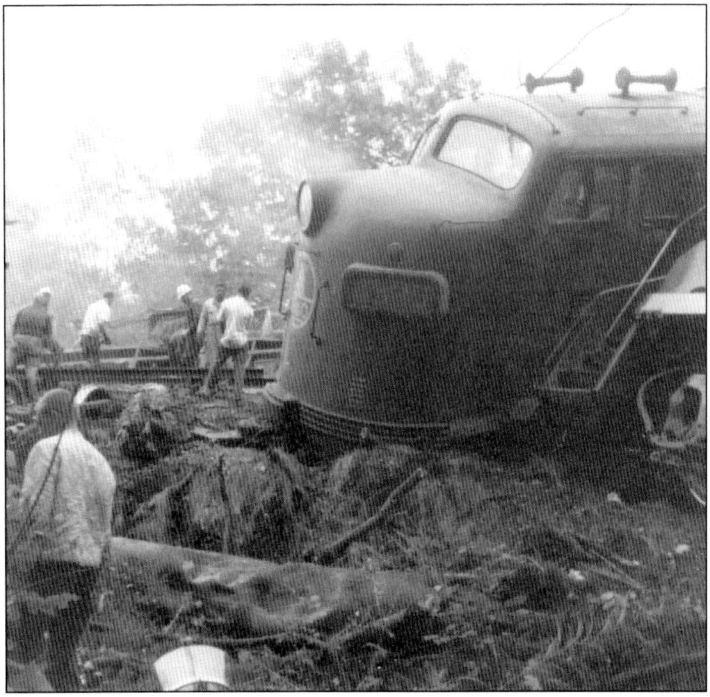

In 1968, when word spread that a Baltimore & Ohio train had jumped the tracks between Chippewa Road and Lions Park, it did not take long for locals to check it out. To their delight, cartons of Nabisco cookies had spilled, and residents were given the nod to take what they wanted if the boxes were broken open. The retrieval was halted when searchers found that another boxcar contained beef hides. (Carla Thomas.)

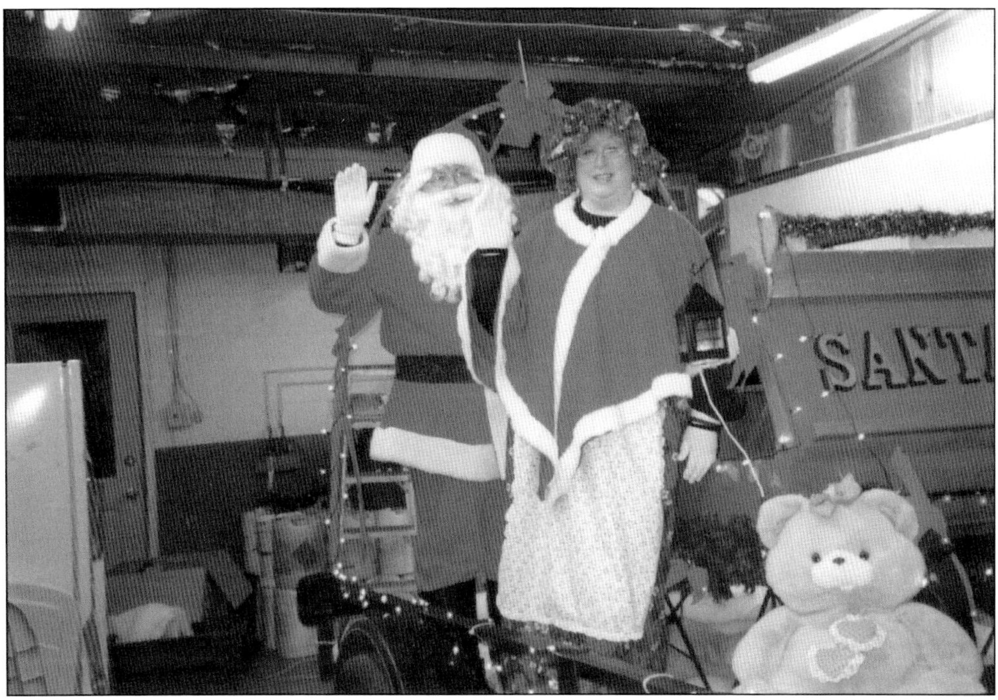

Ken McBride (left) and Jane Highman, an EMT, are preparing to play Santa and Mrs. Claus in this 1999 photograph. This started as a fundraiser in 1988 suggested by April Winter as part of the fire department's Explorer program. The Lafayette Township Firefighters Association took over in 2002. Ken McBride purchased the sleigh and donated it to the Chippewa Lake Fire Department. (Brad and April Winter.)

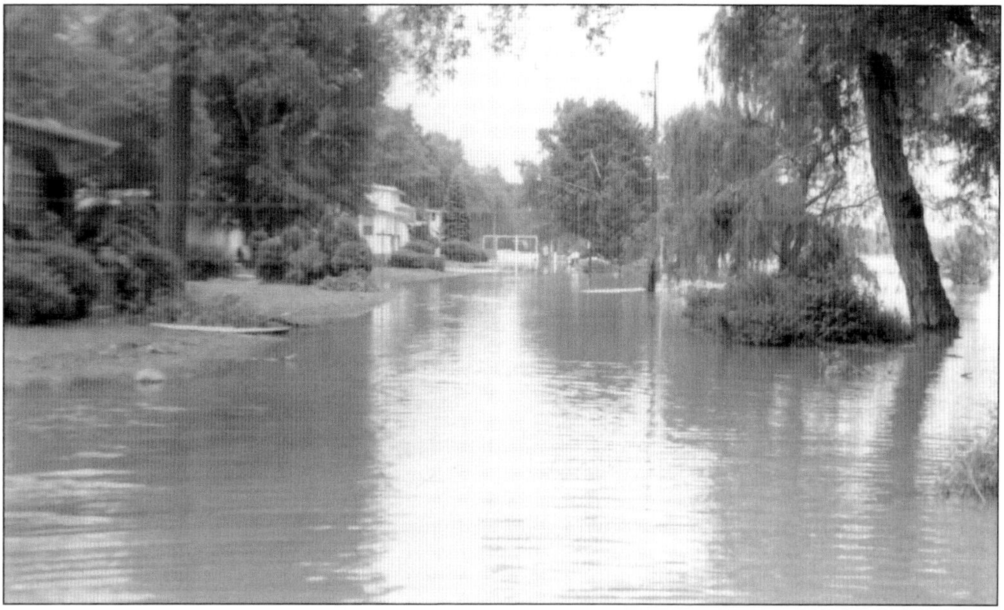

The waters of Chippewa Lake have been known to overflow their banks, usually due to a combination of lake ice thaw and spring rains. The most severe flooding came in the aftermath of a storm on July 4, 1969. Beaches were inundated, and residents used canoes in the water that flooded Beachside Boulevard as neighbors helped neighbors with the cleanup after that memorable storm. (James and Eleanor Pojman.)

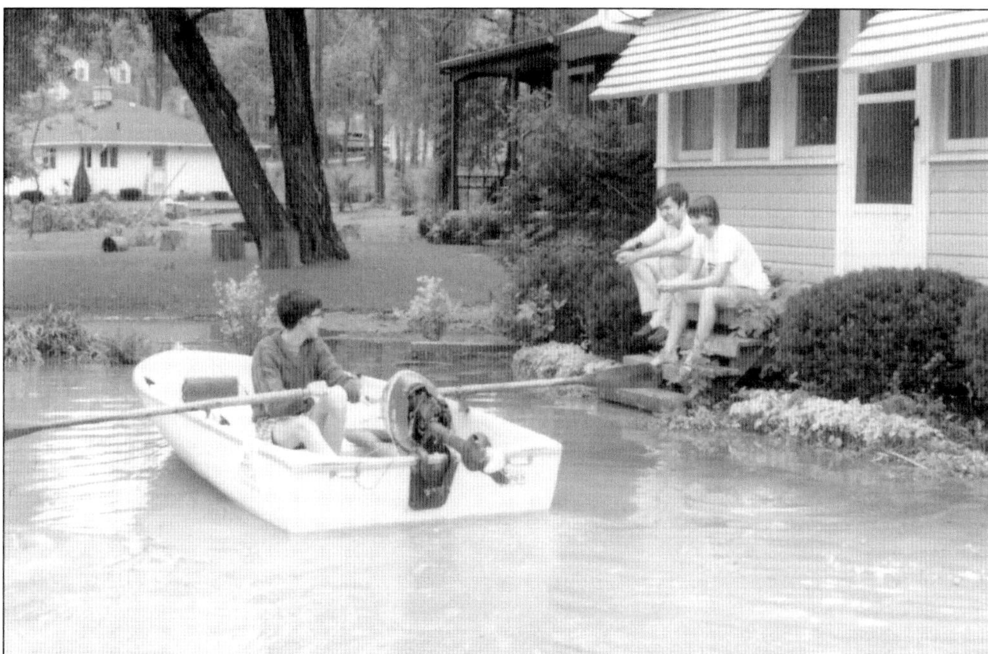

Looking north, Mike Pojman rows along Beachside Boulevard to check on neighbors Dick Cruse and his sister Diane, who are sitting on the steps of their cottage at 209 Beachside Boulevard. During the July 4, 1969, storm, the lake level rose five inches, and it took three weeks for the waters to recede. (James and Eleanor Pojman.)

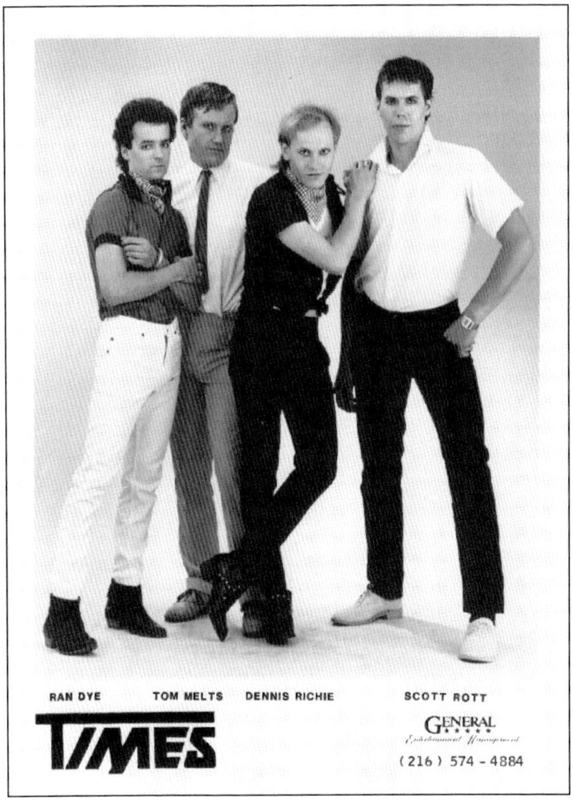

The band Fragile Eyeon was created out of a friendship between three members of the Chippewa Lake Ski Team. Throughout the seven years the band was together, they had various drummers. Pictured here in 1980, the band then known as the Times included, from left to right, Randy Meatz (drummer), Tom Melter (bassist), Dennis Yurich (lead guitarist) and Scott Walchli (rhythm guitarist and keyboardist). Below, Scott Walchli is shown playing the bass guitar when the band was known as Fragile Eyeon. They were performing their first public gig at the Gloria Glens Town Hall in 1977. They played original New Wave music. (Both, Scott Walchli.)

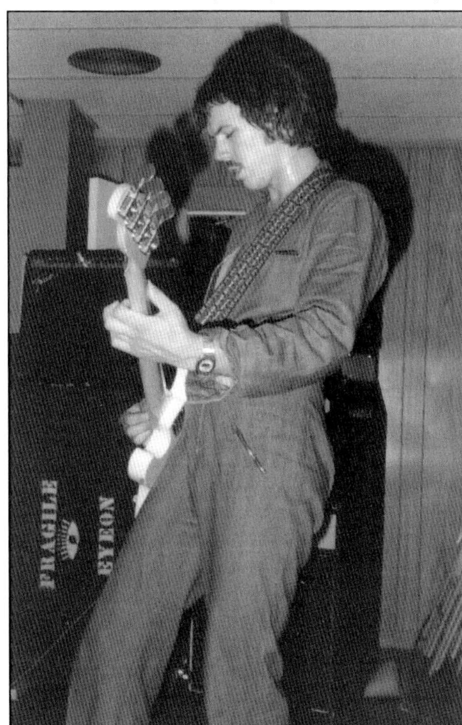

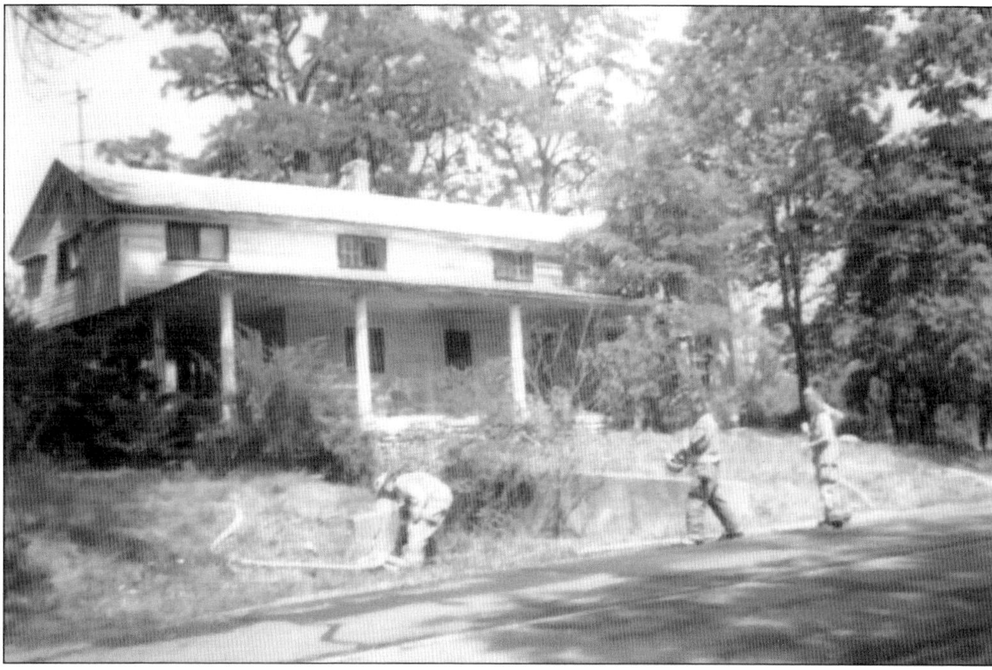

Much to the chagrin of the loyal locals who loved Chippewa Lake Park and the Beach family, Parker Beach's house on Lake Road was burned in a training fire by the Chippewa Lake Fire Department in the early 1990s. Each building that disappeared was another nail in the coffin for any dreams of resurrecting the grand old lady that was Chippewa Lake Park. (Brad and April Winter.)

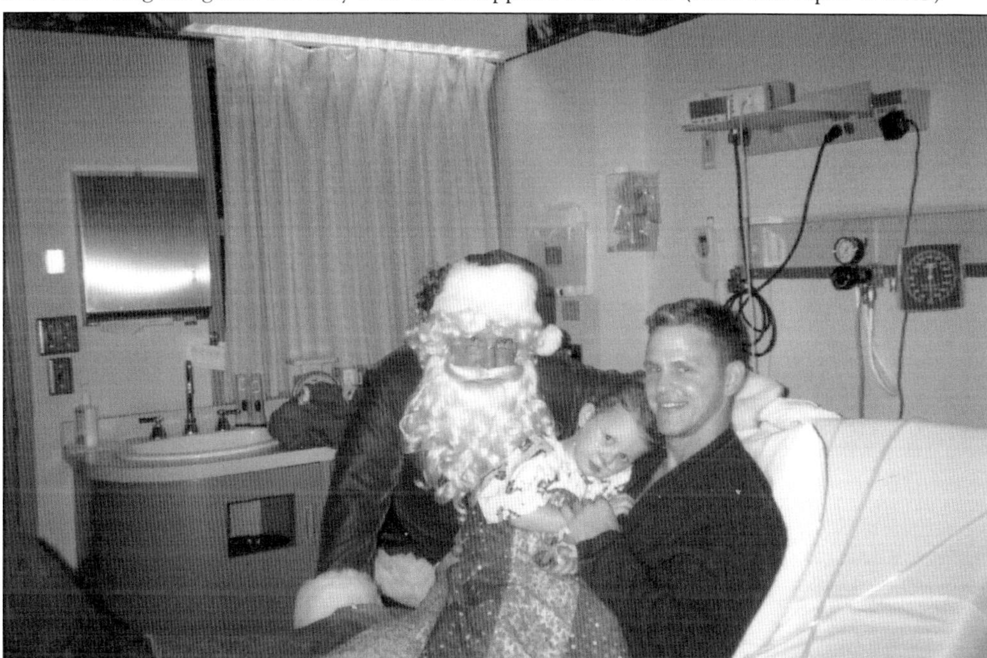

Chippewa Lake Fire Department's Santa visits Medina Hospital on Christmas Eve bearing gifts for the children. Santa also delivered candy canes and coloring books to the children of Chippewa Lake. (Brad and April Winter.)

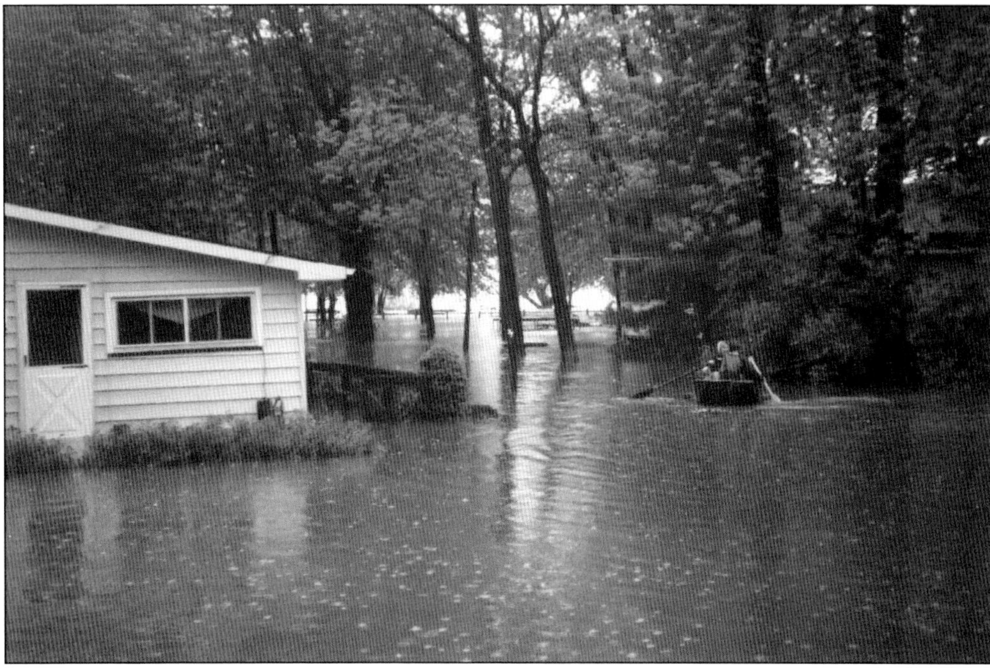

Chippewa Lake has overflowed its banks many times over the years. One of the hardest-hit areas has been the south end of Gloria Glens. Chuck and Joan Armbruster's cottage, located at 605 Twilight Trail, is pictured on the left with residents using boats to get through their community following one of three floods in 2003. FEMA finally recognized the need to intervene through the Repetitive Loss Program, and in January 2007, the Armbrusters' cottage was demolished. All the cottages and homes along Twilight Trail have been removed, and a pavilion was constructed and completed in 2014. (Both, Joan and Chuck Armbruster.)

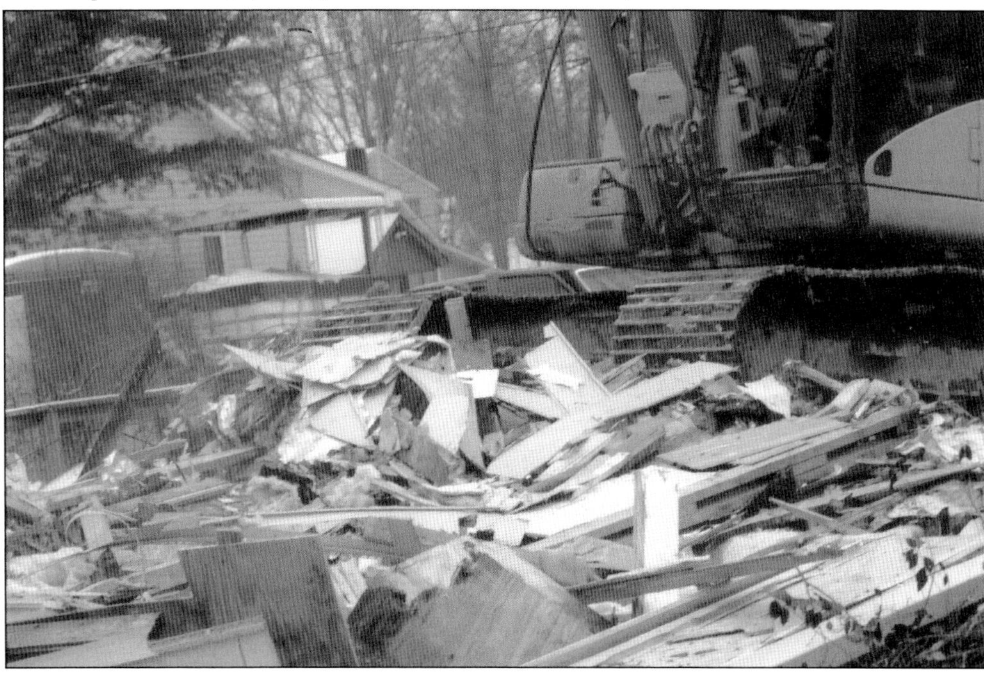

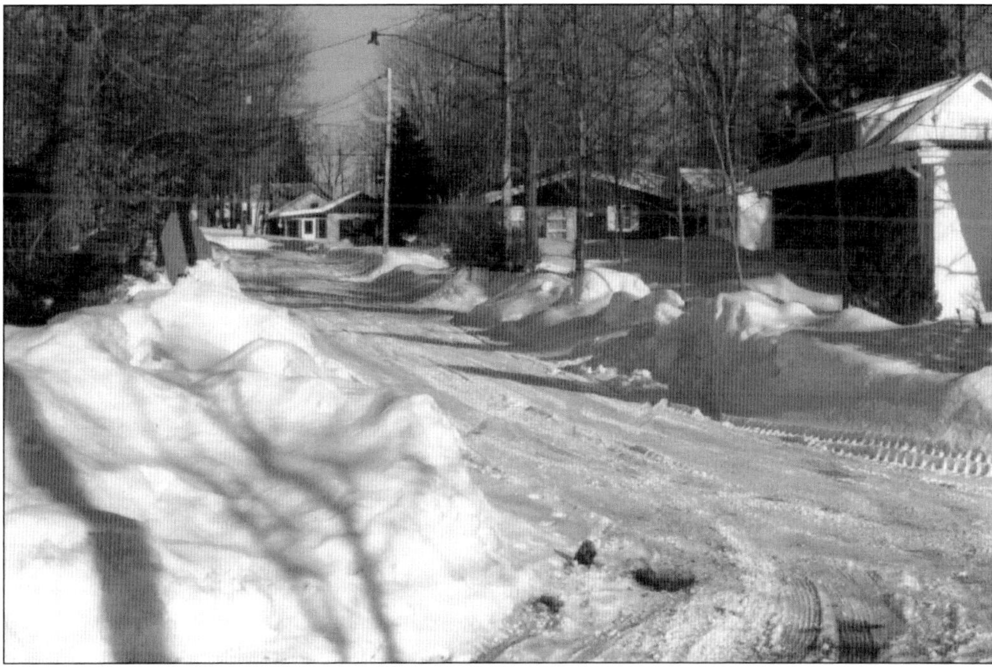

The Great Blizzard of 1978, also called the "white hurricane," hit Ohio on January 26, 1978, and brought residents to a standstill. As the storm passed over Cleveland, a record low barometric pressure was set for the state at 28.28 inches, which is lower than most hurricanes. Winds were over 50 miles per hour, with gusts as high as 82 miles per hour and wind chills reaching -100 degrees. The drifting snow stranded many motorists, and 51 people died in Ohio during the storm. Cottage Cove Drive, looking towards Rockridge Road, is shown above in the aftermath of the storm. Below, near the bridge crossing McCabe Creek on Beachside Boulevard, Carla Thomas shows just how deep the snow was. (Above, Melter family; below, Carla Thomas.)

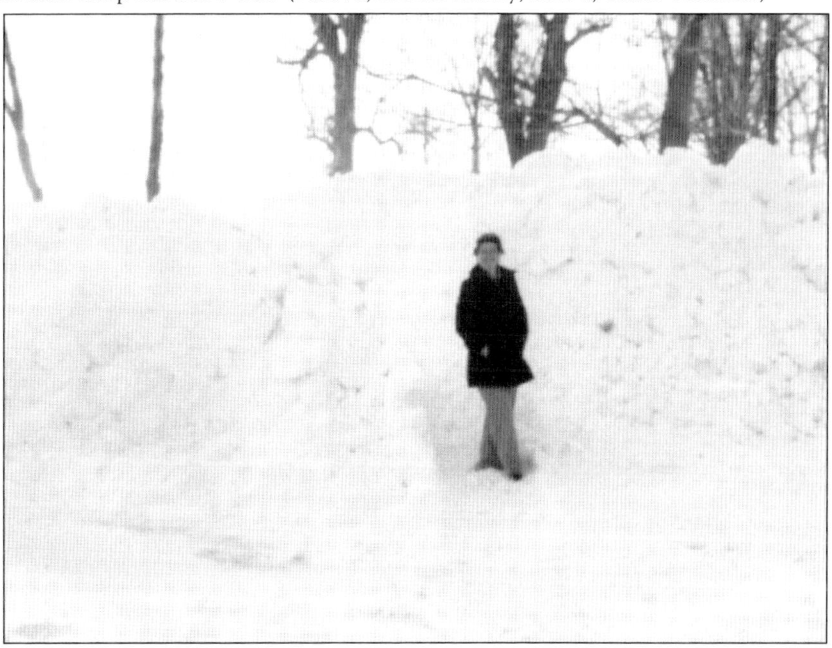

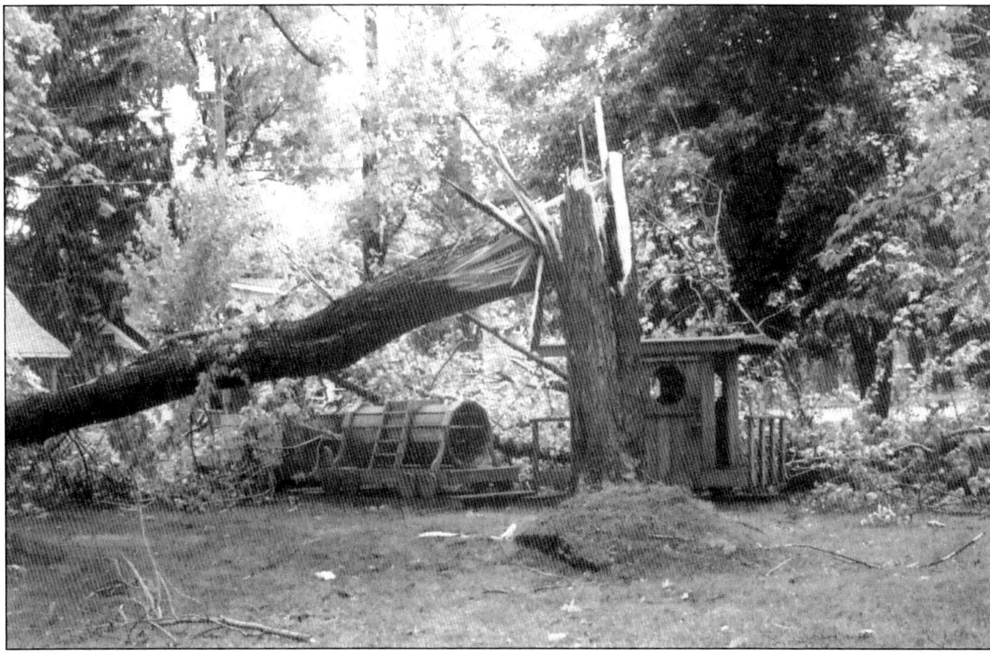

Is there something about the weather in Chippewa Lake? A tornado struck on July 9, 1999, causing considerable damage from a storm that toppled trees and knocked out power for days. Destruction in the Bungalow Bay circle is evident in this photograph. (Gayle Baxter Foster.)

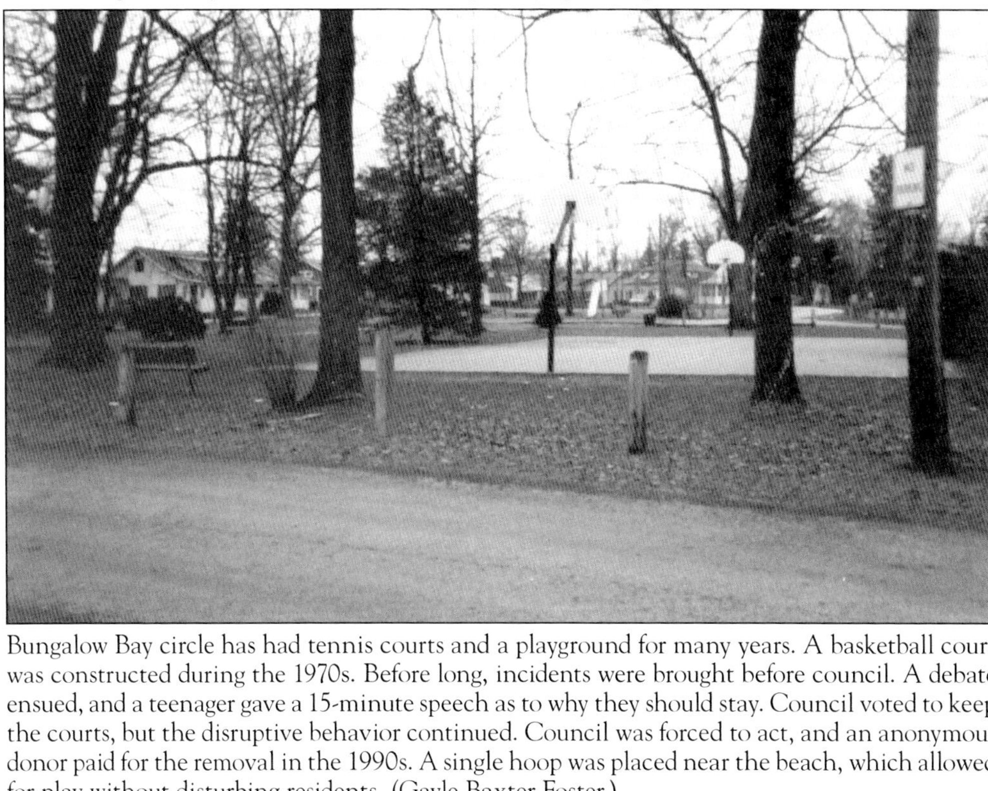

Bungalow Bay circle has had tennis courts and a playground for many years. A basketball court was constructed during the 1970s. Before long, incidents were brought before council. A debate ensued, and a teenager gave a 15-minute speech as to why they should stay. Council voted to keep the courts, but the disruptive behavior continued. Council was forced to act, and an anonymous donor paid for the removal in the 1990s. A single hoop was placed near the beach, which allowed for play without disturbing residents. (Gayle Baxter Foster.)

Three

CLUBS AND ORGANIZATIONS

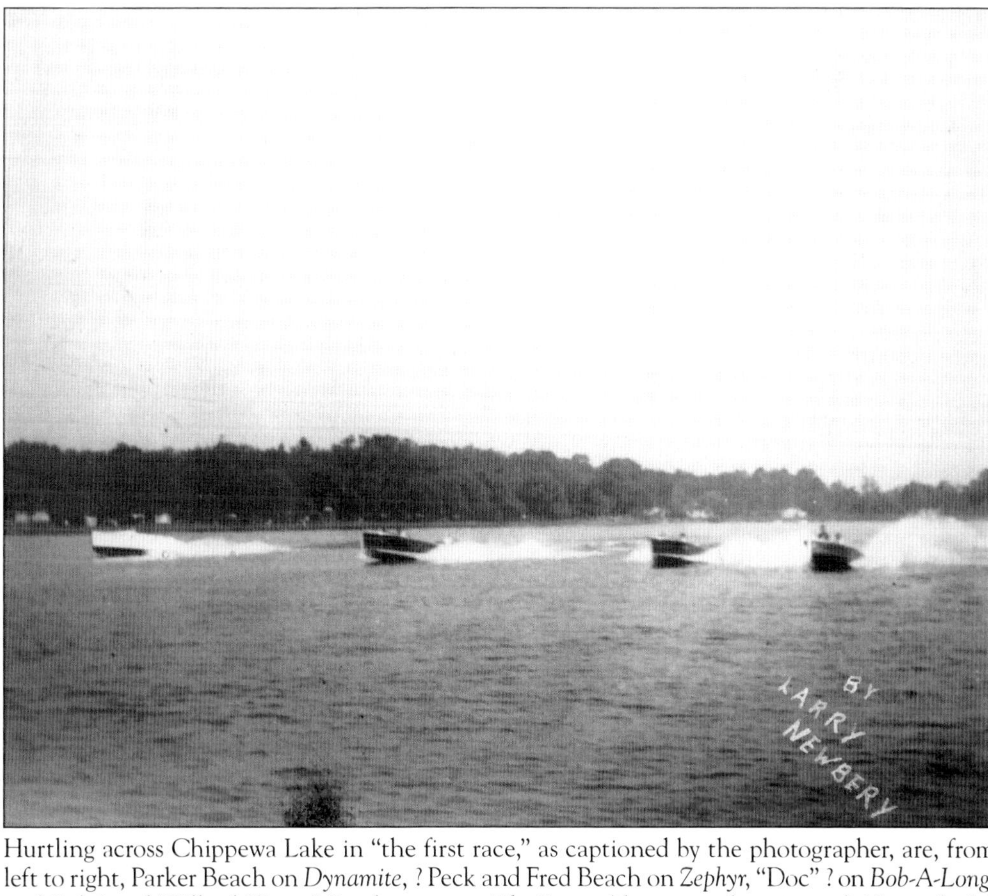

Hurtling across Chippewa Lake in "the first race," as captioned by the photographer, are, from left to right, Parker Beach on *Dynamite*, ? Peck and Fred Beach on *Zephyr*, "Doc" ? on *Bob-A-Long*, and Bob ? and Willard "Steve" Stephenson on *The Rogue* (they were the winners). Not only did Beach enjoy the thrill of speedboats, he supported the founding and construction of the Chippewa Lake Yacht Club. (Stephenson collection.)

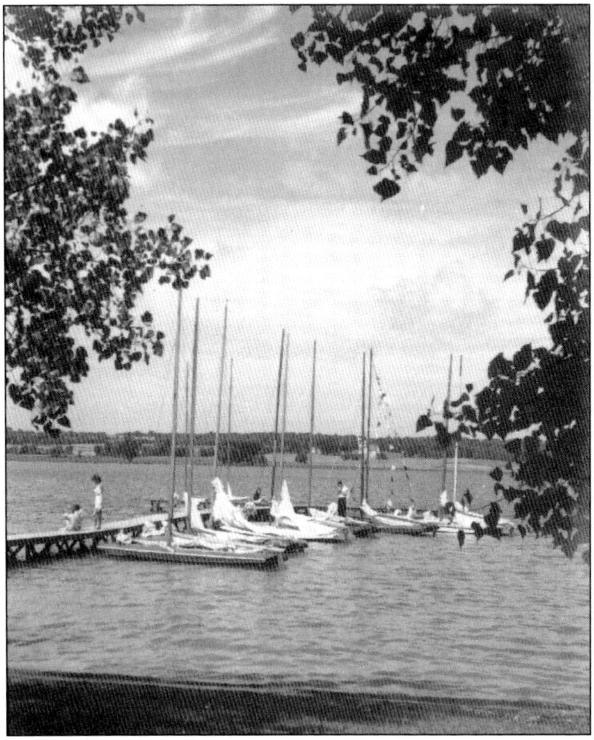

The Chippewa Lake Yacht Club was founded in 1939. The first commodore was Rev. John Quinton of St. Paul's Episcopal Church in Medina. He constructed the first Y-Flyer to sail on Chippewa Lake. Sailboats such as Y-Flyers, Snipes, Sunfish, and Lasers raced on Sunday mornings during the season. The yacht club sponsors a Y-Flyer regatta featuring 15 to 24 boats a few times per season, with sailors coming from all parts of the United States and Canada. The club is strictly a sailing club—no motorized boats. The boats must be less than 22 feet long and have a single mast and a centerboard. This is an early photograph of the yacht club's dock. (Beach family.)

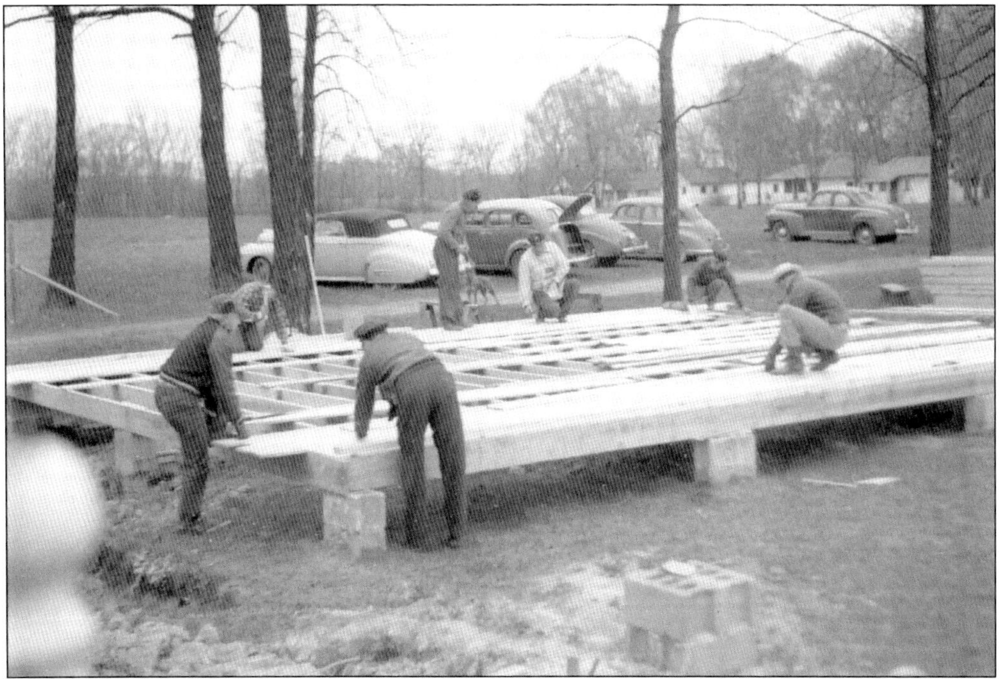

Founding Chippewa Lake Yacht Club members are shown beginning construction of the club in 1942; it was completed in 1943. The locker rooms and kitchen were added in 1956. Euclid Avenue is in the background. This is the area where the earliest cottages of Chippewa Lake Park were built, with some dating to the 1800s. (Stephenson collection.)

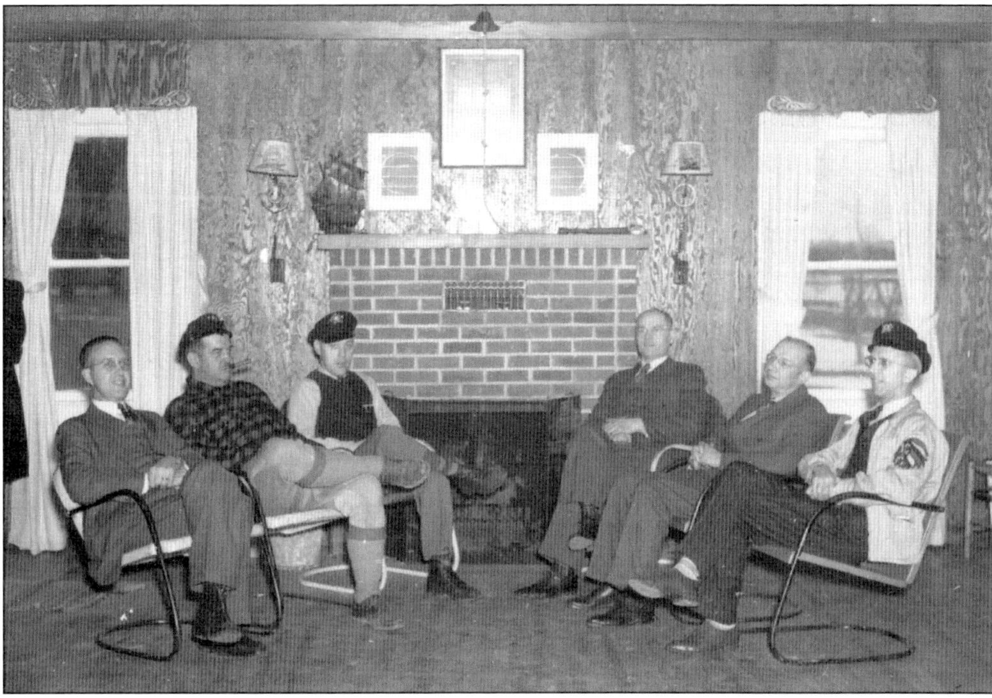

Pictured inside the yacht club shortly after construction are, from left to right, the first Chippewa Yacht Club commodore, Rev. John Quinton; Dan Krug; Clyde Ambrose; Frank Jensen; Larry Newberry Sr.; and Milton Busch. All the men served as commodore except Busch. Beginning in 1940, a new commodore was elected each year, with some serving more than once. The only commodore to serve two consecutive terms was Willard "Steve" Stephenson, in 1941 and 1942, with a term cut short when he left to serve in World War II. Three women have been commodores, with Sheila Denison being the first in 2001. Below are the sailboats that Parker Beach reportedly thought people would enjoy seeing during their visits to the park. (Above, Stephenson collection; below, Beach family.)

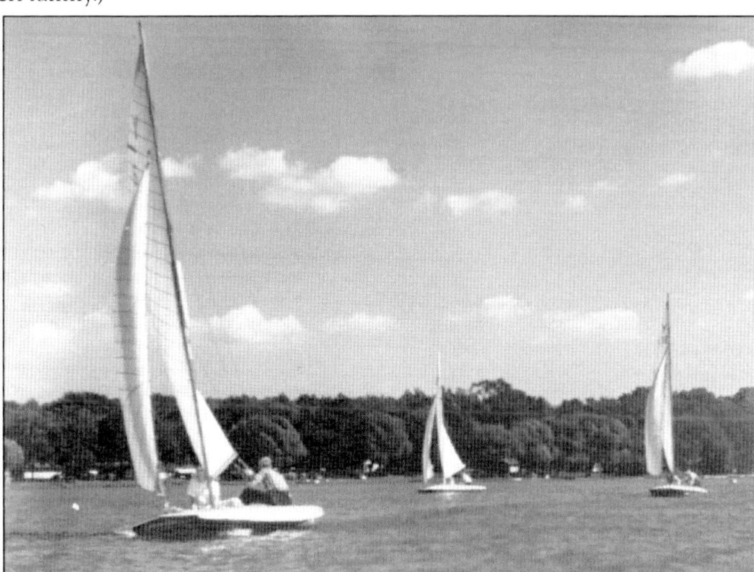

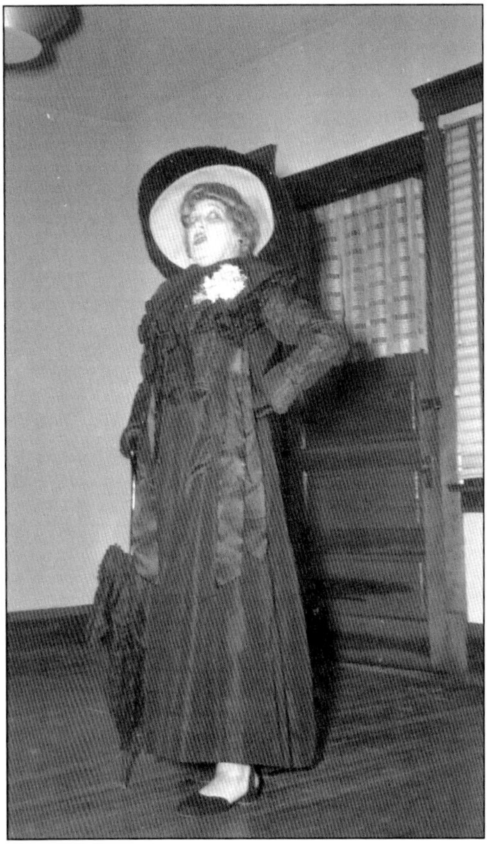

The Chippewa-on-the-Lake Women's Club was established in 1928 by Etta Branch. They met at the homes of members until 1932, when Mayor George Moses told the women about a piece of property for sale that soon became the Women's Club. One of the members paid upfront for the house, and Swiss steak dinners were held to raise money for repayment; within two years, they had paid back the money. Dinners, card parties, plays, ice cream socials, and country bazaars were among the activities used to raise money for maintenance. The club did charitable work as part of its agenda. In 1985, it began giving annual scholarships to Cloverleaf High School seniors and a donation to Chippewa Lake Rescue Squad. The club closed its doors in 1999 and sold the clubhouse to Randy Baird, who established a patio over the basement of the house so residents could sit and watch the evening sunsets. It became known as Friends of the Circle. At left, Bernice Bostwick is singing "She's Only a Bird in a Gilded Cage" for a play in 1948. Pictured below in 1999 are, from left to right, Vivian Baxter, Theresa Lias Enderle, Pearl Novak Frontz, and Helen ?. (Both, Barbara Grubb Whitlam.)

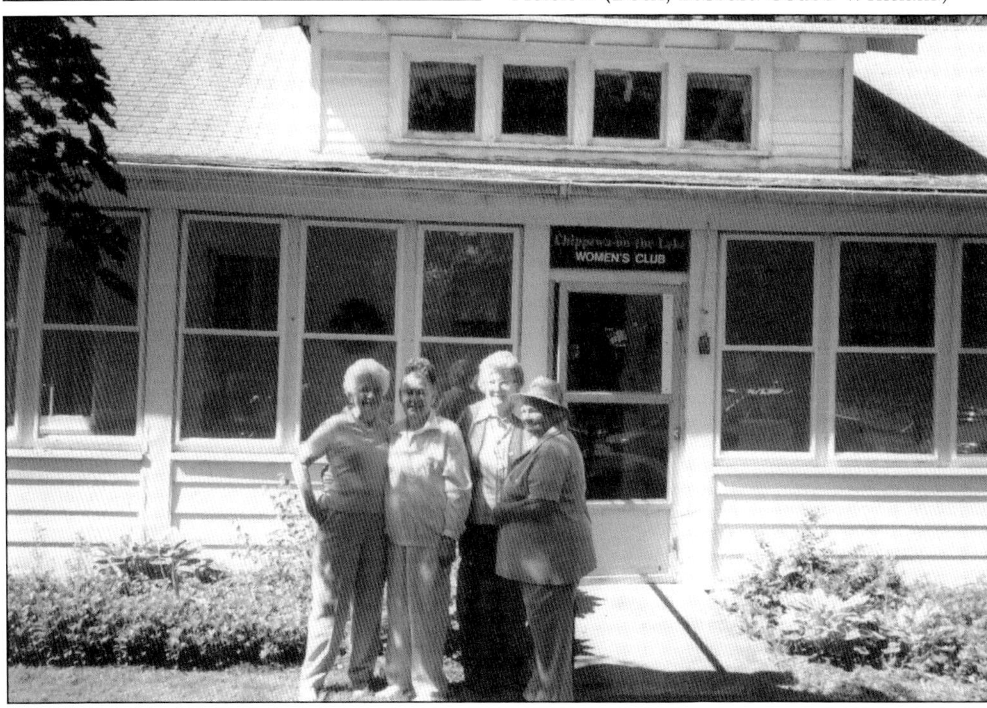

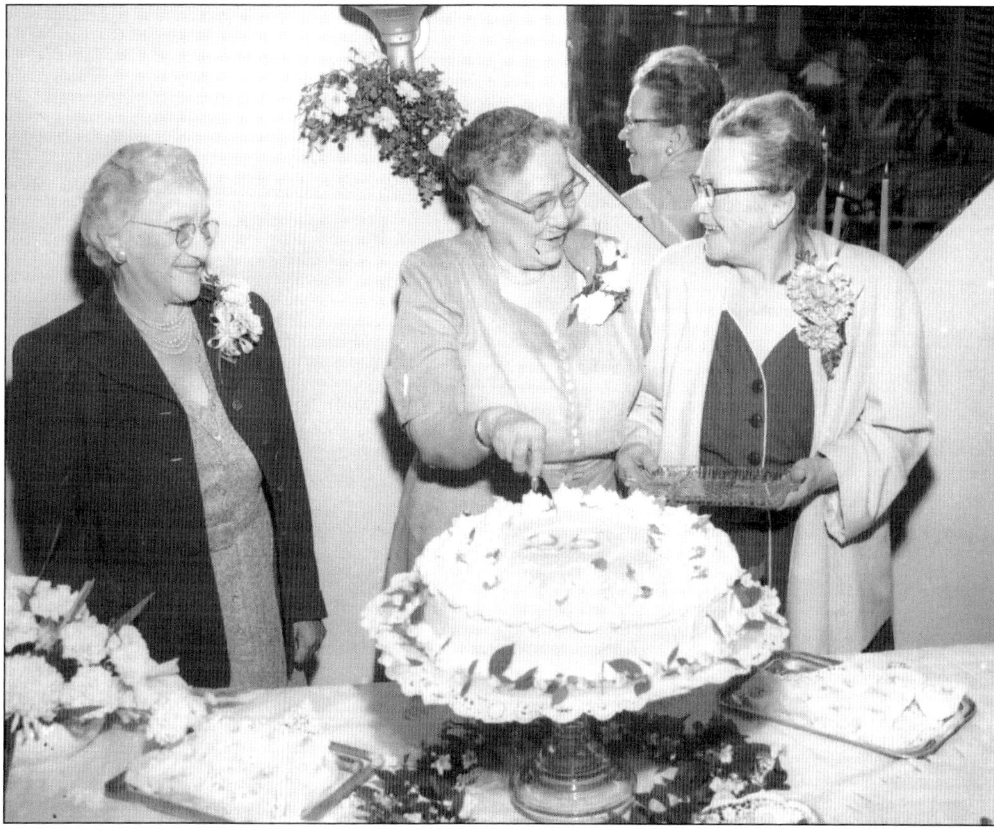

Pictured here at the 25th anniversary of the Chippewa-on-the-Lake Women's Club in May 1953 are, from left to right, Martha Wiedenman, Minnie Moses, and Bessie Lees. The Women's Club was incorporated in October 1933—the original incorporators were Anna Wiedenman, Carrie Curtis, Ida Doering, Etta Branch, Elizabeth Hulland, and Bessie Lees. (Barbara Grubb Whitlam.)

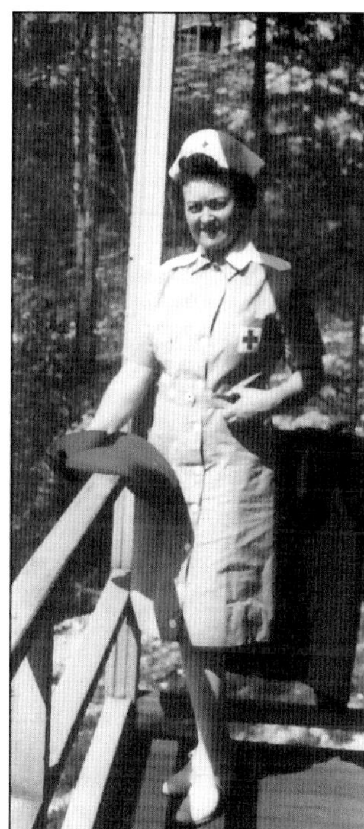

Bernice Bostwick was a devoted member of the Women's Club and Garden Club. From her humble beginnings as the daughter of an Arkansas circuit preacher, Bostwick learned the value of hard work, being thankful, and giving back to others. She was a Red Cross volunteer during World War I and at Medina General Hospital, receiving an award for her 50 years of service. During World War II, she worked at the Pentagon decoding messages. She was a teacher, suffragist, Colonial Dame, member of the Eastern Star Order, and Daughter of the American Revolution. Bernice collected cultural costumes from her vast world travels and gave numerous presentations on Women Around the World to schools and civic groups. She was an avid historian and earned a master's degree in history. She wrote a history of Medina County and served as president of the Medina County Historical Society. She is buried at Mound Hill Cemetery in Seville, and her marker reads "Medina County Historian." (Jeffrey Schmitt.)

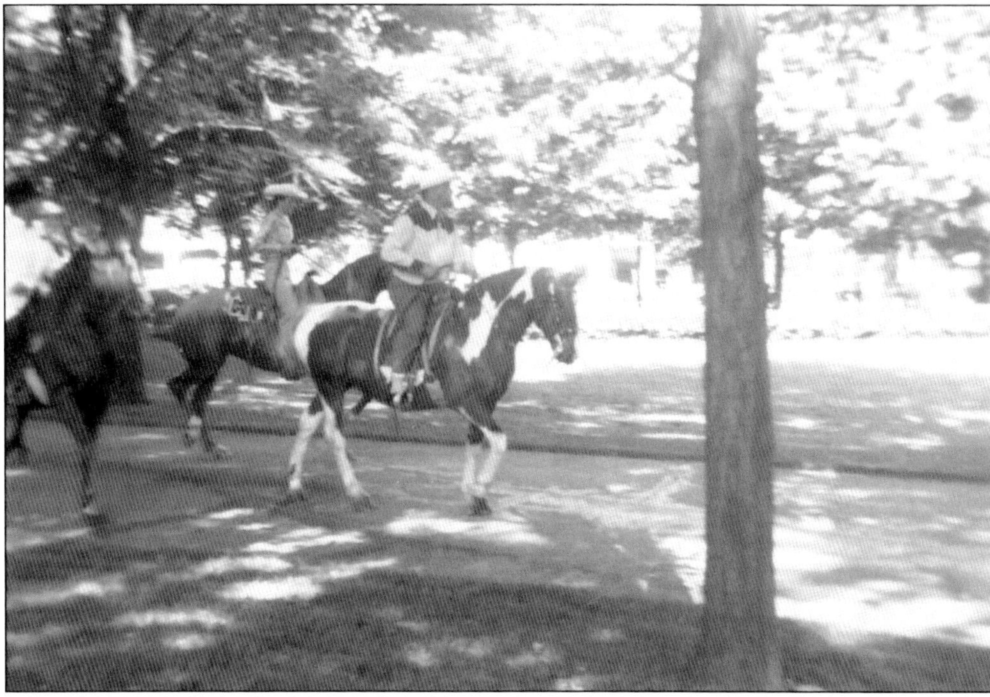

The annual Fourth of July parade had its beginnings in the mid-1950s with a parade that traveled the Bungalow Bay circle. The parade continues today, following a route on Lake Road that culminates at Lions Club Park, where trophies are presented. Later in the afternoon, the award-winning Chippewa Lake Water Ski Show Team presents a free ski show. A popular Cardboard Boat Race, presented by the community's Chippewa Village Pride Program, follows the ski show, with entrants demonstrating imagination and talent. Above, Parker Beach is leading one of the early Fourth of July parades in 1956. Pictured below is Ken Walters Sr., who made this parade float that won first prize at the Fourth of July parade in 1958. (Above, Carla Thomas; below, Barbara Grubb Whitlam.)

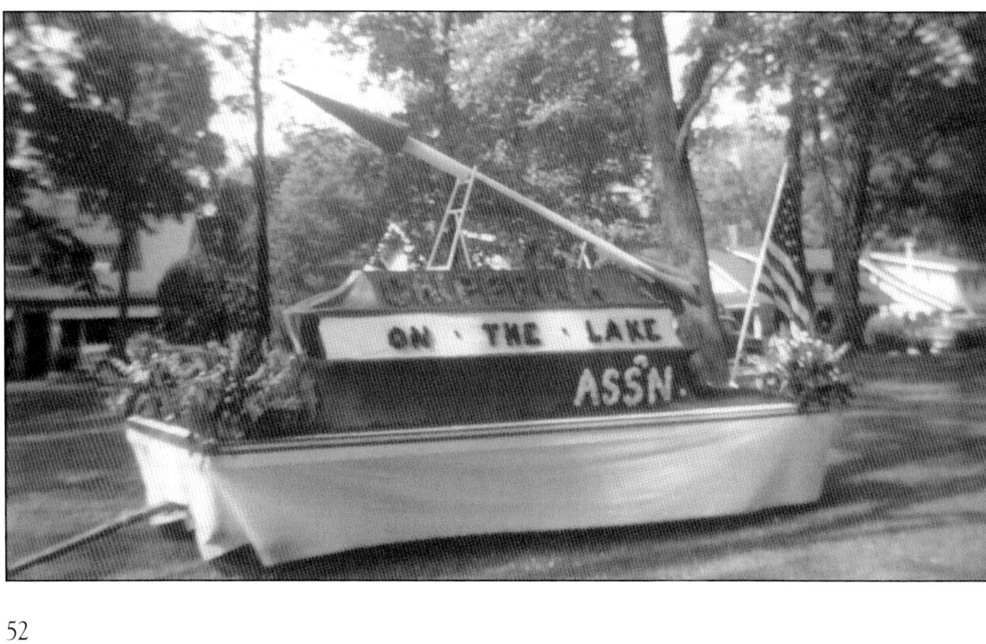

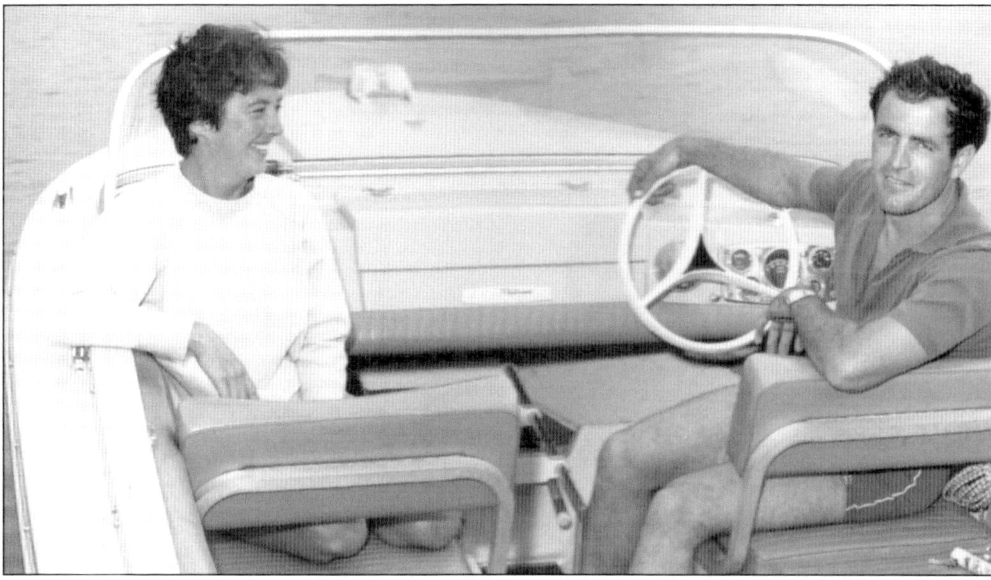

The founders of the Chippewa Lake Ski Team, Daryl (right) and Joanne Gibbs, are pictured in their boat in 1969. Some of the first skiers on the team included Jim Pojman, Tom Melter, Martha Melter (Tom's sister), and Bruce Lovejoy. Prior to the ski team, Parker Beach permitted waterskiing on the lake for those who had lake rights. Ski boats could have no larger than a 90-horsepower engine, and Parker required they have a yellow ski flag on their boat while skiing. This flag cost the property owners $25 per year. (Margaret Glenn.)

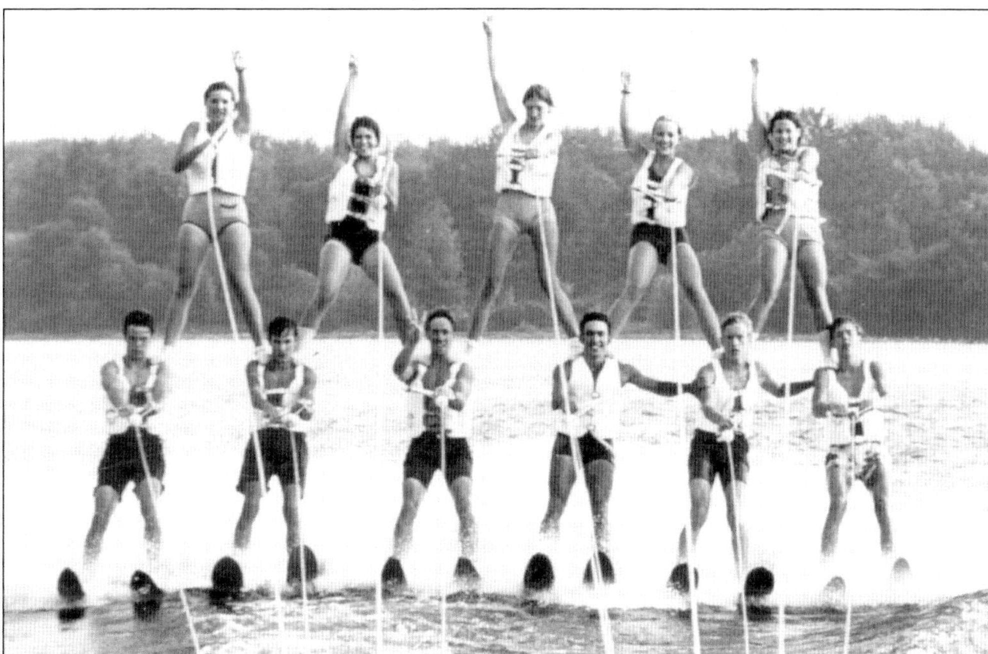

The Chippewa Lake Ski Team performs during the summer of 1970. From left to right are (first row) Mark Lovejoy, Jim Pojman, Bruce Lovejoy, Dan Trausch, Tom Melter, and Scott Walchli; (second row) Diann Cruse, Ellen Leahy, Margaret Pojman, Martie Melter, and Mary Jo Murajda. (Margaret Glenn.)

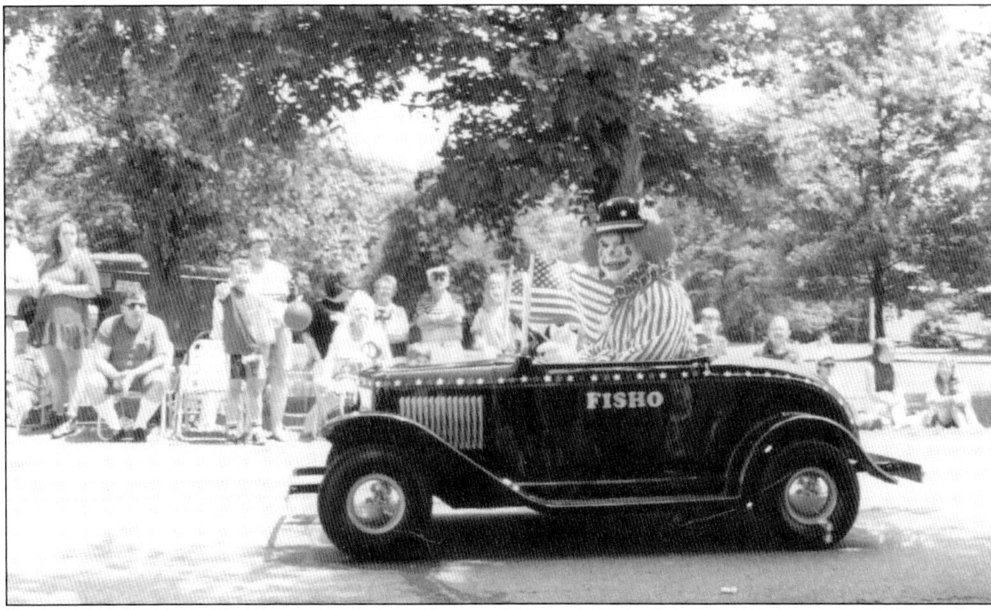

Eventually, Parker Beach, owner of Chippewa Lake Park, moved the Fourth of July parade from Bungalow Bay circle to Lake Road. Once the park was sold, the Lions Club continued the tradition. Certain folks made a point of being in the parade every year, including Don Fisher. For many years, he dressed up as a clown and rode his little car in the parade while everyone cheered him on. (Ruth Lees Napier.)

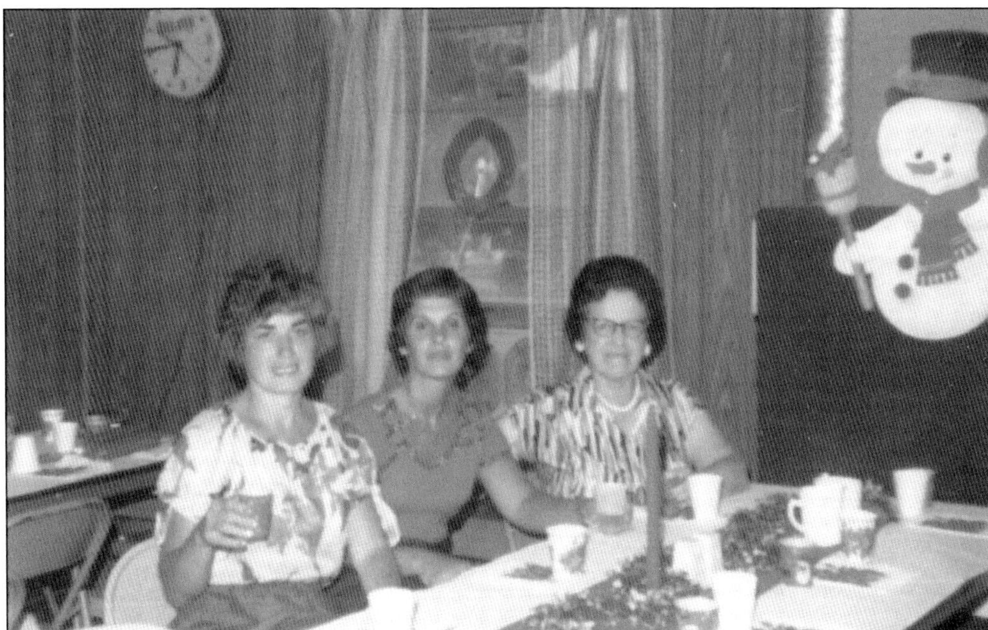

The Gloria Glens Women's Club was active in maintaining and beautifying Gloria Glens, sponsoring an annual Easter Egg hunt and participating in various activities to support the community. This is a Gloria Glens Women's Club gathering at Christmastime at their town hall. From left to right are Ann Simatacowlos, Donna Yurich, and Elinore Yurich. (Jan Harmon.)

Grant money from the Stephenson Foundation enabled the construction of Stephenson Park in 2014. Located in the unused intersection of Willow Wood Drive and Rockridge Road, the small garden recognizes Willard "Steve" Stephenson, a longtime resident. Members of the Briarwood Beach Garden Club and Chippewa Village Pride Program worked to beautify the little section of the village by including plantings, stone walkways, and a stone bench. Steve Stephenson is pictured below in 1933, the year that he purchased Oatman's Hardware from Lyman Oatman and changed the store's name to Medina Hardware, which is now run by his son Rick. (Right, Amber Dalakas; below, Stephenson collection.)

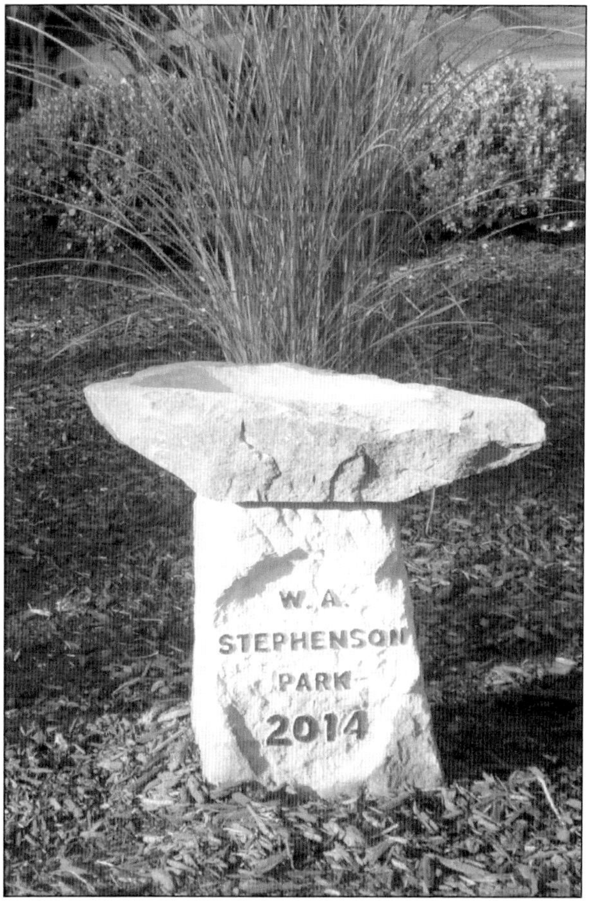

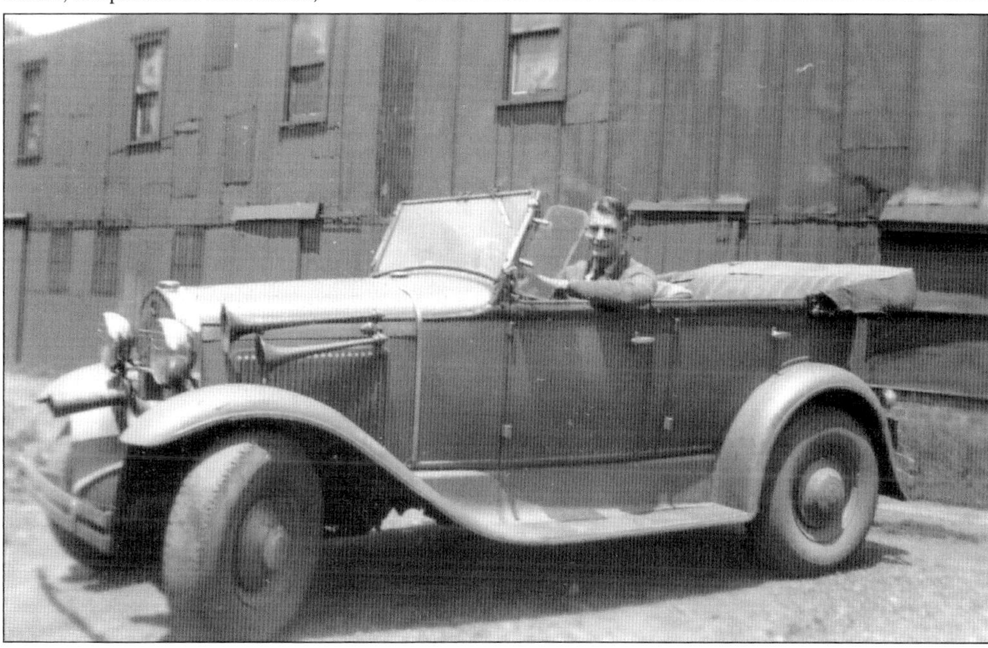

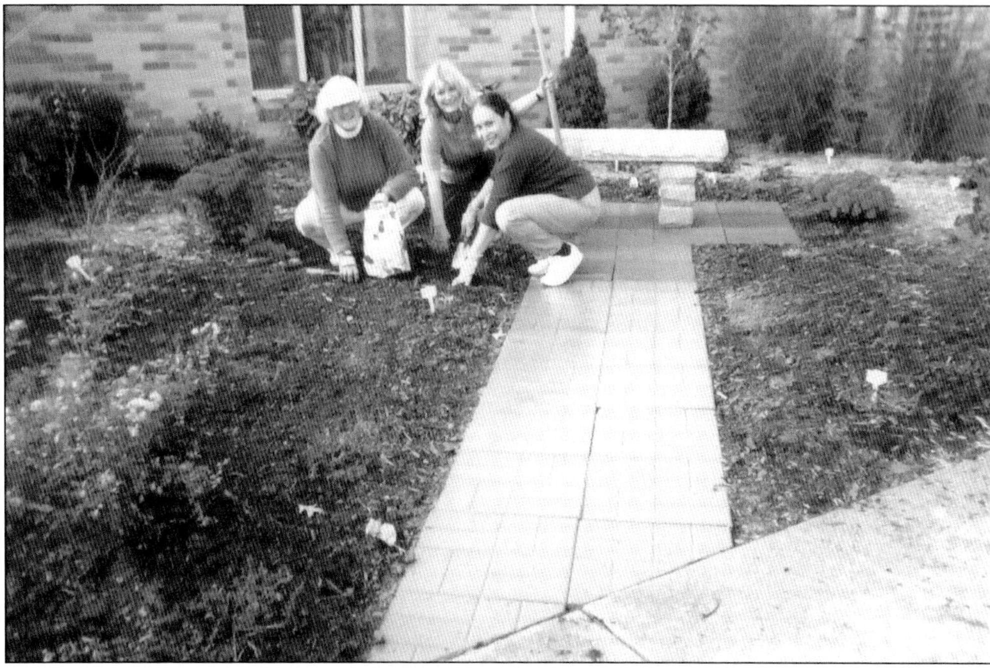

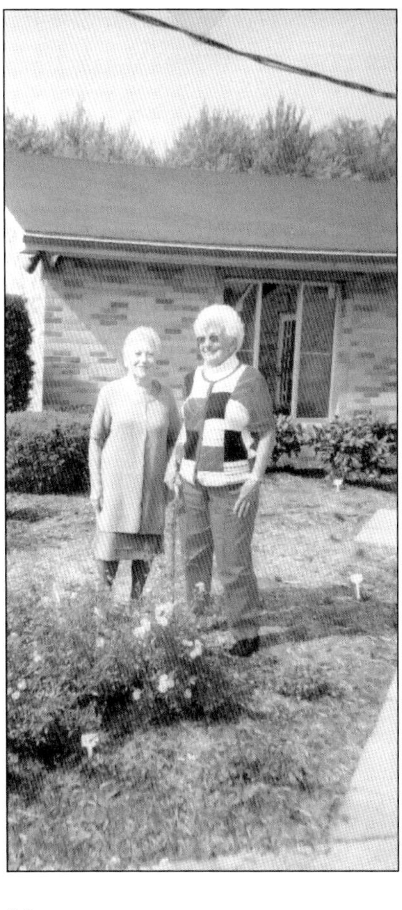

In November 2005, Briarwood Beach Garden Club members (from left to right) Jan Harmon, Gisela Mattingly, and Nora Purdon planted fall bulbs for the next spring bloom at Chippewa Church at the Lake United Methodist's Memorial Garden. Other garden club members who worked on the project included Sherry Ostrowski, Sherry Dunn, and Grace Romis. (Briarwood Beach Garden Club.)

The memorial garden at Chippewa Church at the Lake United Methodist was completed by the Briarwood Beach Garden Club. Funding was provided by special memorial donations made to the church. Roberta Humbel (left), a church and garden club member, and Vivian Baxter, a church member, are shown enjoying the garden. In July 2006, the garden club received an award at the Ohio Association of Garden Clubs' state convention for their work completing this civic beautification project. (Briarwood Beach Garden Club.)

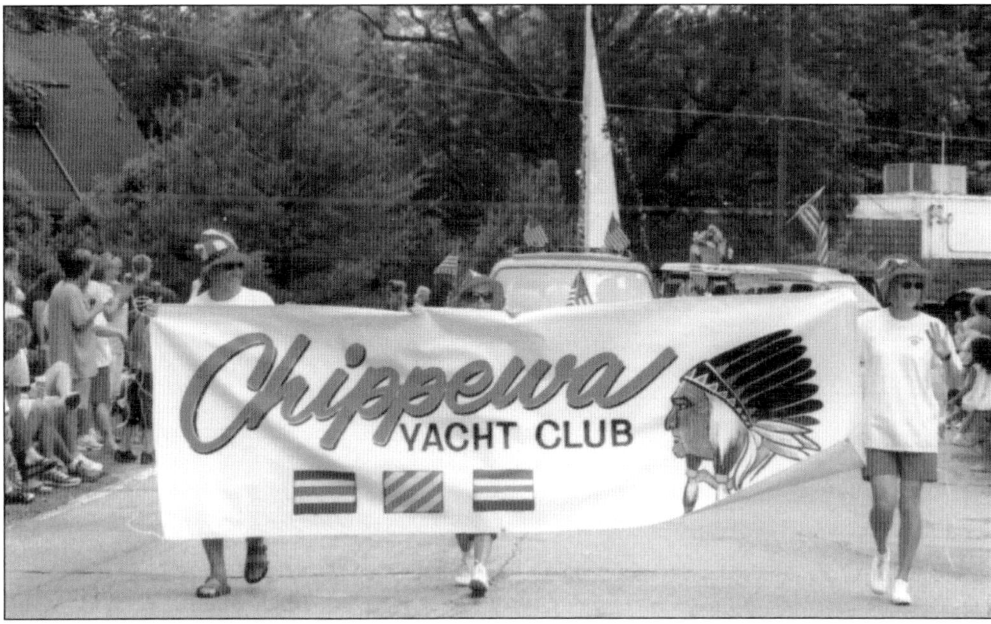

In 2008, the Chippewa Yacht Club participated in the Fourth of July parade. Pictured carrying the banner are, from left to right, Bob Williams, Sheila Denison, and Alice Horwath. (Chippewa Yacht Club.)

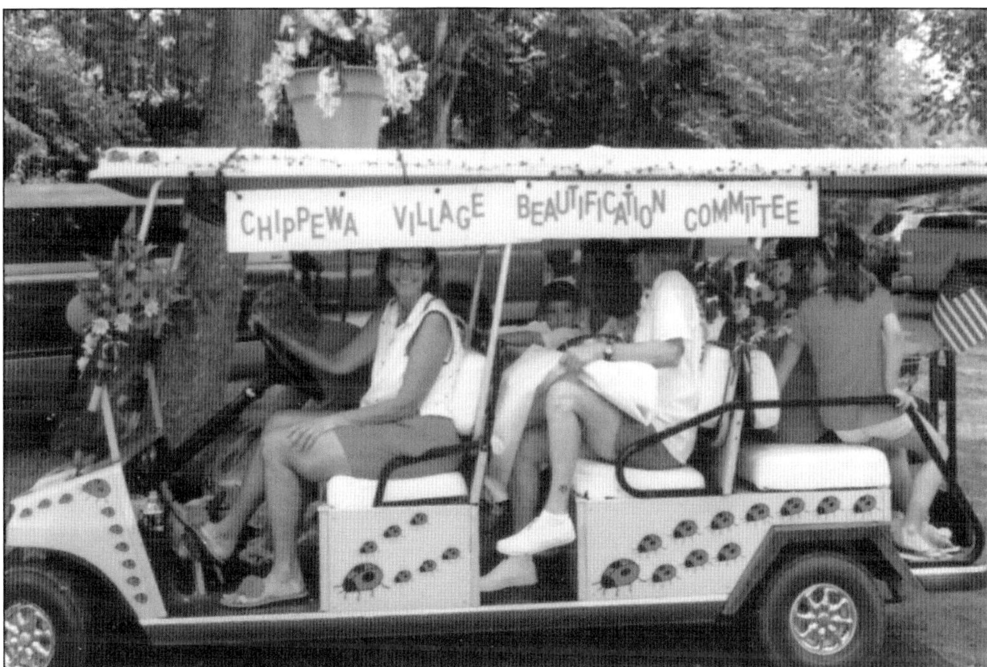

The Chippewa Village Beautification Committee, which later became the Chippewa Village Pride Program, made its appearance in the parade on July 4, 2008. This organization was formed by a small group of residents to encourage others to take pride in their community by beautifying Chippewa Lake. Contests are held in the summer for the nicest yards and in winter for the best Christmas light displays. (Chippewa Yacht Club.)

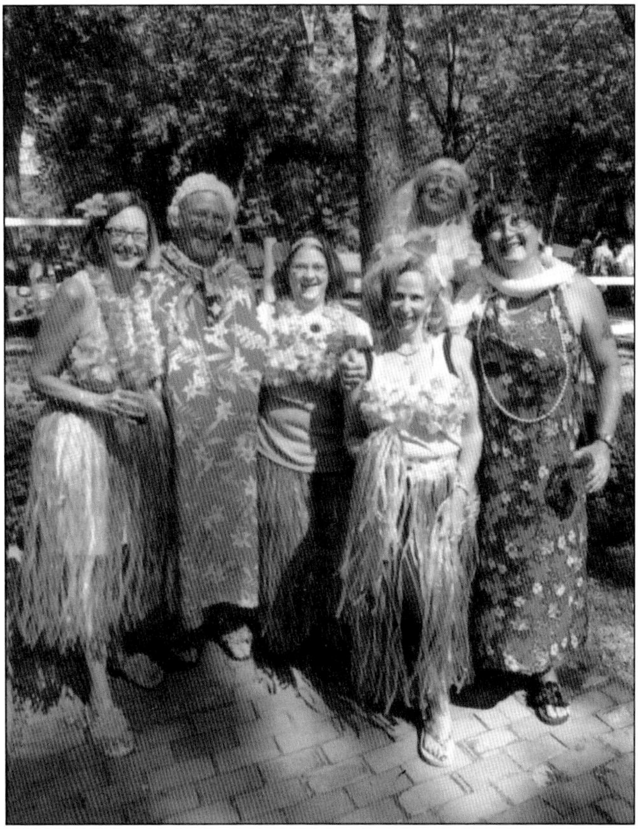

It seemed like a good reason for a party, so good friends (from left to right) Pam and Bob Williams, Mary and John Baker, and Sheila and Bob Denison threw a party in July 2008 to celebrate their 20 years as members of the Chippewa Yacht Club. (Chippewa Yacht Club.)

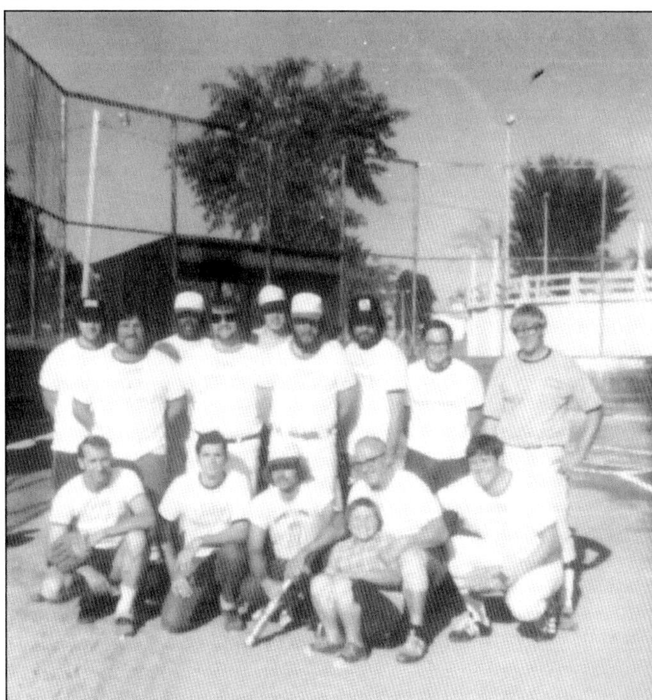

Leohr's Chrysler dealership in Chippewa Lake sponsored a slow-pitch softball team managed by Bill Baxter (front row, second from right). They won the Wadsworth Division championship in 1973. The team's home field was at the entrance to Chippewa Lake Park. (Gayle Baxter Foster.)

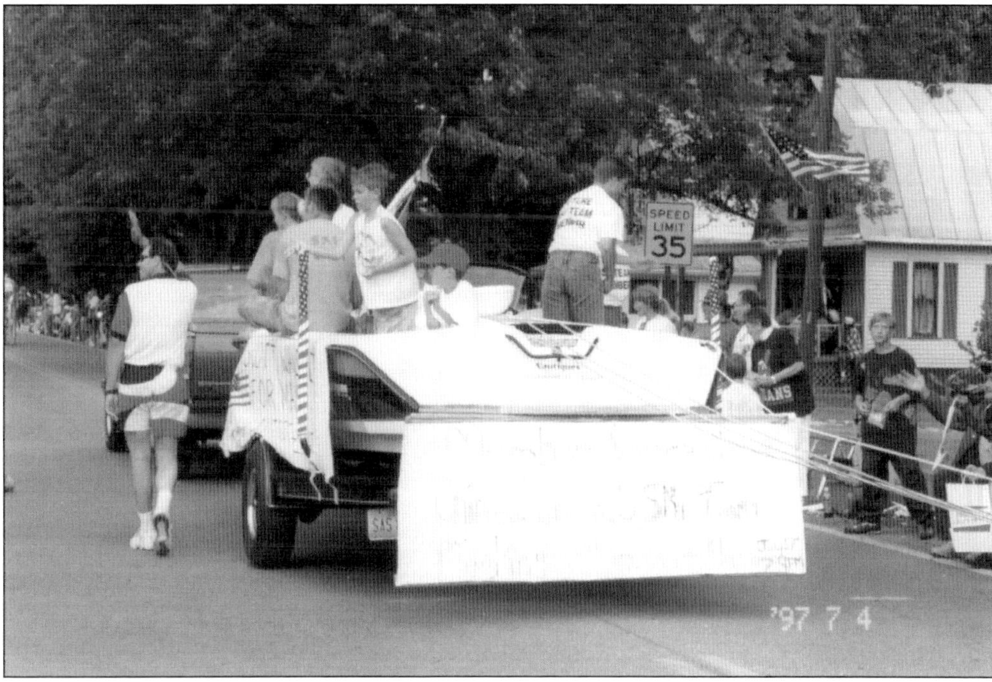

On July 4, 1997, recruiting was underway to revive the Chippewa Lake Water Ski Show Team. Scott Walchli and Tom Melter, former team members from the 1960s and 1970s, led the effort with a float in the Fourth of July parade. Walchli is shown walking next to the boat. Below is the back of the float with children who are already planning to participate on the new ski team. The team will celebrate the 20th anniversary of this revival in 2017. From left to right below are Chase Gregory, Zach Melter, unidentified, and T.J. Leahy. (Both, Scott Walchli.)

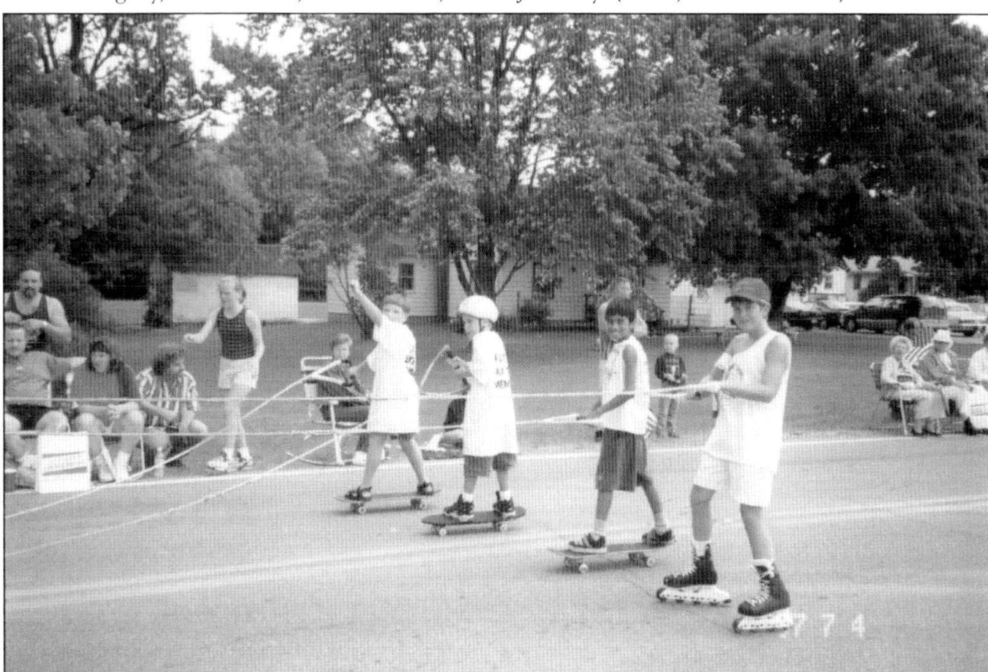

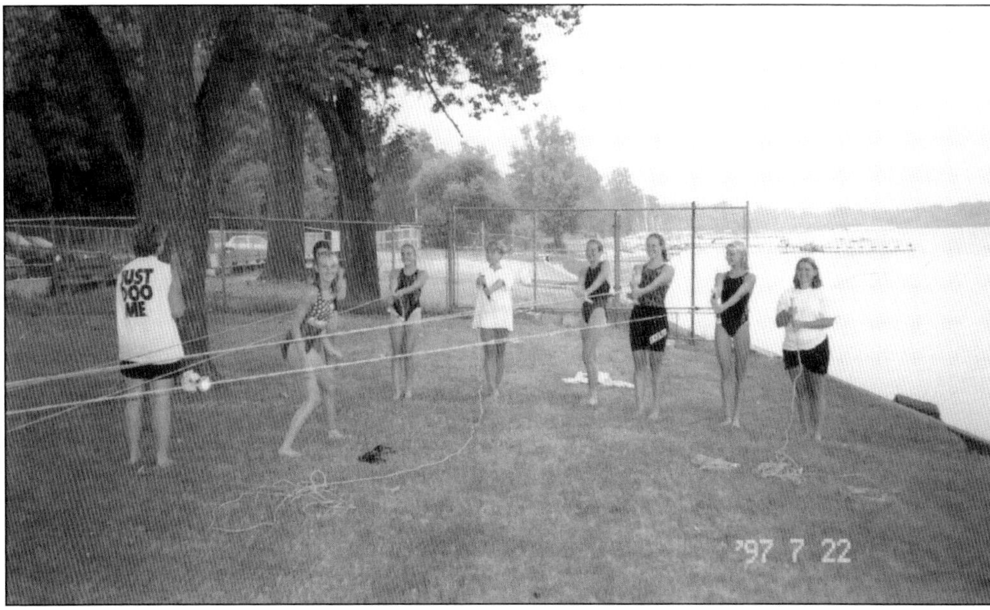

The first practice for the revived Chippewa Lake Water Ski Show Team took place on July 22, 1997. Their first full year was completed and their first competition took place in 1998 at the regional qualifier. They qualified for and won the Division II nationals in 2004 and have been competing in Division I since. This is the only competitive water ski team in Ohio. From left to right are Sue Snow, Toni Snow, unidentified, Jessica Wills, Tonya Cobb, Sarah Wills, Jenny Cochrane, Laura Armbruster, and Helle Knudsen. (Scott Walchli.)

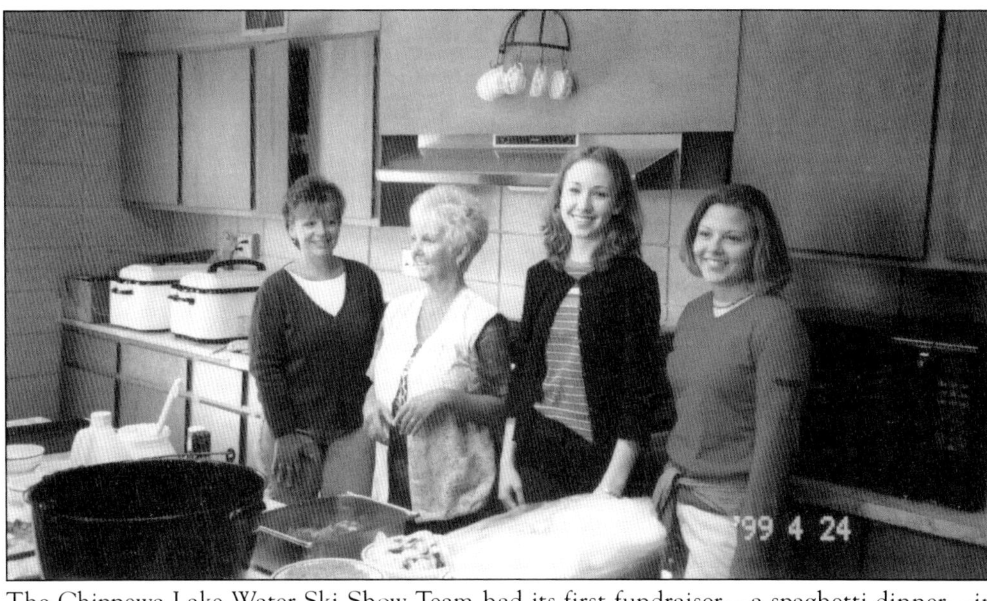

The Chippewa Lake Water Ski Show Team had its first fundraiser—a spaghetti dinner—in 1999. Since then, they have held an annual steak dinner during the summer at Emerald Lake in Norton, Ohio, and an auction each spring. Fundraisers would not be possible without the help of parents and grandparents and support from the community. Pictured from left to right are Cindy Cobb (ski mom), Garlene Gregoire (ski grandmother), and ski team members Jade Melter and Tonya Cobb. (Scott Walchli.)

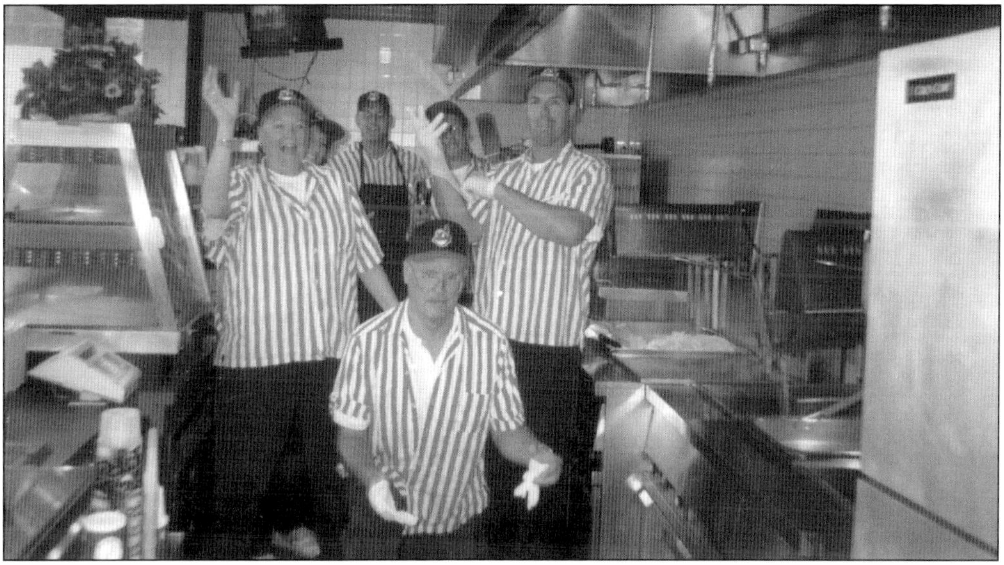

Becoming a member of the Chippewa Lake Water Ski Show Team not only offered an opportunity to learn how to ski, it taught life lessons and leadership skills, led to a couple of marriages, and even produced professional skiers who now work at Sea World. Helping make that happen at a fundraiser at the Cleveland Indians' stadium in 1999 are, from left to right, (first row) Gary Fowls; (second row) Cheryl Walchli and Scott Walchli; (third row) Karen Fowls, Eric Langenfeld, and William Adamczyk. (Scott Walchli.)

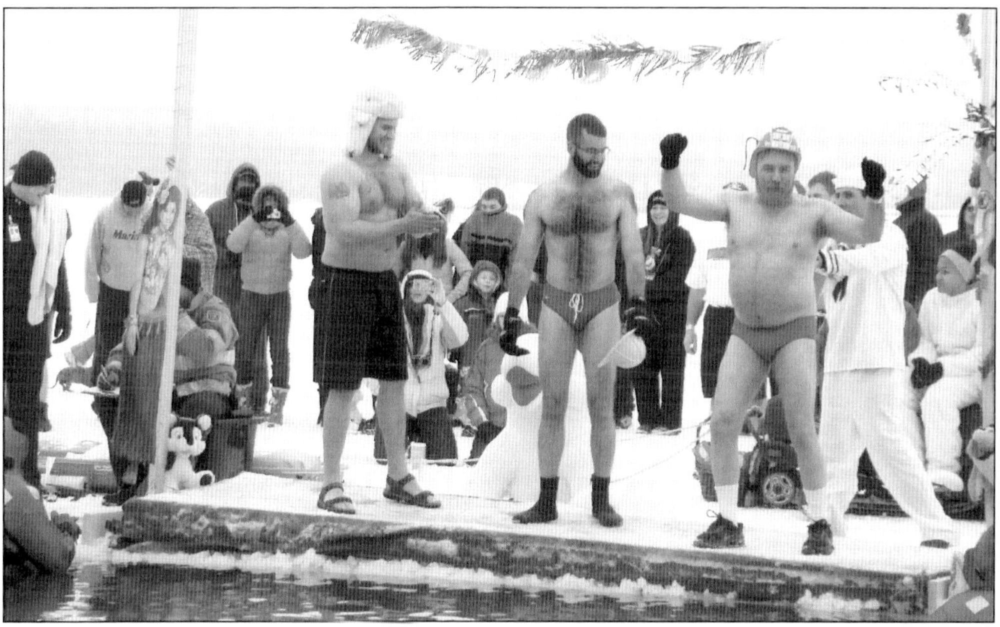

Every January, members of the local fire department cut a large hole in the ice of Chippewa Lake for those who dare to jump in as a fundraiser for local services such as food pantries, churches, and the Lions Club. Jumpers go into the water individually or as a team. The Polar Bear Jump is preceded by a 5K run/walk. Participants are encouraged to obtain sponsors in addition to paying their entry fees. Pictured at the 2011 jump are, from left to right, Brian Ryncarz, Chippewa Lake fireman Adam Nilson, and Scott Romanoff. (Amber Dalakas.)

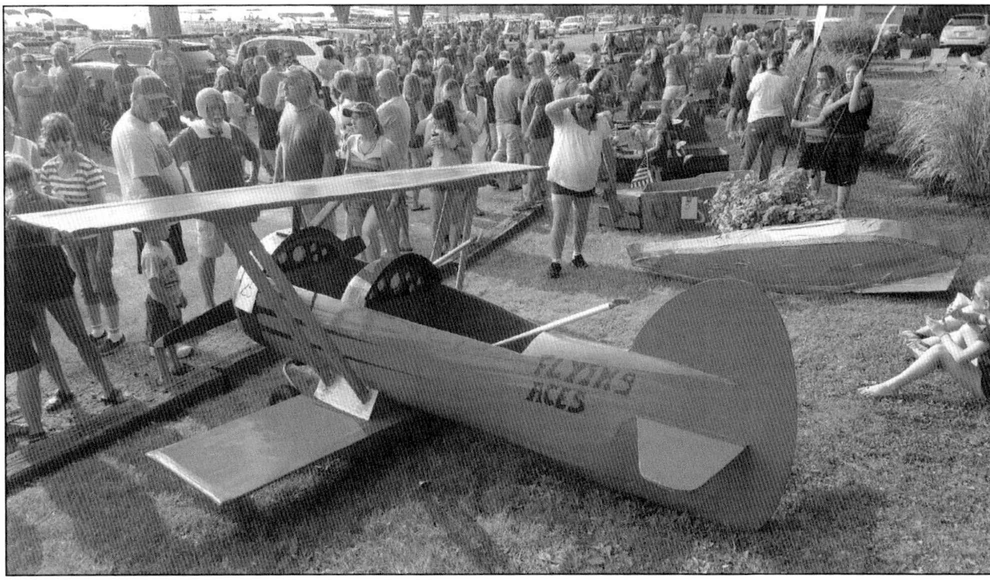

The Chippewa Village Pride Program began sponsoring the Cardboard Boat Race in 2010. It is now a highly anticipated Fourth of July event, with hundreds of people flocking to the beach area to watch the race. Above is Bud Hardesty and his son-in-law Chris Ryk's airplane entry, *Flying Aces*, in 2015. Pictured below at the 2013 event are Jim Christenson (right) and his children Jack and Alex. Jim won the race in 2015 with his recycled boat, *Second Time Around*, from the 2014 race. (Above, Sharon Sefl Karhan; below, Amber Dalakas.)

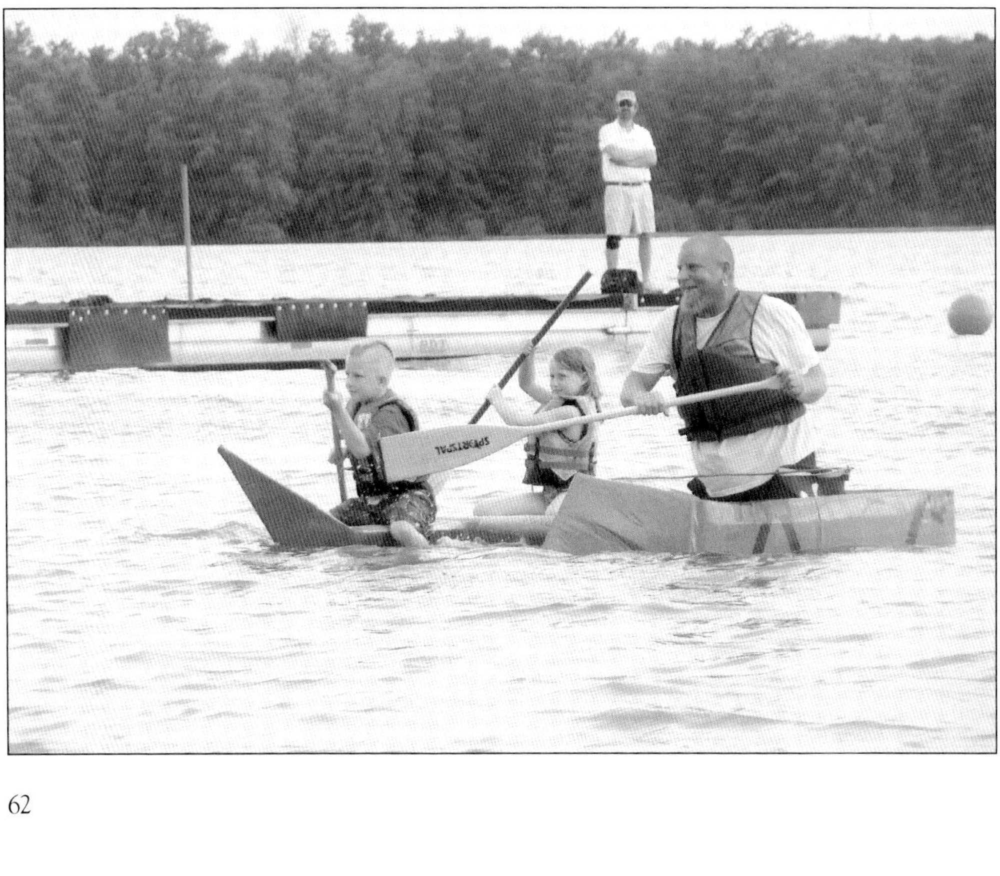

Four

FAMILIES

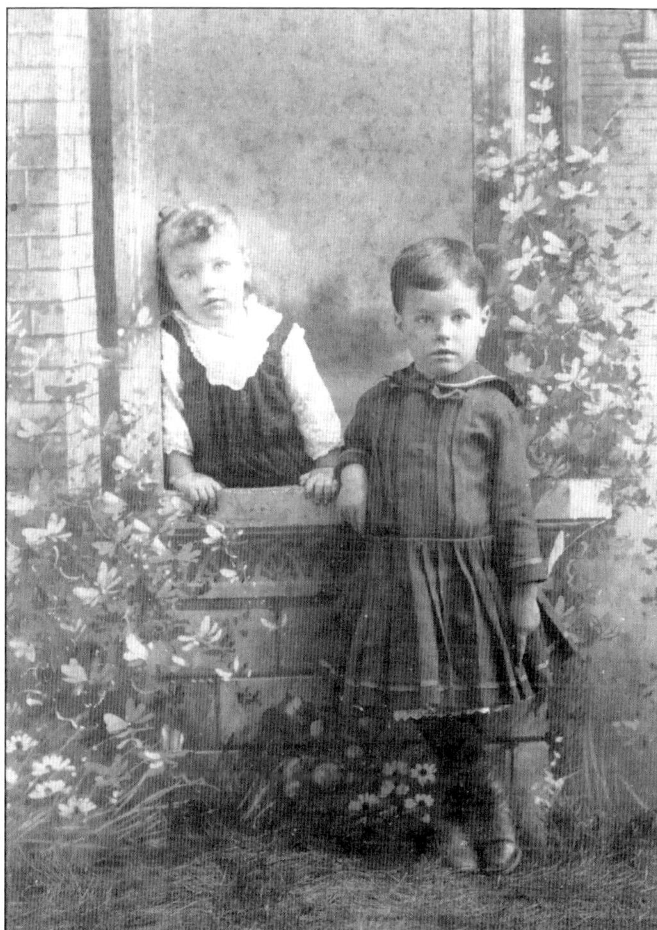

Clara Barrett was born in Chippewa Lake in 1867 to Joseph H. and Margaret Barrett. Their farm was located on present-day Lake Road south of Chippewa Road in what would eventually become the early "grove." Clara married Sam Palmer at age 16 in 1882. Their two children, Roy (right) and Relia, are pictured here. Clara and Sam Palmer divorced in 1889, and she married Gideon Markle in 1890. Clara's father, Joseph, claimed that the first public gathering took place on July 4, 1847, just north of the future Andrews Pleasure Grounds. A group from Canaan Township in Wayne County came to celebrate Independence Day on the banks of Chippewa Lake. Joseph Barrett, an accommodating man, brought his old hewed-out log canoe so that the group might enjoy rides on the lake. (Helen Riehm.)

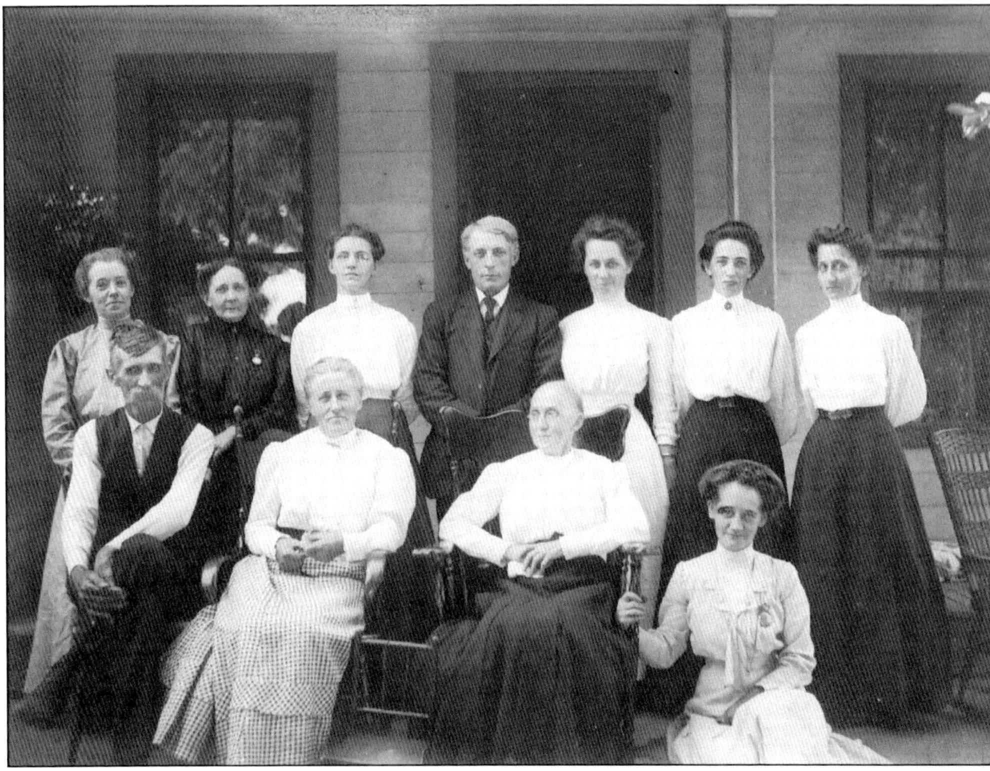

The Barrett family is pictured at T. Sherman Barrett's house on the north side of Chippewa Road just west of the railroad tracks at 5759 Chippewa Road. Pictured are Clara Barrett Palmer Markle (second row, far left) and her brother Sherman (second row, center). (Helen Riehm.)

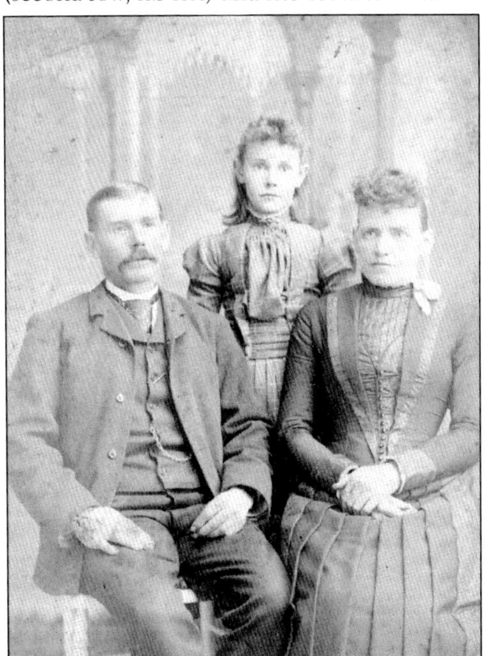

Nathan Harper worked for the railroad. Each day, he would pass through Seville and see a beautiful girl, Delilah Jane "Jennie" McCabe, brushing out her long hair on the steps of the restaurant near the tracks. Harper told his coworkers that he would marry that beautiful girl. One day, he asked the conductor to slow down so he could meet his future wife, and he did. She ran inside, he followed, and she had to wait on him. After doing this a few times, he proposed, and she accepted. Jennie's mother, Harriet Morton McCabe, wife of Allen McCabe, was not happy and called Nathan a "dandy." Nathan and Jennie married, and the family remained estranged for years. After Jennie died, Nathan died eight months later, it is told, of a broken heart. Jennie is pictured here with her parents, Allen and Harriet. (McDonald family.)

Mabel Delight Harper, pictured here with her husband, Robert McDonald, and their daughter Roberta (Humble), was one of several children of Jennie and Nathan Harper. Their house, one of the first wooden homes built in Chippewa Lake, was located on Chippewa Road. Many children who grew up in the area remember sledding on McDonald Hill. (McDonald family.)

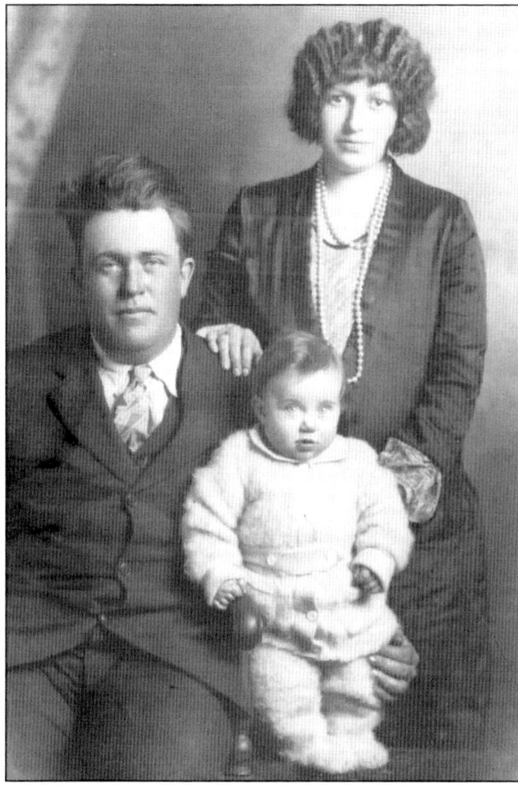

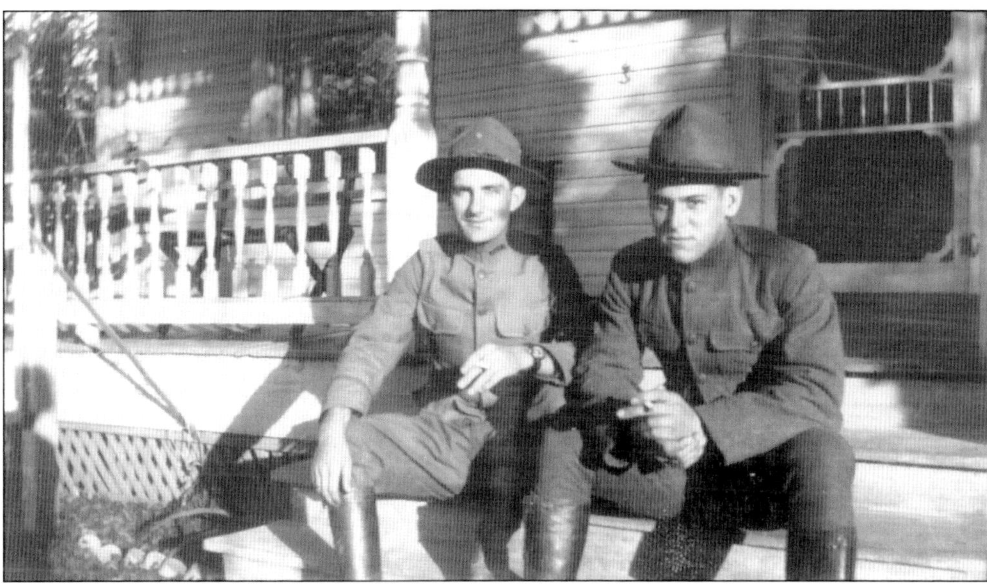

Romy Reese Laughlin (left) was born in Chippewa Lake in 1891. He graduated from veterinary school at the University of Toronto and went on to serve in World War I as a second lieutenant working with cavalry medical corps horses in the Army Veterinary Corps. He started one of the first small-animal clinics in the Chagrin Valley. His practice was not limited to small animals, though, and he was a very successful cattle and horse veterinarian. He was the son of Thomas and Minnie Reese Laughlin. (Lorinda Laughlin.)

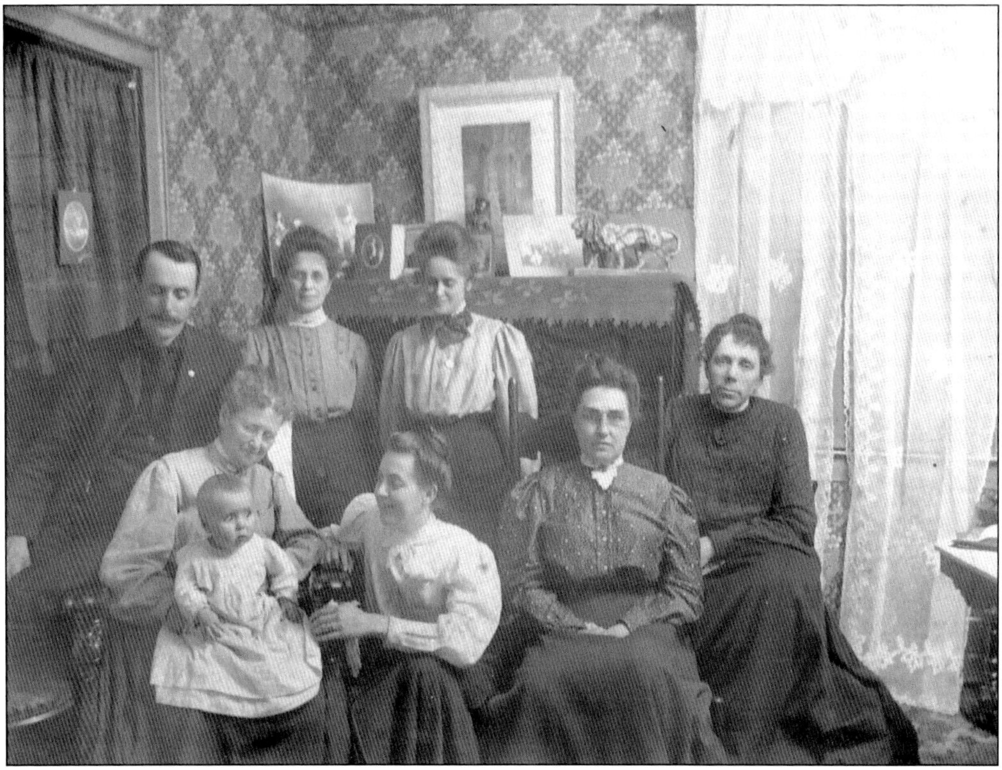

The Beach family is pictured here in December 1905, shortly after their arrival in Chippewa Lake. They are, from left to right, (first row) Parker Beach (eight months old and held by his grandmother Margaret McDowell Beach), Bertha Beach, and two unidentified; (second row) Albert McDowell "Mac" Beach and two unidentified. (Beach family.)

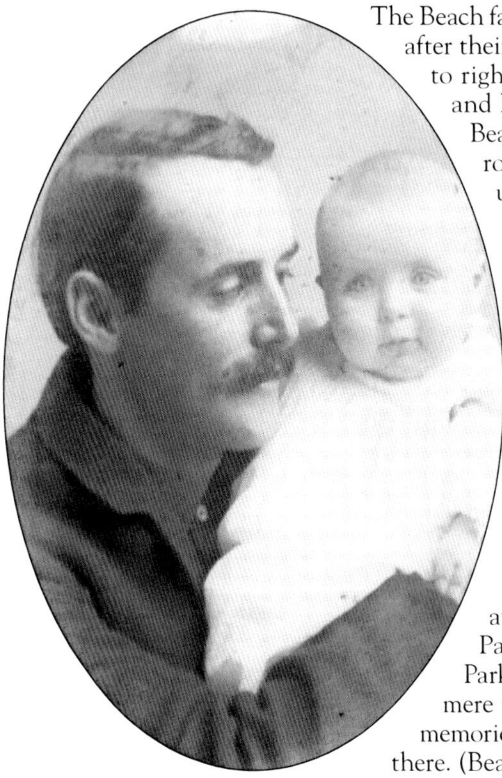

Albert McDowell "Mac" Beach is shown holding his young son A. Parker Beach in 1905. What began as a job at a fledgling "pleasure resort" for Mac would turn into a lifelong love affair and passion for Parker. First Mac and then Parker would go on to develop Chippewa Lake Park into a place that touched the lives of many. A mere mention of the park can elicit a smile and fond memories that come flooding back to those who visited there. (Beach family.)

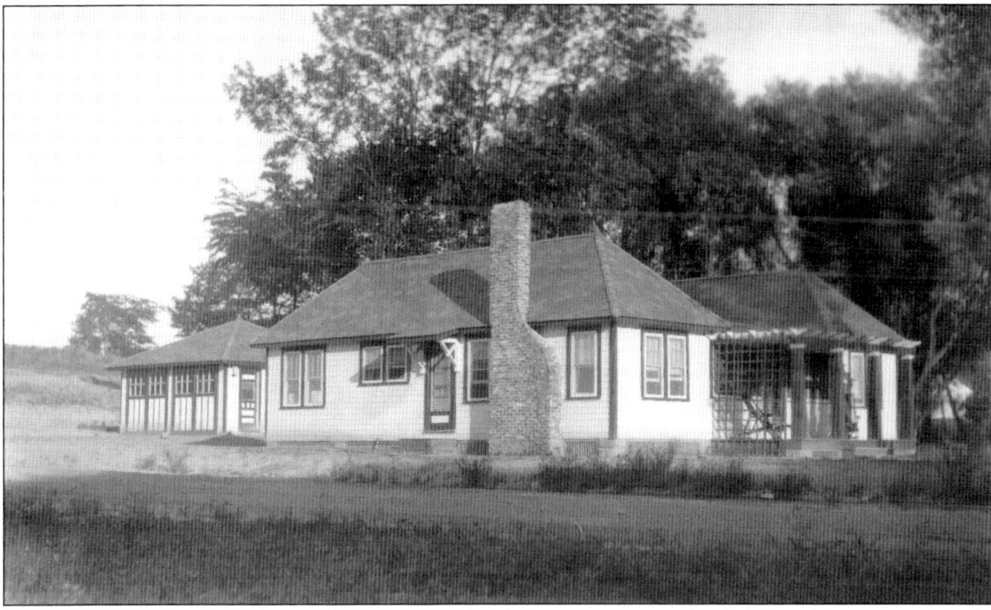

This is an early photograph of the Pojman cottage at 242 Clover Cliff Drive at Beachside Boulevard on the lakefront. It was built by a man named Gove, who made his living in oil. Joseph F. and Cecilia (Krbec) Pojman purchased the cottage in 1942 and are pictured at right. Their son James and his wife, Eleanor, own the cottage today. This was one of the early cottages built in Chippewa Lake, and was originally painted white with red trim. (Both, James and Eleanor Pojman.)

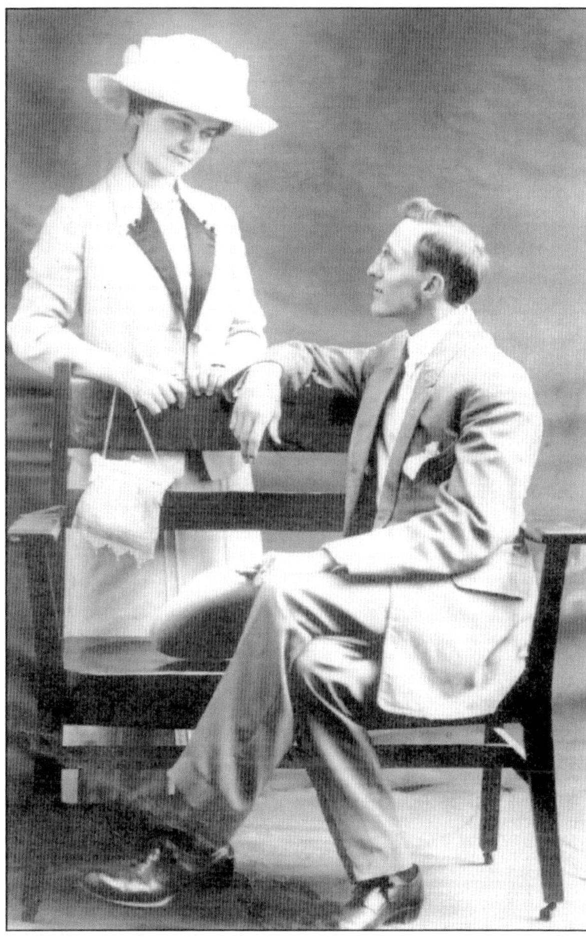

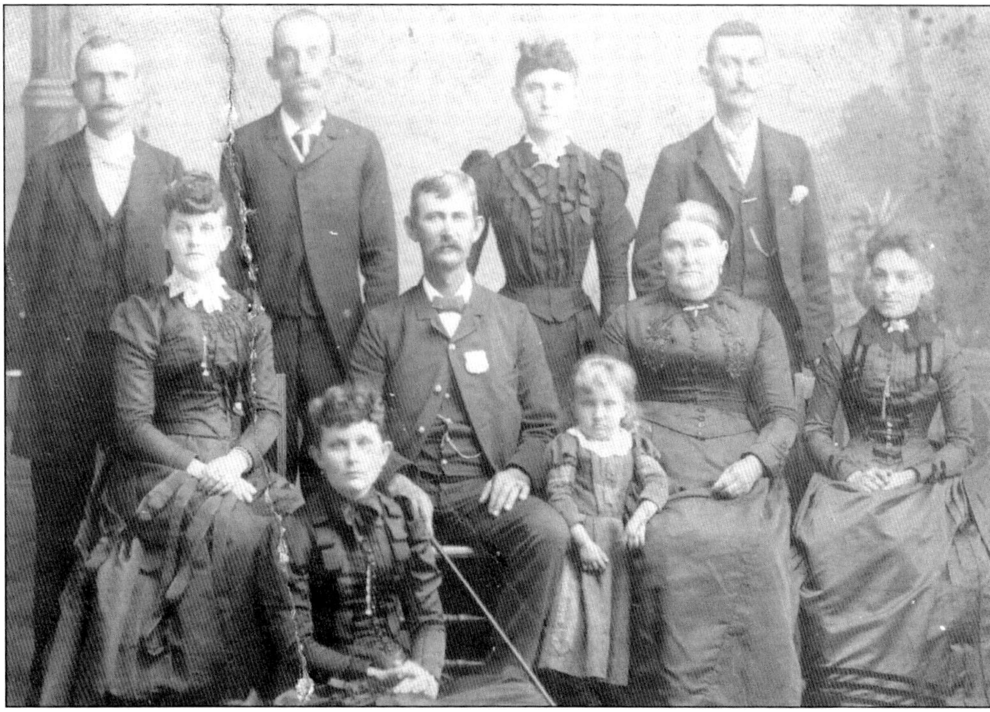

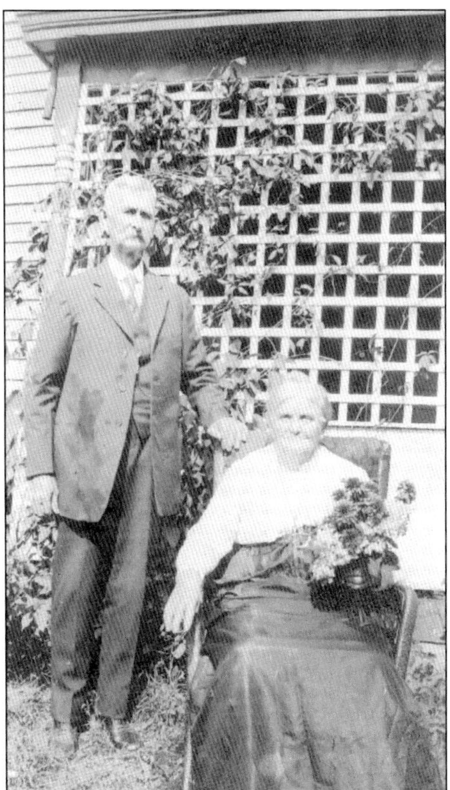

The Reese family, pictured here in 1890, included, from left to right, (first row) Maggie Reese (daughter) and unidentified; (second row) Jeannette Reese (daughter), Newton N. Reese (father), Maria Beck Reese (mother), and Josephine C. Erhart Reese (wife of Melville); (third row) two unidentified, Minnie Reese (daughter), and Melville Reese (son). Newton Reese was the first owner of the Tiles Works in Chippewa Lake in 1884, selling his interest in the company to the firm Rickard and Nye in 1885. Newton Reese had many pursuits, including his Chestnut Grove Park in Chippewa Lake, which mainly catered to church groups and small reunions—it never offered any real competition for Chippewa Lake Park. (Lorinda Laughlin.)

Newton N. and Maria Beck Reese are pictured here at their 55th anniversary celebration in 1920. Their four children, along with their families and friends, were present to enjoy a special dinner on the lawn. Newton was born in Sharon Township in Medina County and eventually settled in Chippewa Lake. Newton held a large tract of land in Chippewa Lake that is still known as Reese's Grove. (Lorinda Laughlin.)

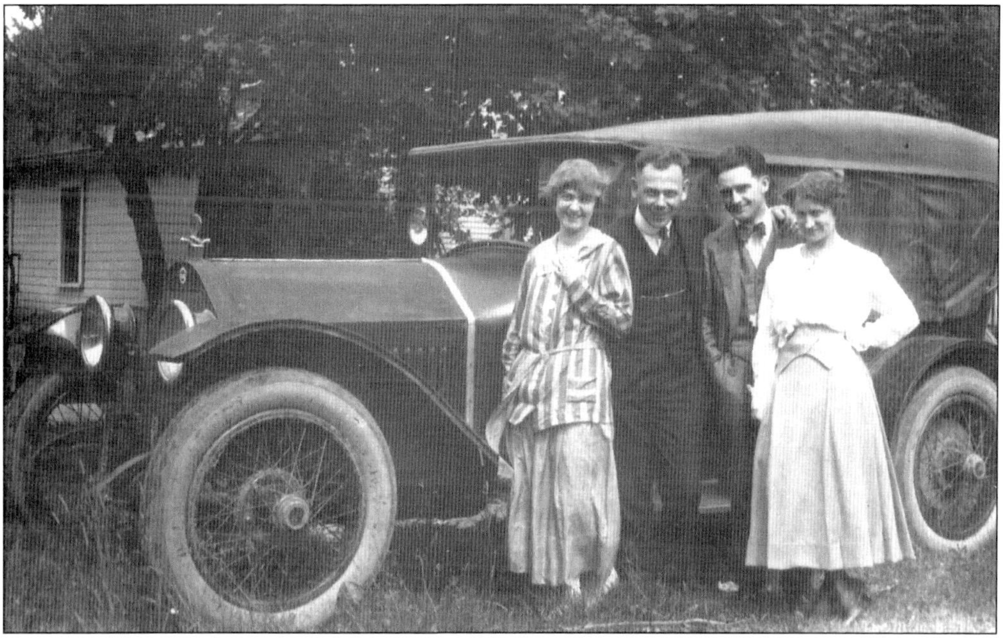

Ralph Ivory Bostwick, a native of Seville, Ohio, and Bernice Stoaks were married on January 1, 1918. Ralph descended from the prominent Bostwick family of New York and Pennsylvania. Pictured here with Ralph's Stutz Bearcat are, from left to right, Emma Bostwick (Ralph's mother), Ralph, Charlie Stoaks (Bernice's brother), and Bernice. The couple built their home in 1920 on the Bungalow Bay circle overlooking Chippewa Lake just north of the Townsend estate. Ralph was an attorney, engineer, and a brilliant mathematician who worked on the Manhattan Project in Oak Ridge, Tennessee, during World War II. (Jeffrey Schmitt.)

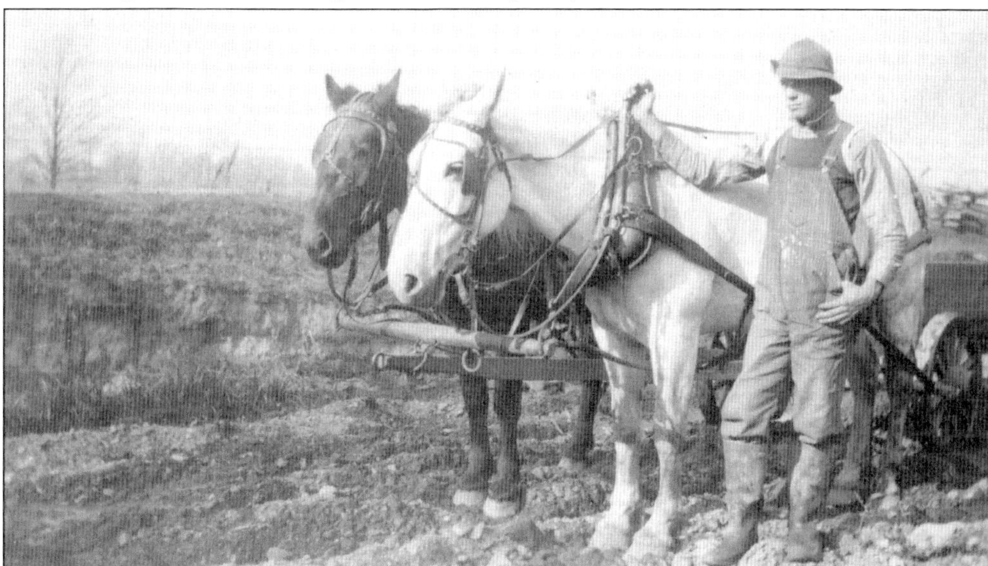

Milton George Ruder was born in Chippewa Lake in 1898 to William M. and Katherine Ruder; he was one of 10 children. His grandparents emigrated from Germany and settled in Berea. He attended the two-room Chippewa Lake schoolhouse and worked on his family's farm on Chippewa Road just west of the Inlet. He spent his entire life in the Chippewa area. (Jeffrey Schmitt.)

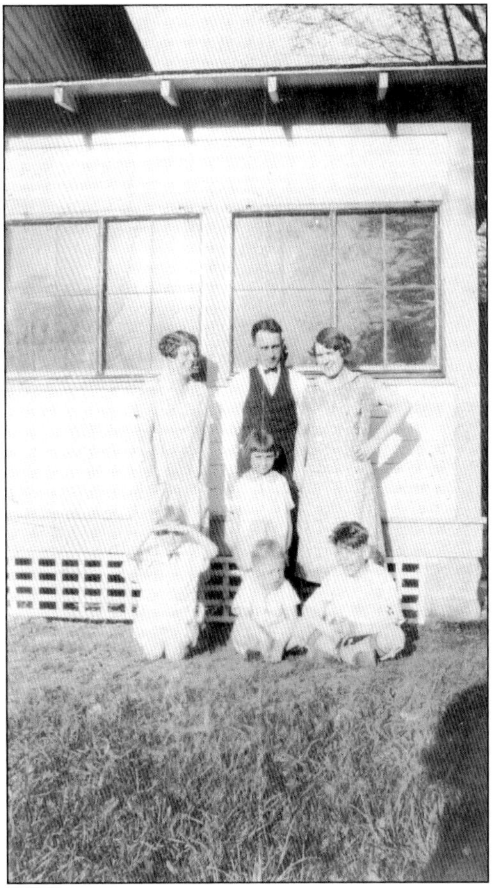

Esther Grubb is standing at left with her friends Irvin (center) and Dorothy Morris. Betty Morris is standing behind the Grubb children, from left to right, Vivian, Glenn, and "Herbie." The group was visiting Bert and Esther Grubb's cottage on Parkway Path around 1929. (Barbara Grubb Whitlam.)

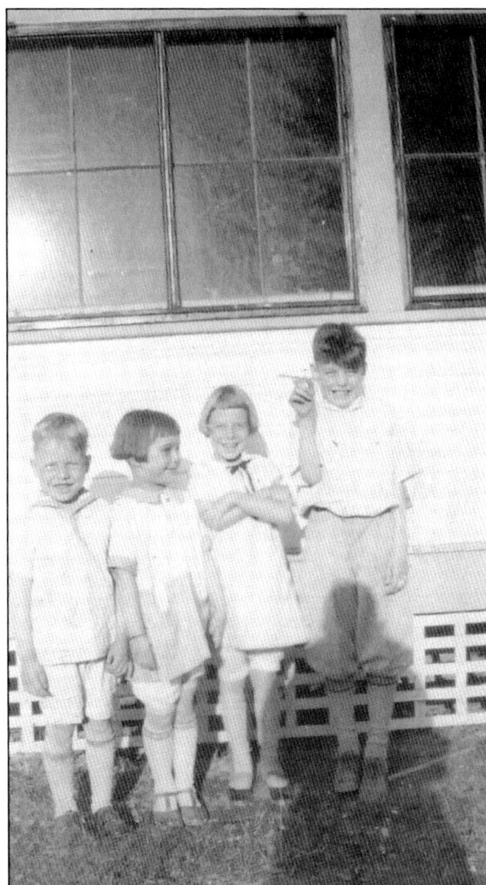

Pictured in front of Bert and Esther Grubb's cottage at 12 Parkway Path are, from left to right, Glenn W. Grubb, Betty Morris (family friend), Vivian E. Grubb, and "Herbie" P. Grubb at Chippewa-on-the-Lake in 1929. Many Cleveland families summered at Chippewa Lake. (Barbara Grubb Whitlam.)

Mere days before his wedding in June 1930, Parker Beach, age 25, penned this letter to Janet Klove, his betrothed, after a long day of work at the park. He shared his anticipation for their future together and how much he loved and missed her. Plans were made for his duties to be handled during his absence, and he looked forward to their homecoming to Chippewa Lake Park as husband and wife. Their marriage spanned 62 years, although according to all who knew them, their love for one another was timeless. (Beach family.)

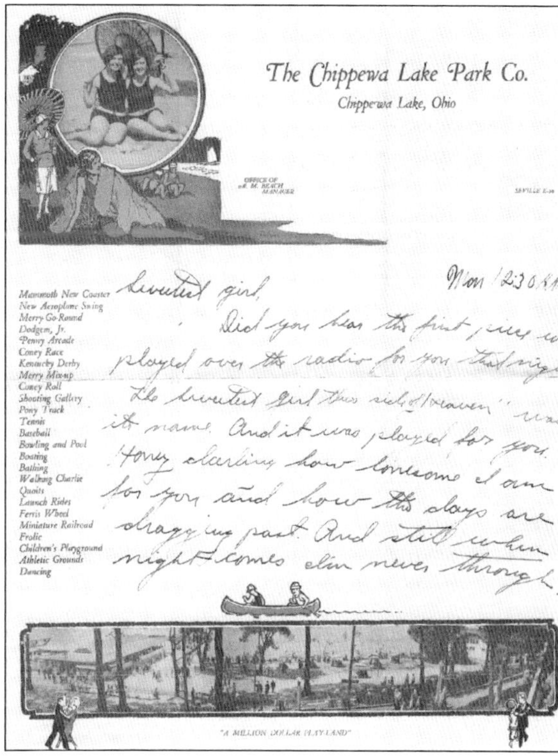

The Chippewa Lake Park Co.
Chippewa Lake, Ohio

OFFICE OF
M. BEACH
MANAGER

Mammoth New Coaster
New Aeroplane Swing
Merry-Go-Round
Dodgem, Jr.
Penny Arcade
Coney Race
Kentucky Derby
Merry Mix-up
Coney Roll
Shooting Gallery
Pony Track
Tennis
Baseball
Bowling and Pool
Boating
Bathing
Walking Charlie
Quoits
Launch Rides
Ferris Wheel
Miniature Railroad
Frolic
Children's Playground
Athletic Grounds
Dancing

Mon 12:30 AM

Sweetest girl,

Did you hear the first piece we played over the radio for you tonight "The Sweetest Girl this side of Heaven" was its name. And it was played for you. Honey darling how lonesome I am for you and how the days are dragging past. And still when night comes I'm never through.

"A MILLION DOLLAR PLAYLAND"

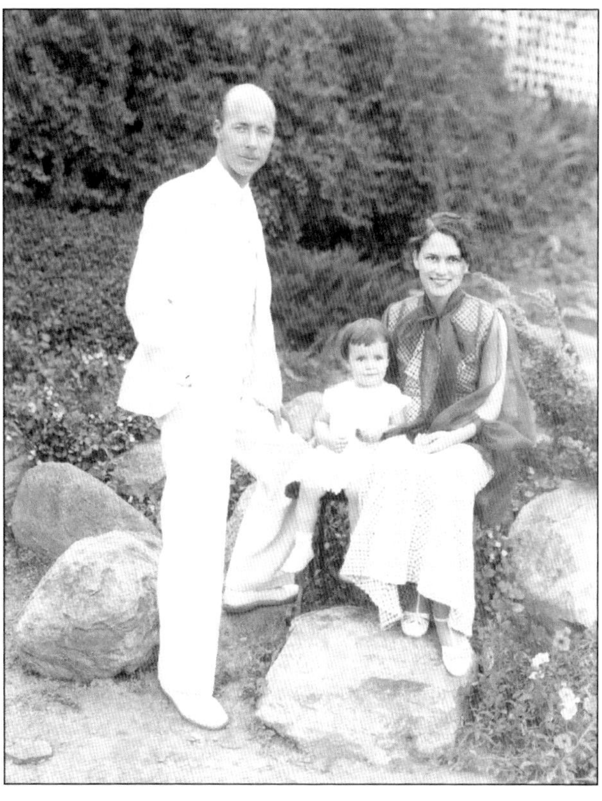

The Beach family poses on Labor Day in 1934 near the hill by Stand A. At the time, the United States was in the throngs of the Great Depression, and the park was not without its troubles. This was the year that Chippewa Lake Park Company went into receivership. Parker Beach is pictured with his wife, Janet, who is holding their daughter Lynn. (Beach family.)

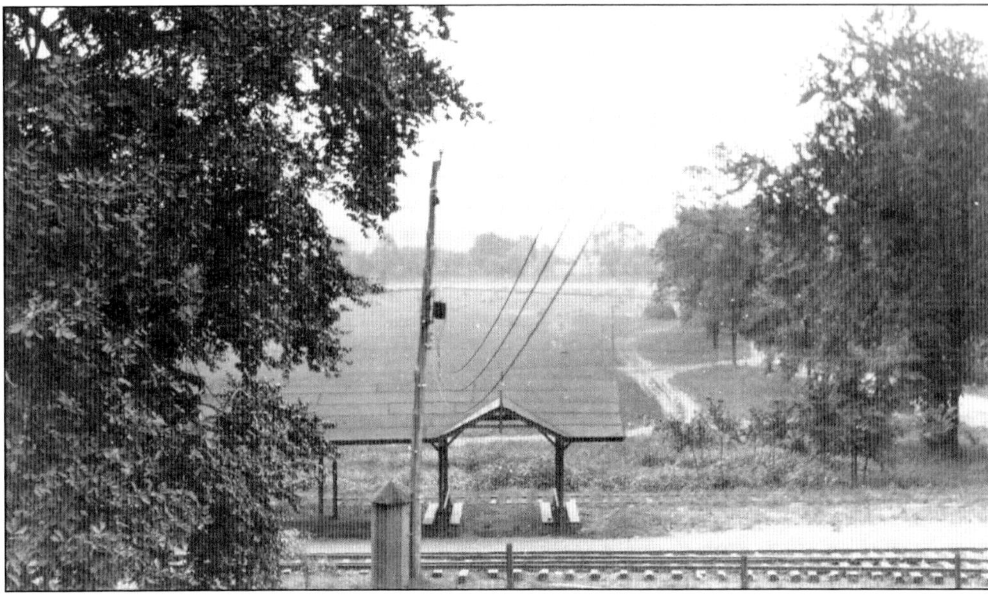

The decline of ridership on the Cleveland & Southwestern Interurban resulted in revenues dropping 50 percent in 1929, which sent the company into receivership. It was becoming more difficult to compete with the automobile in addition to dealing with decreasing revenues and increasing costs. With the entire country immersed in the Depression, the Green Line made its last trip on February 28, 1931—a change that would greatly affect the Beach family and Chippewa Lake Park. (Beach family.)

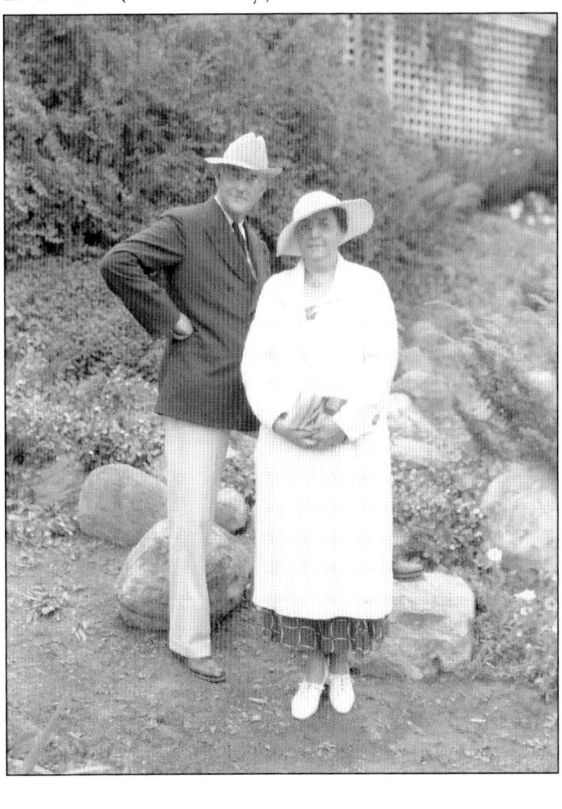

Albert McDowell "Mac" Beach was the son of a prominent Seville physician, Dr. Albert Platt Beach, and his wife, Margaret. Mac had worked as a painter, cigar maker, and salesman before he was pursued by Chippewa Lake owners and partners Oscar Townsend and W.H. Hawley; Beach joined the management team in 1898. While he was inexperienced in resort management, he proved to be a key factor in the development of Chippewa Lake Park. A quick study, Mac leased the Lower Grounds around 1900 and began redevelopment, implementing strict bans on liquor and bad behavior. As the Lower Grounds became more popular, the competing Upper Grounds' popularity faded. In 1921, Mac, along with several other investors, formed the Chippewa Lake Park Company, purchasing the lake and the resort area. Albert "Mac" Beach and his wife, Bertha, are pictured near Stand A on Labor Day in 1934. (Beach family.)

Fred Beach (left) and his niece Lynn were quite close. They are pictured near the Chippewa Lake Park pier in 1939. (Stephenson collection.)

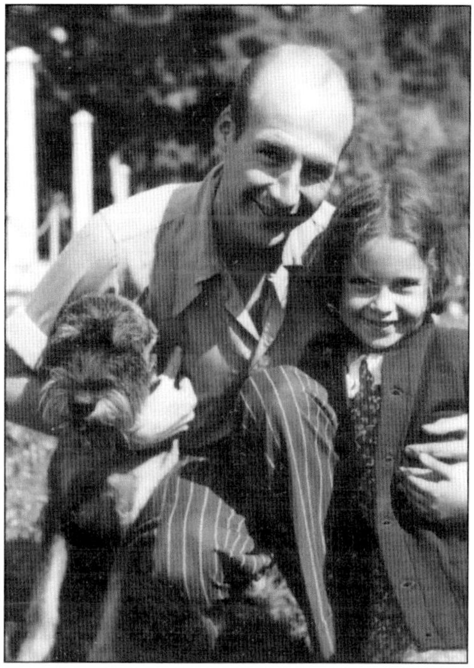

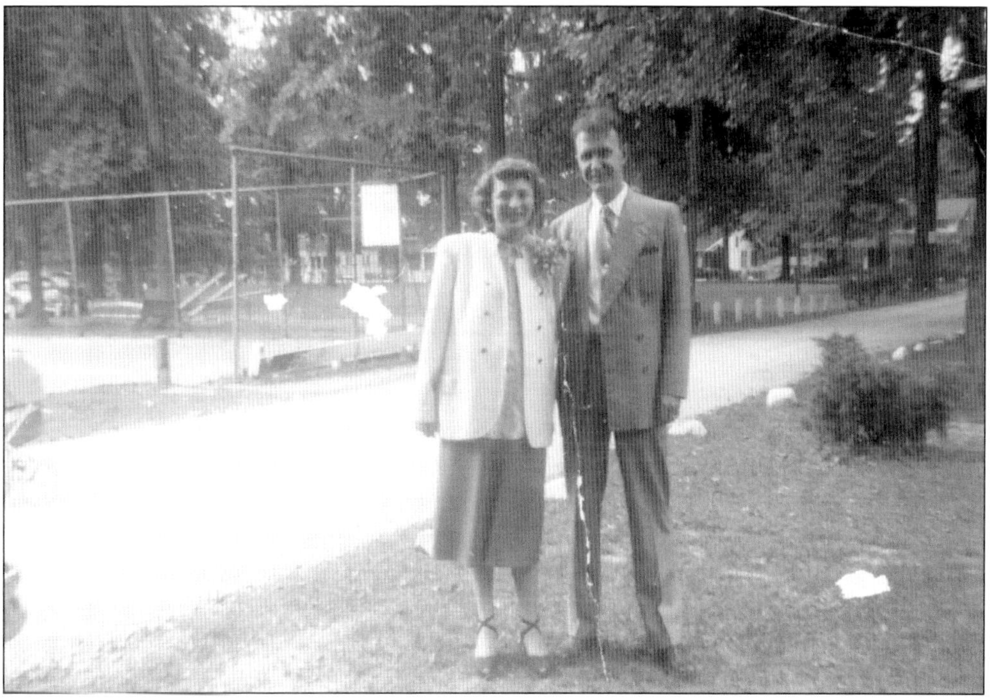

Over the years, Chippewa Lake became a special place for celebrations, including family birthdays, weddings, anniversaries, ice cream socials, or just an opportunity to get together with family on a Sunday afternoon. Here, Ralph and LaVerne Sefl are arriving at their cottage at Bungalow Bay Boulevard to spend their honeymoon night in 1950. Ralph purchased the cottage from Cleo Losh in 1942. Many folks drive through this area to reminisce about their memories of the past, while others come to enjoy the beauty of Chippewa today. (Sharon Sefl Karhan.)

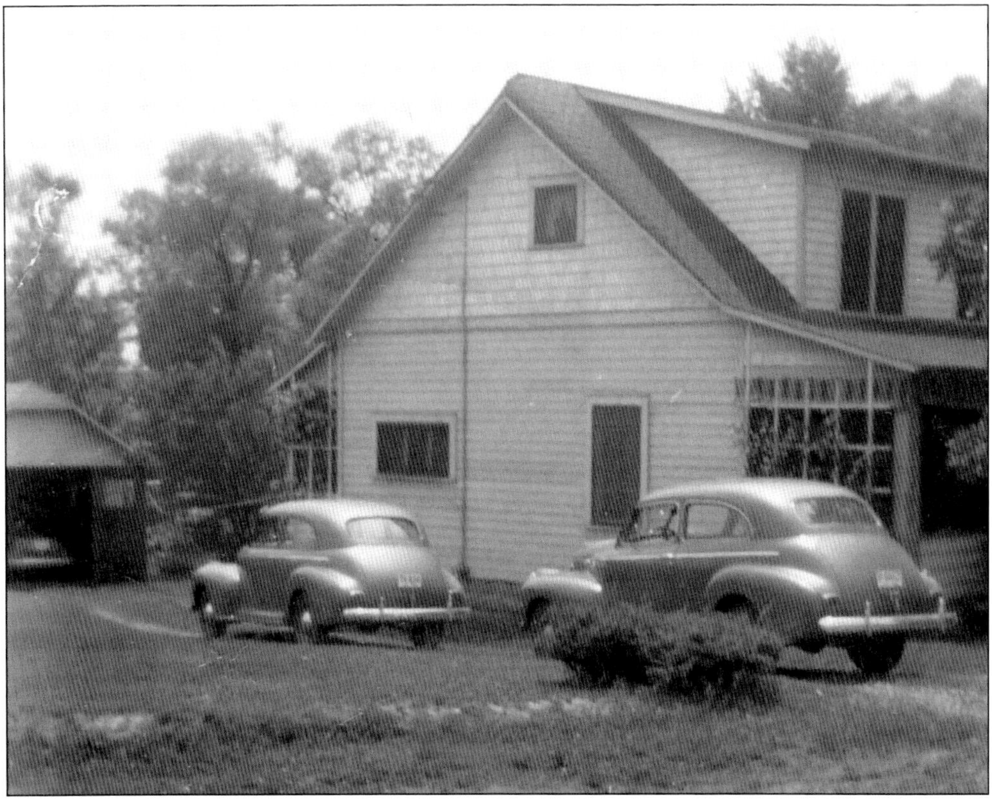

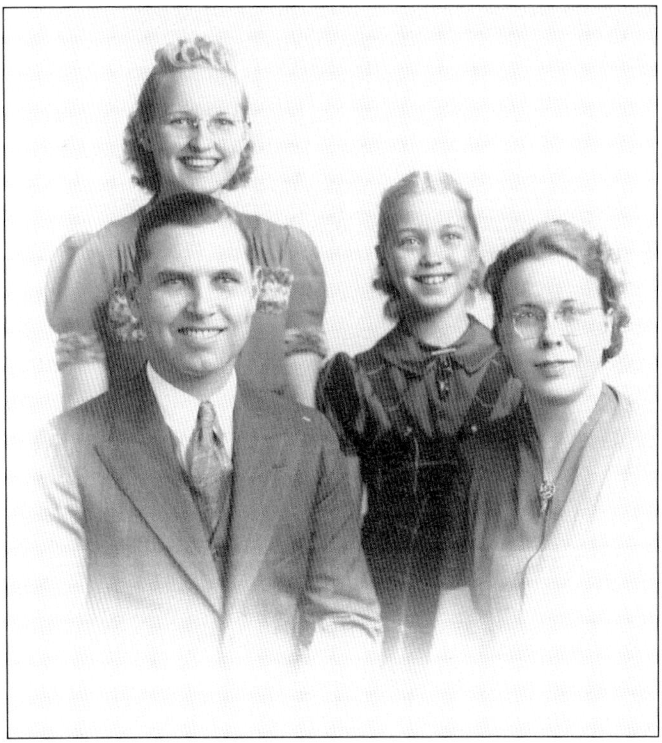

Clyde and Cornelia Dague purchased this cottage at 229 Willow Wood Drive in 1941. They heated the cottage with a potbelly stove that they affectionately called "Myrtle." They later upgraded to a furnace in 1946, when they made the cottage their full-time residence. Cornelia lived here until 1985. Clyde and Cornelia and their daughters Janet (left) and Shirley are pictured at left in 1939. (Jim Favri.)

Pictured at their home at 64 Bungalow Bay Boulevard during the summer of 1950 are, from left to right, siblings Jim, Jerry, and Julie Favri. They lived here until their parents, Clyde and Janet Favri, built a home on Beachside Boulevard. (Jim Favri.)

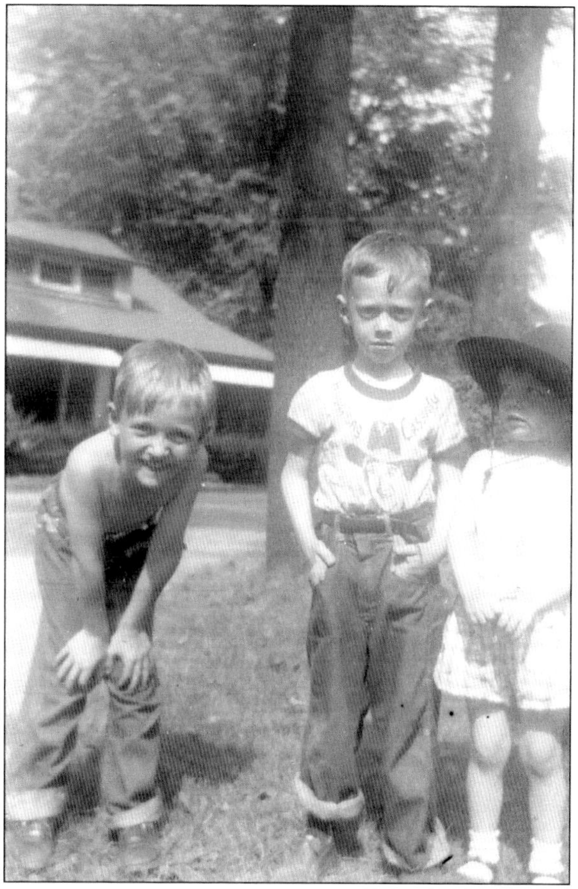

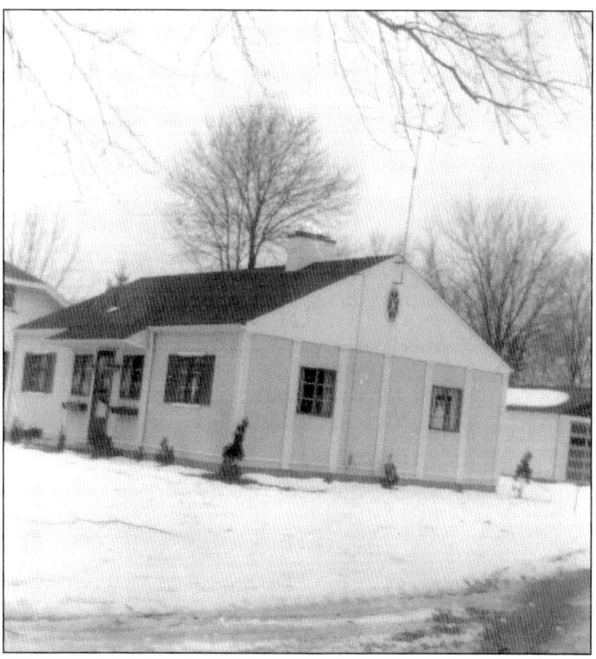

This Gunnison home, built in 1950 by Robert and Janet Dague Favri, is located at 250 Beachside Boulevard. Gunnison homes were unique for having a distinctive metal chimney that made them easily identifiable. They were quite popular after World War II, as they were affordable, well built, and could be erected in a relatively short span of time. (Jim Favri.)

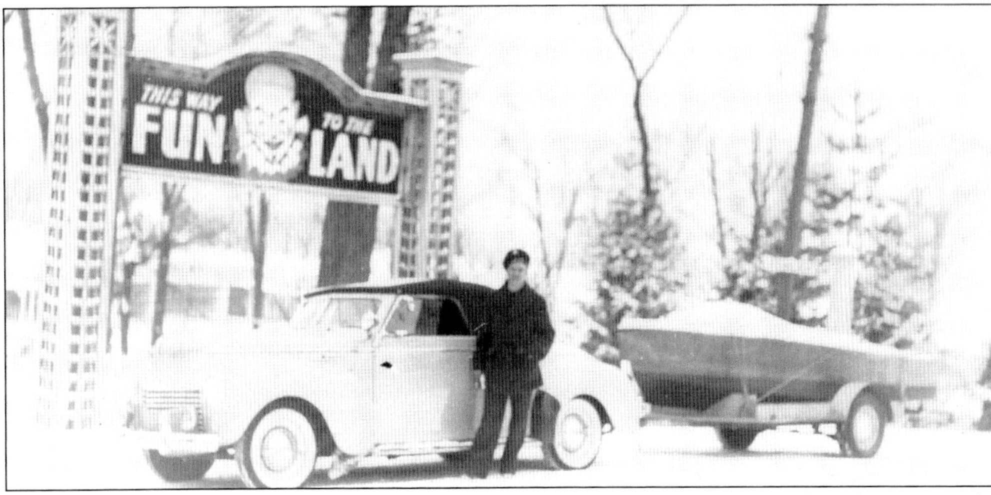

Williard "Steve" Stephenson's family was from Zanesville, Ohio. He first arrived in Chippewa Lake in 1933 after graduating from college in 1932. He bought his first cottage at 105 Euclid Avenue, later purchasing a home on Beachside Boulevard. Steve is shown here in 1940 heading off on his annual trip to Florida. (Stephenson collection.)

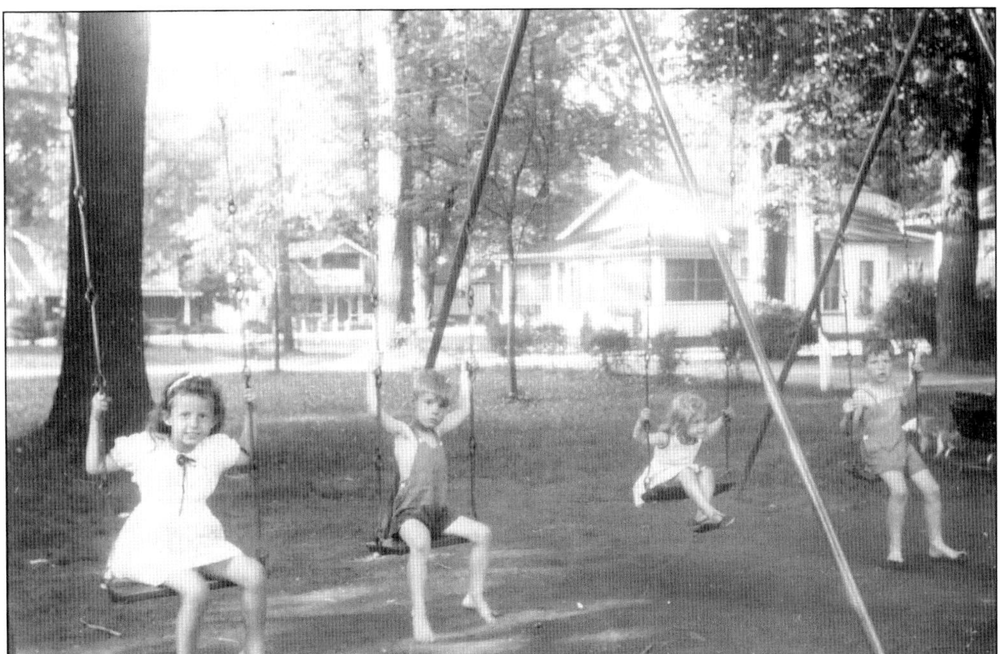

From left to right, cousins Gayle Baxter, Jeff Grubb, Nancy Grubb, and Chad Grubb spent many hours on the playground on the Bungalow Bay circle during the 1950s. The park and tennis courts are encircled by Bungalow Bay Boulevard. The swings consisted of hard wooden seats and metal rods before the chains and flexible rubber seats of later years. (Gayle Baxter Foster.)

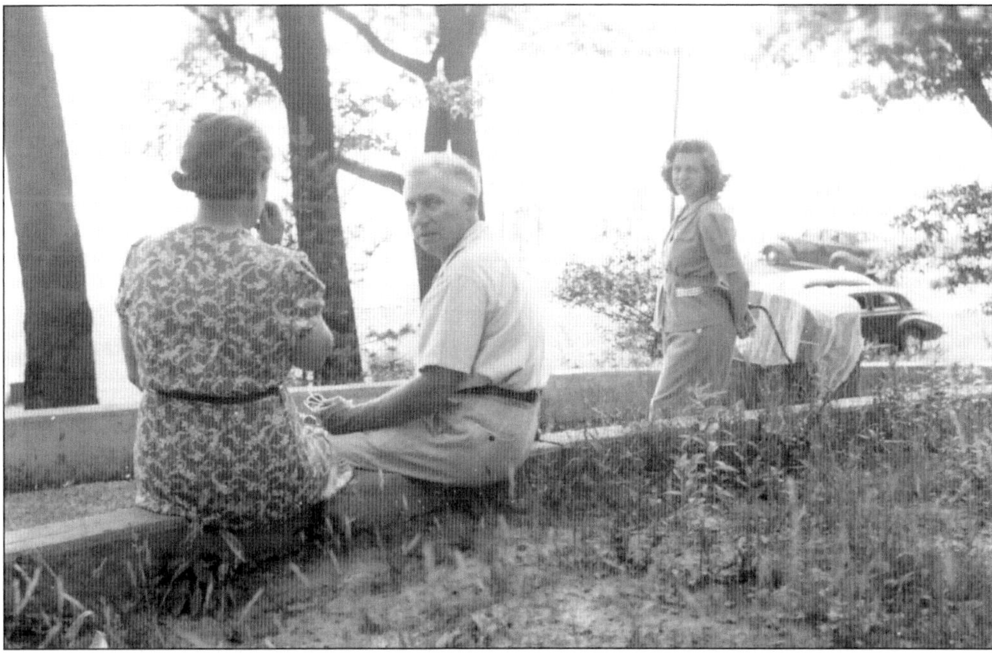

Esther (left) and Bert Grubb, cottage owners at Chippewa-on-the-Lake, sit on the stone wall of the ramp leading to the beach while they await their daughter Vivian Baxter as she pulls a baby buggy up from the beach. Since the ramp was steep, it was much easier to pull a buggy or stroller than to push it. As a safety measure, the hill was off-limits to motorized vehicles of any sort. Residents often sat on the wall to enjoy the view of the lake or a sunset without making the climb. The Grubb cottage, The Vivian (pictured at right), was located at 12 Parkway Path—an easy stroll from the beach. (Both, Gayle Baxter Foster.)

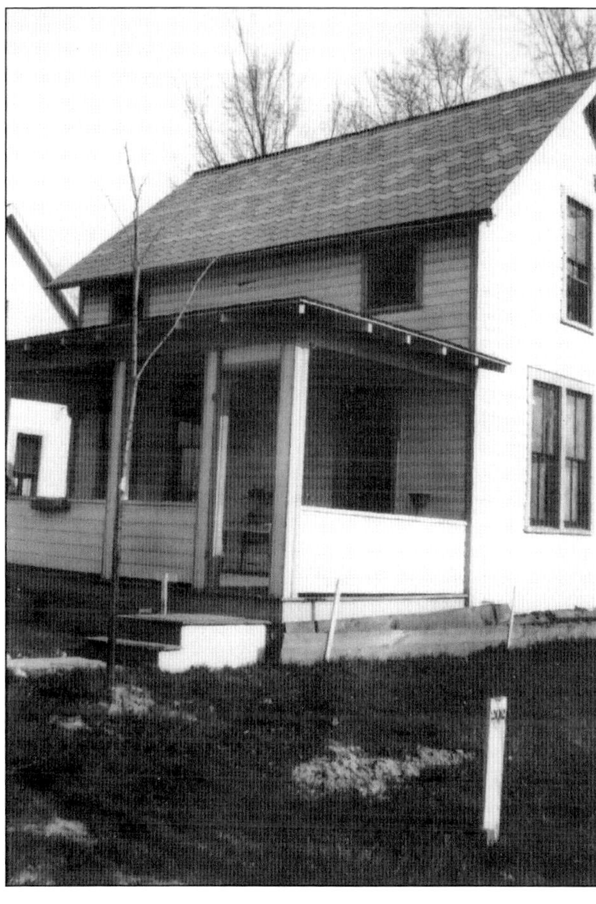

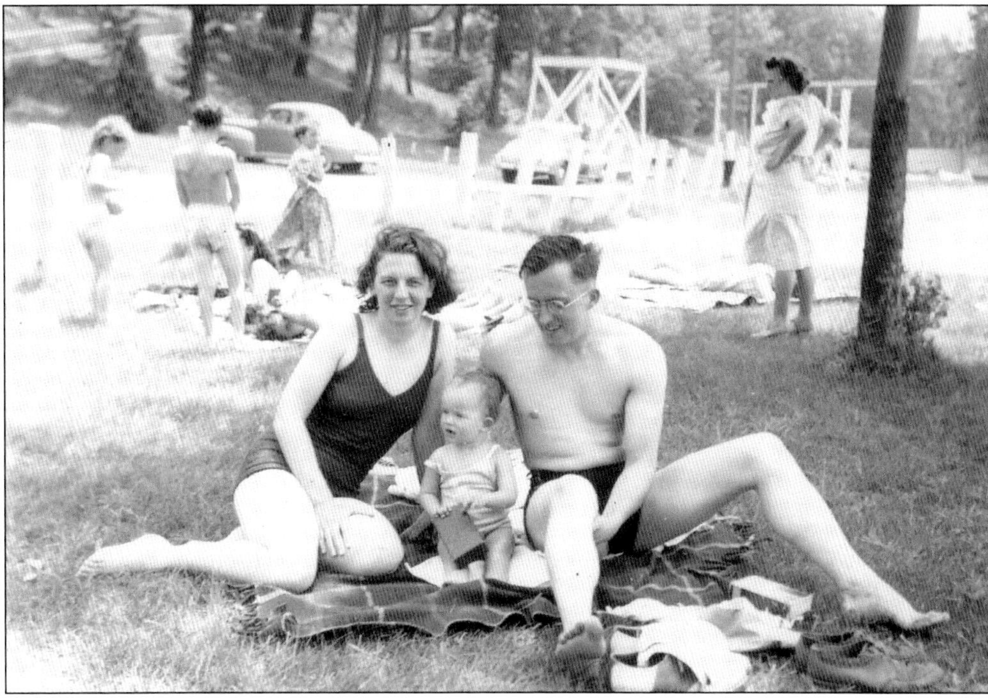

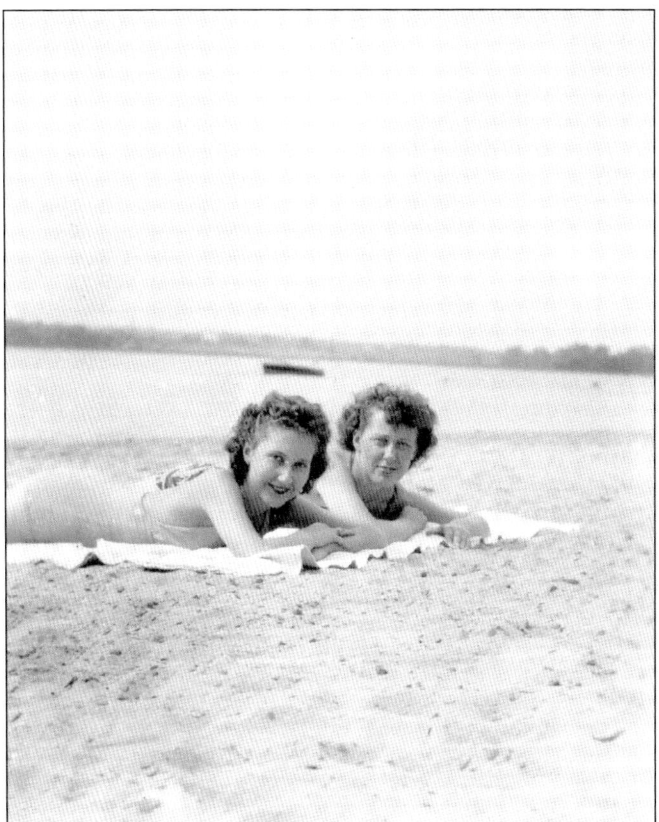

In this 1943 photograph, Vivian and Bill Baxter enjoy a day at the beach at Chippewa-on-the-Lake with their first child, Gayle. After a lifetime of summer vacations at Chippewa, the Baxter family eventually moved from Garfield Heights to make Chippewa their permanent home; they lived at the lake from 1953 to 2011. (Gayle Baxter Foster.)

Dorie Callihan (left) and an unidentified friend sunbathe on the beach at Chippewa-on-the-Lake in the 1940s. Dorie's parents, Eb and Florence Callihan, had a cottage next door to Florence's brother Bert Grubb on Parkway Path. The Callihans and Grubbs lived two doors apart in Garfield Heights, Ohio, when they were not vacationing at Chippewa. (Gayle Baxter Foster.)

Parker Beach, born in 1905 to "Mac" and Bertha Beach, came to Chippewa Lake at the age of one month; Mac was the general manager of what would one day be known as Chippewa Lake Park. As boys, brothers Parker and Fred worked as vendors in the park. Parker graduated from Seville High School and attended Ohio University, where he met his future wife, Janet Klove. They married in 1930 and lived in the park hotel for the first 16 years of their lifelong marriage. Taking the opportunity to buy the lake, park, and farm for $3,500 at auction in 1937, Parker turned the place into a popular family playground, delighting hundreds of thousands of visitors, including entertainers and politicians. However, faced with inflation and exorbitant insurance costs, Beach sold the properties to Continental Business Enterprises of Cleveland for $1.5 million in 1969. Parker and Janet moved to a horse farm in York Township for a number of years, ultimately retiring to Florida, where Parker passed away in 1992. Janet and Parker are pictured at right outside their hotel apartment. (Beach family.)

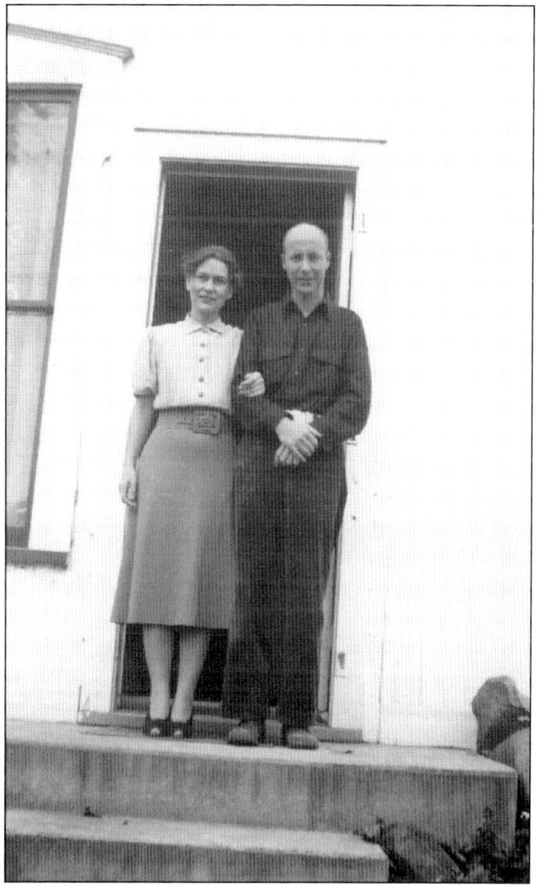

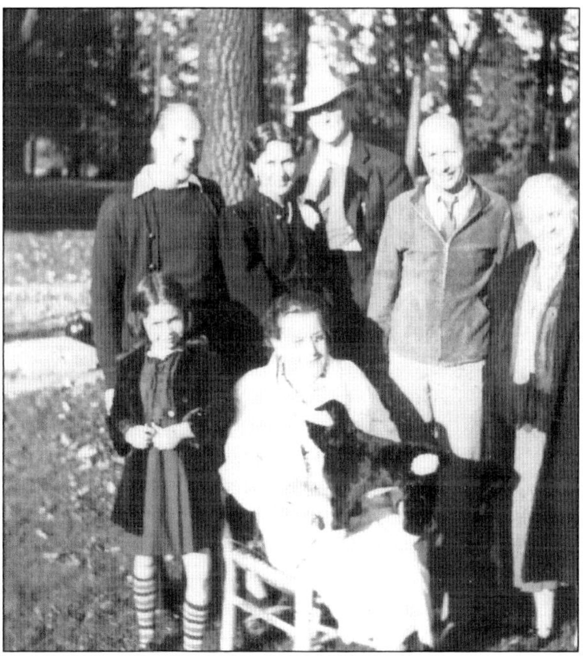

The Beach family is pictured here in 1939. From left to right are (first row) Lynn and Bertha; (second row) Fred, Janet, Mac, Parker, and Margaret. (Beach family.)

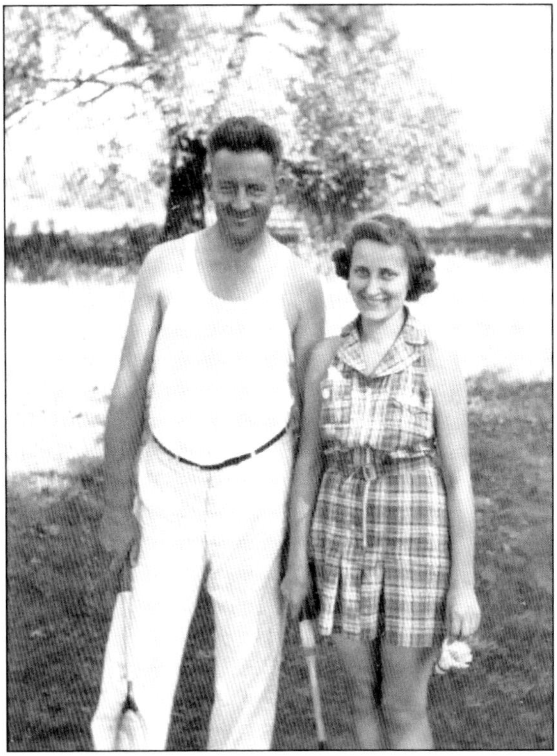

Harold (left) and Helen Stephenson married in 1938. They came to Chippewa to run the hardware store belonging to Harold's brother, Williard "Steve" Stephenson, while he served in World War II. Prior to relocating, Helen did her student teaching at New Concord Elementary School, where she was John Glenn's kindergarten teacher, and Harold owned an Indian motorcycle dealership in Zanesville. After moving to the lake, Helen soon became a very prominent member of the community and lived to 103. She was involved with Chippewa Church at the Lake United Methodist, Garden Club, and Women's Club, and was a Brownie leader and a writer for the *Medina County Gazette*. Harold worked in the hardware store with his brother and managed the business while Steve traveled. Harold and Helen's residence was located on Bungalow Bay Boulevard. (Stephenson collection.)

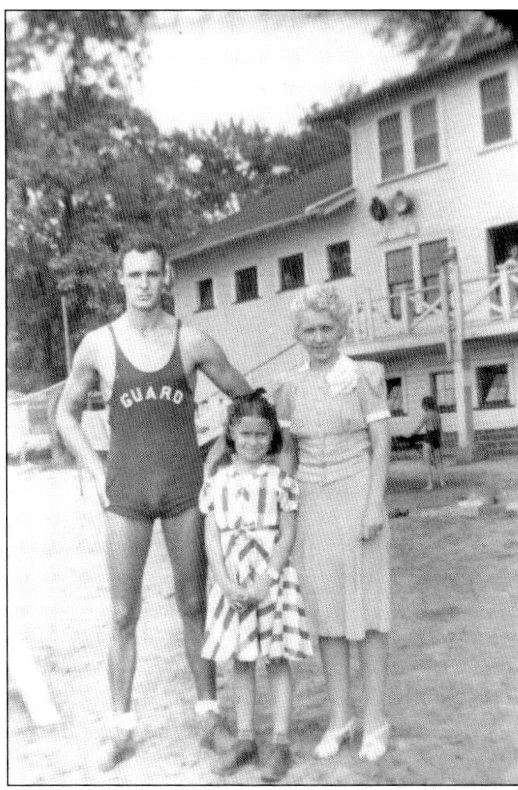

Al Tanner was a fixture at the park for many summers. He not only guarded swimmers at the beach, he spent his later years on the pier entrusted with driving the speedboats. He loved to sail his Y-Flyer on Chippewa. Away from Chippewa, he was a physical education teacher at Miami University of Ohio, where he became a close friend of famed Notre Dame football coach Ara Parseghian. Al (left) and Helen Tanner are pictured with Lynn Beach on August 27, 1940—Lynn's eighth birthday. (Beach family.)

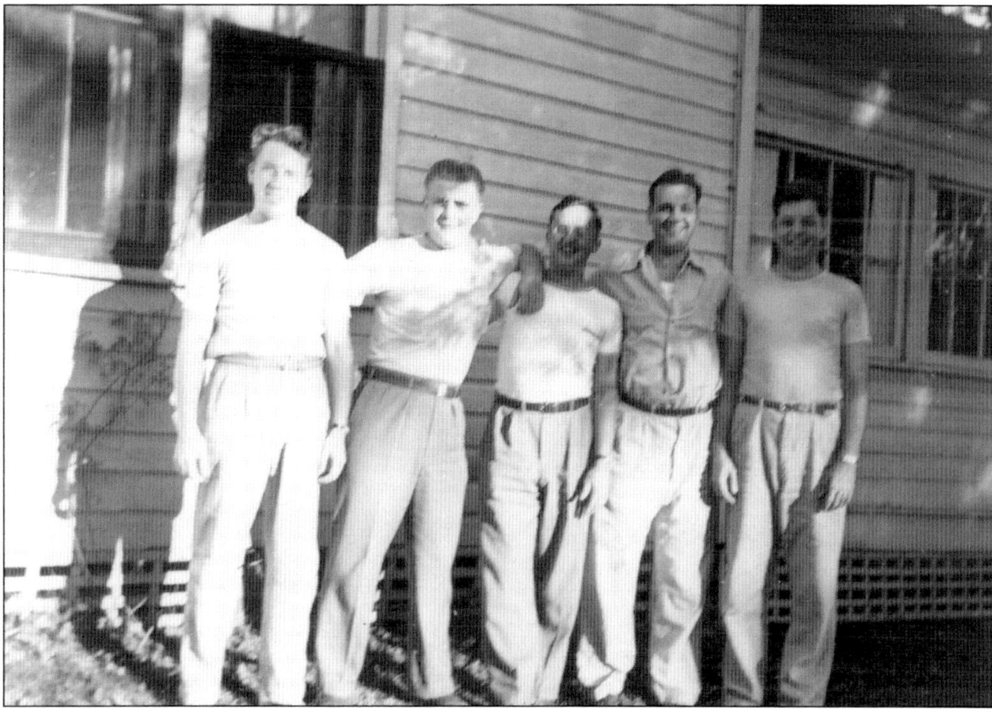

Manly men, taking a break from manly things, pose for a photograph outside the Bert Grubb cottage on Parkway Path at Chippewa-on-the-Lake in 1940. Bill Baxter is in the center with his brother-in-law Herb Grubb at far right. The others are unidentified. The brothers-in-law eventually moved their young families into year-round homes at Chippewa-on-the-Lake. (Gayle Baxter Foster.)

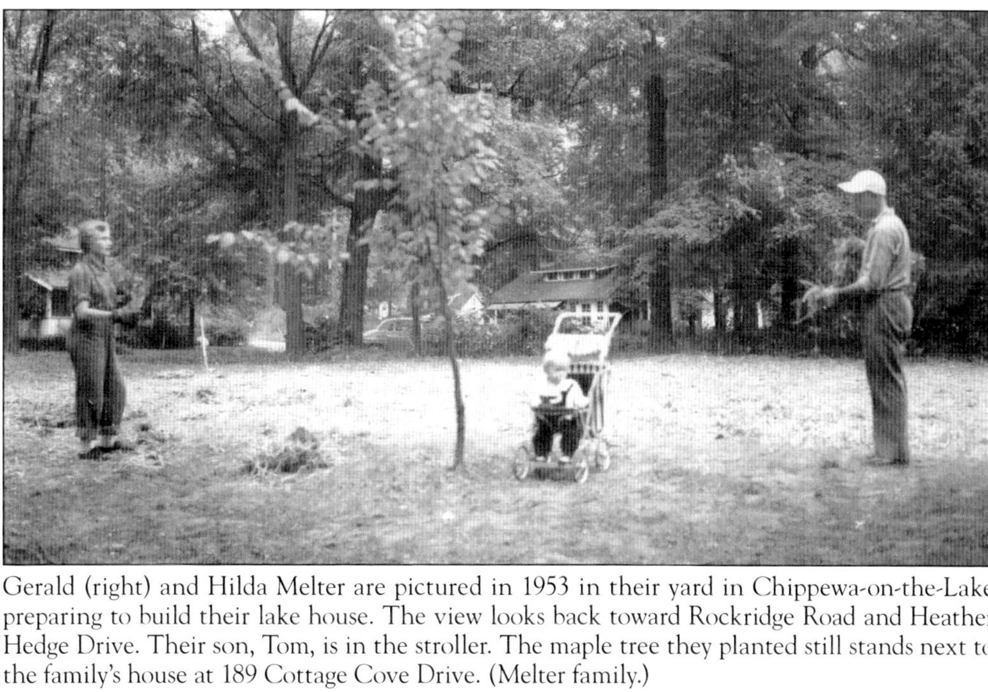

Gerald (right) and Hilda Melter are pictured in 1953 in their yard in Chippewa-on-the-Lake preparing to build their lake house. The view looks back toward Rockridge Road and Heather Hedge Drive. Their son, Tom, is in the stroller. The maple tree they planted still stands next to the family's house at 189 Cottage Cove Drive. (Melter family.)

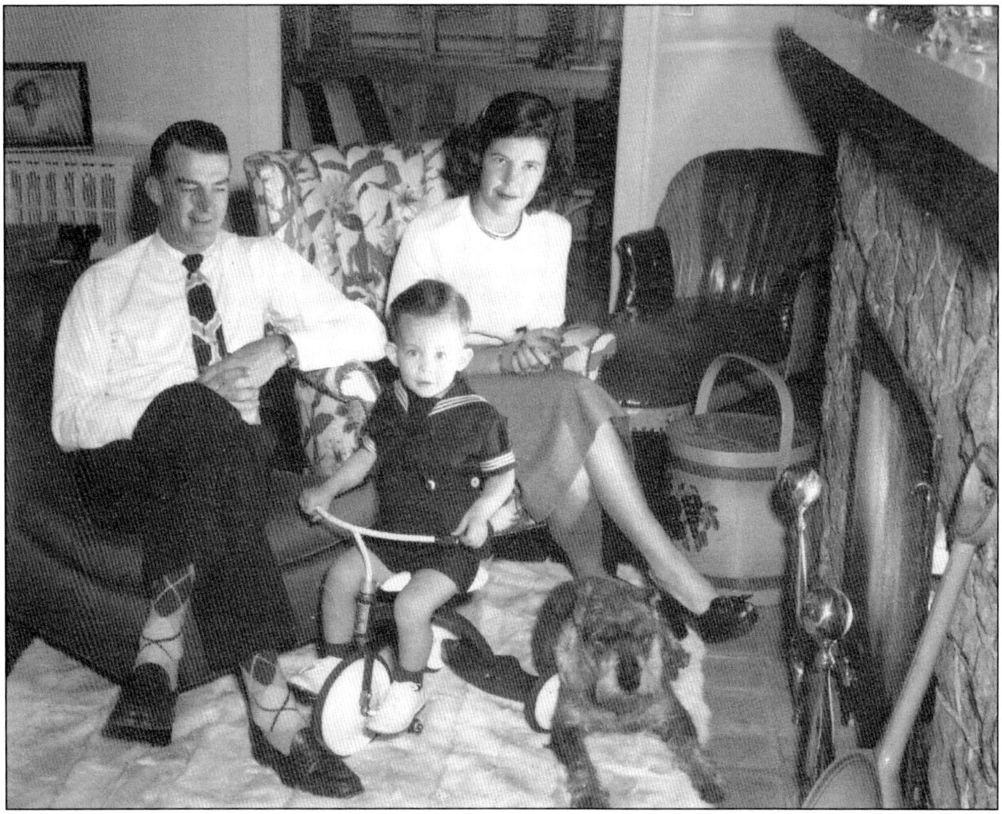

Willard and Helen Stephenson are pictured in their home on Beachside Boulevard with their son Bill. (Beach family.)

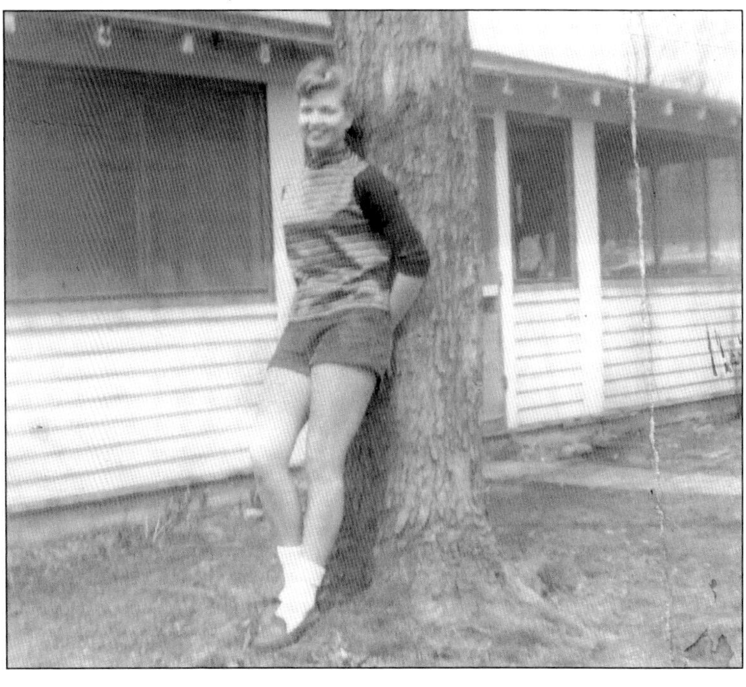

Mary and Steve Antal raised their family of 11 in the Chippewa area after moving there in 1949. In this 1956 photograph, their daughter Betty, age 16, poses in front of 65 Lakefield Lane in Gloria Glens, the home she shared with four siblings (the older children had already moved out). (Beshire family.)

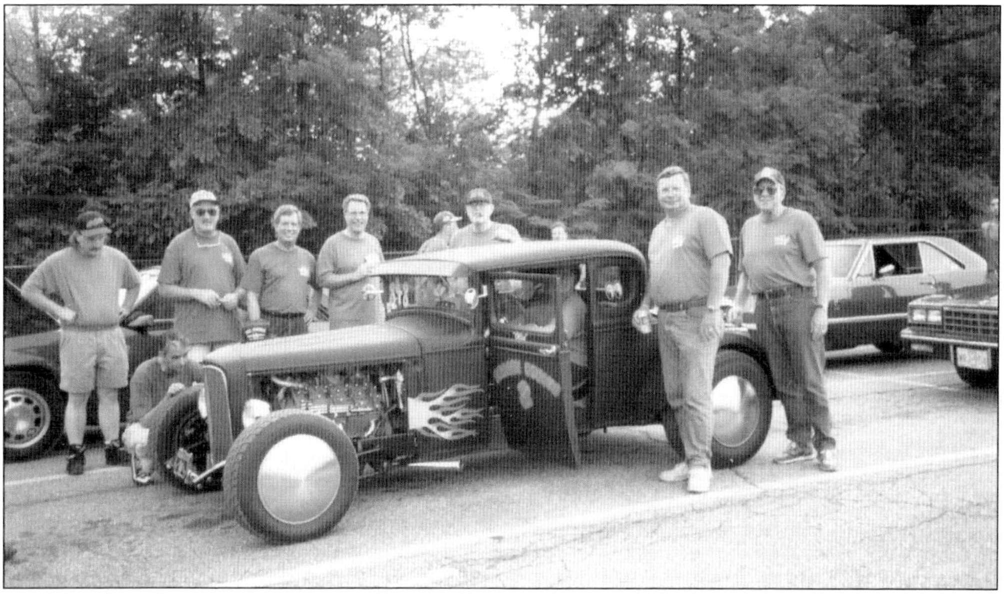

In 1960, the Chippewa Lake Dragon Deuces Hot Rod Club, a group of teenage boys barely old enough to drive, built a 1930 Model A Ford in the basement of Lee Jay Davis's dad's home in LeRoy (now Westfield Center), Ohio. The car had to be dismantled and rebuilt outside. The young Davis created the dragon logo used on club jackets and the plaques each member sported on their personal cars. Thirty years later, Davis happened upon an identical car, got in touch with his old pals to share the purchase price, and bought Ollie II. Taking turns keeping the car at their homes across the country, they worked on it, drove it, took it to car shows, and proudly took "her" for a trip down Dragway 42 in West Salem, Ohio. A 1990 reunion brought the original Deuces together again. Pictured above are, from left to right, unidentified, Jack Whitlam (kneeling), Rick Schmitt, Gary Baxter, Jeff Grubb, Lee Davis, Jim Ponting, unidentified, and Charlie McDermott (in the car). Below, Davis is pictured with Ollie in his dad's basement in 1960. Honorary Deuce Paul Neidart bought Ollie with the promise to bring her out for funerals. (Both, Lee Davis.)

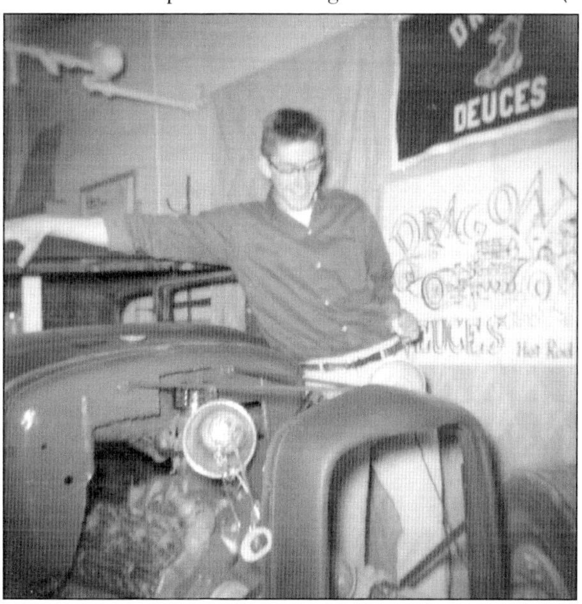

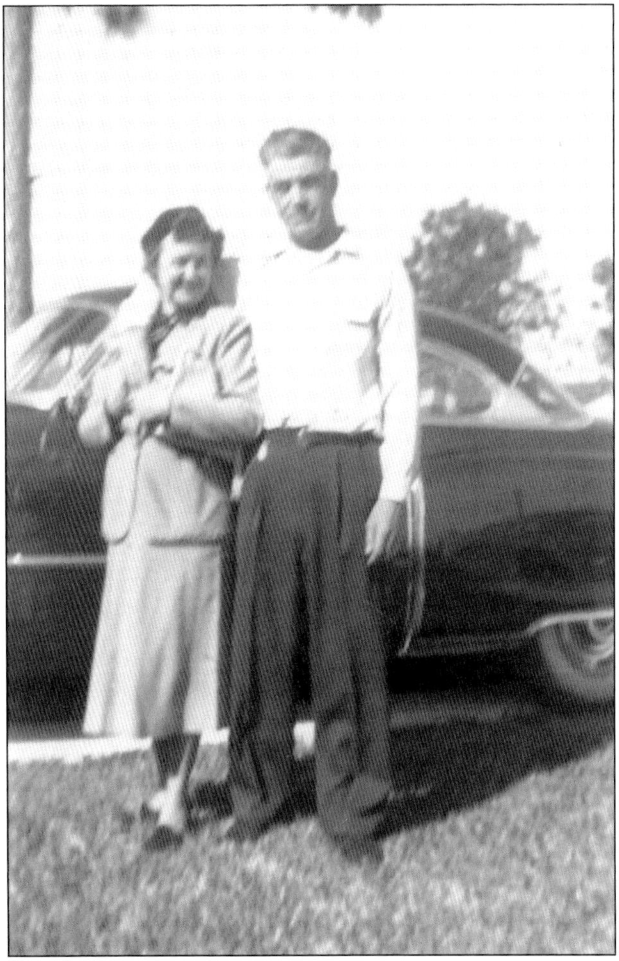

Bernice Bostwick and Milt Ruder were married in Ticonderoga, New York, on September 8, 1950. They spent their honeymoon in Florida before returning together to Chippewa Lake. (Jeffrey Schmitt.)

The Wengatz house is pictured following the flood of January 1959 surrounded by the ice that followed. The house was completed in 1953, and it is located on the southeast corner of Brookshore Drive at 248 Beachside Boulevard. It looks much the same today with the exception of some cosmetic changes. (Carla Thomas.)

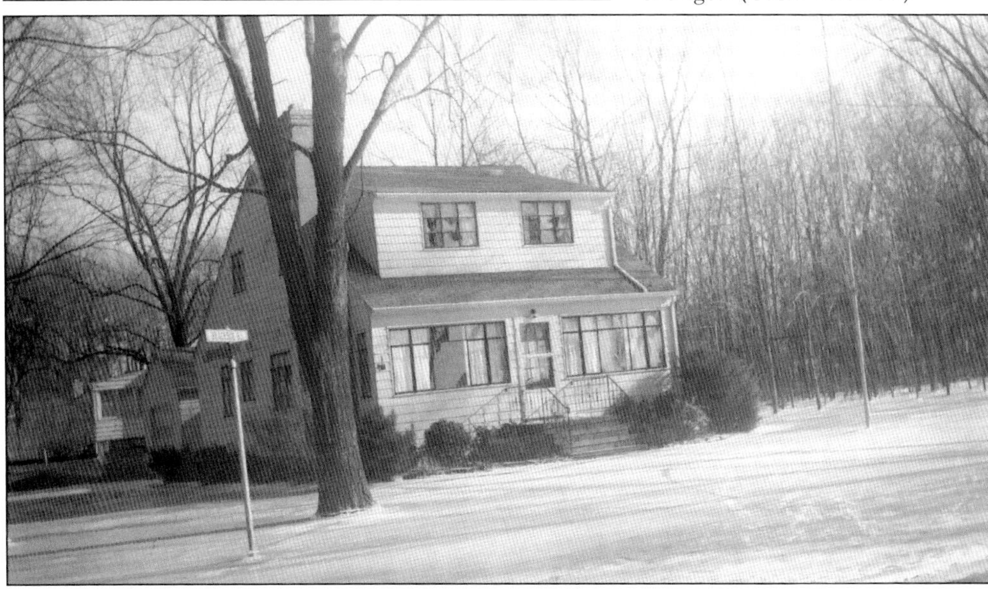

What could be better than growing up with an amusement park next door? Shutting down the road to go sledding in winter! Here, a local gang is riding down Longacre Lane in 1954. From left to right are Mary Van Pelt, Fred Van Pelt, Barbara Grubb, Gary Baxter, Jeff Grubb, Gayle Baxter, Chad Grubb, Jean Edwards, and Bruce Baxter. The cottage at 5891 Longacre Lane is in the background. (Gayle Baxter Foster.)

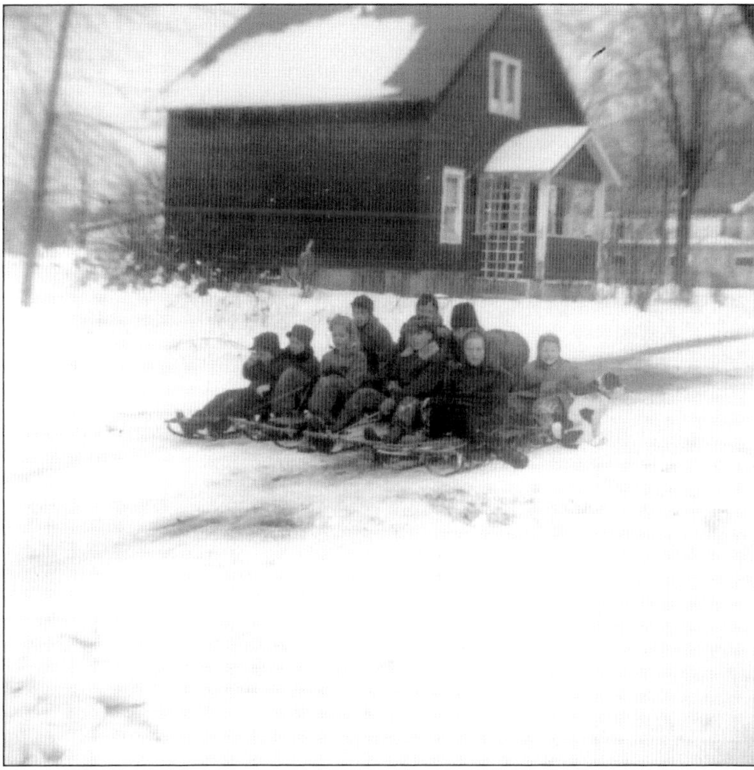

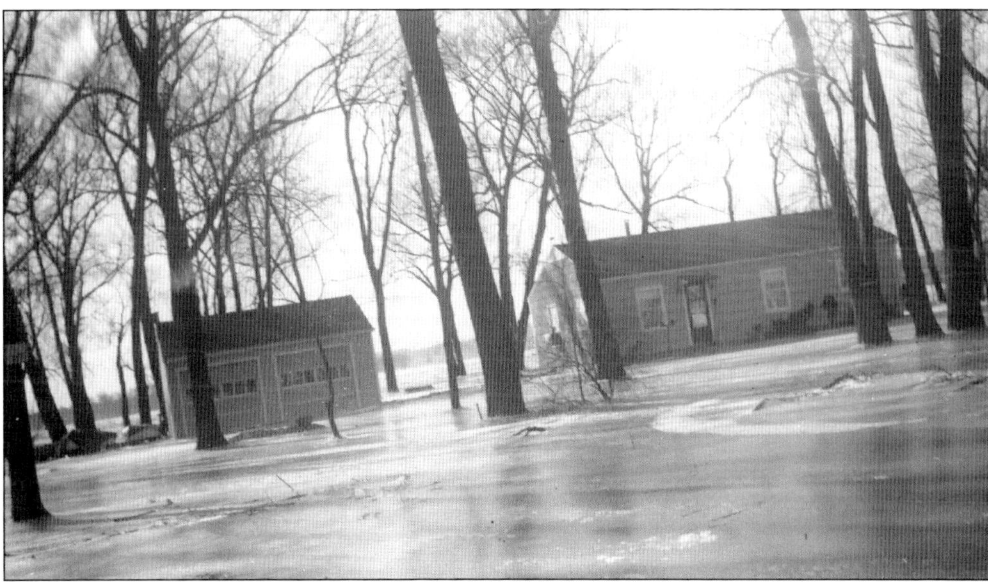

This is the only house built on the lake side of Beachside Boulevard in Chippewa Lake. It belonged to the Soper family in 1959 and is shown surrounded by ice following the January 1959 flood. (Carla Thomas.)

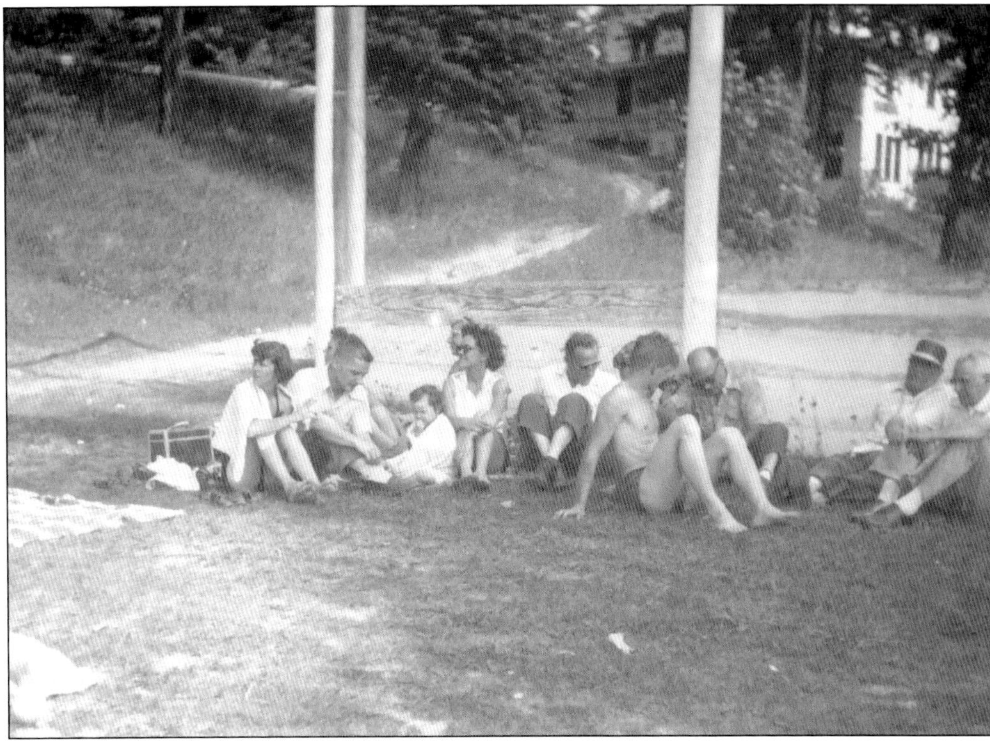

The Gleeson gang is pictured here in 1955 enjoying the beach at Chippewa-on-the-Lake before the fence was installed. The path led up to Bungalow Bay circle. (Barbara Grubb Whitlam.)

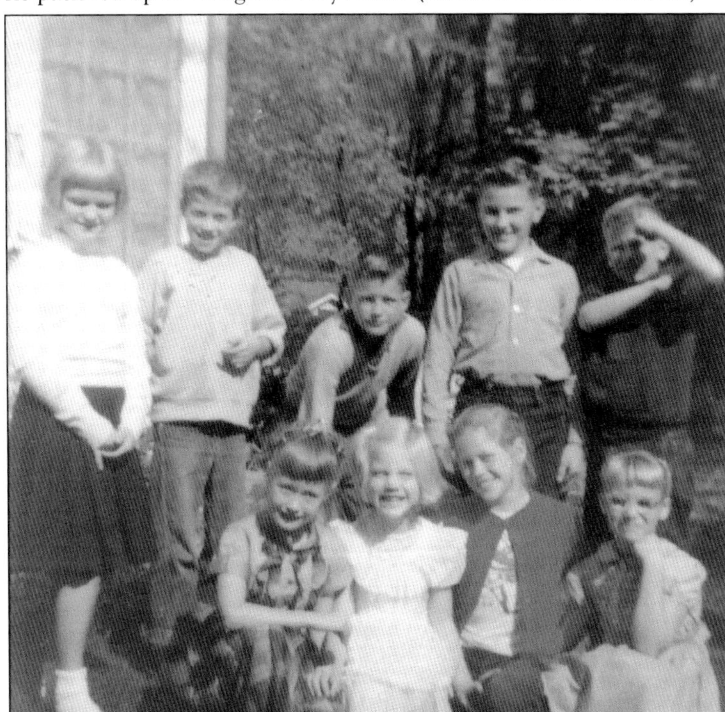

Few things were better than living in Chippewa as a child. In the 1950s and 1960s, young families not only came to the area during summer, but many lived here year-round. They enjoyed the park and beach during the summer and sledding down Longacrce Lane in the winter. From left to right are (first row) Ruth Lees, Nancy Grubb, Mary Van Pelt, and Judy Ambrose; (second row) Susan Ambrose, Fred Van Pelt, Bruce Baxter, Bobby Schmock, and Ricky Rombach. (Gayle Baxter Foster.)

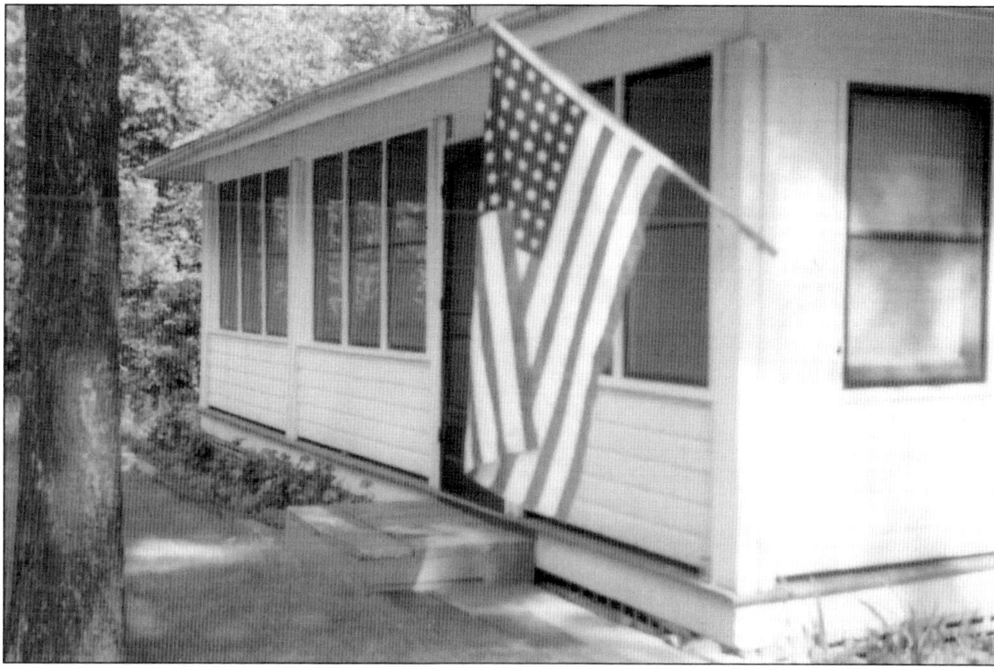

Eb and Florence Callihan named their cottage at 13 Parkway Path The Robin. It sat next door to The Vivian, located at 12 Parkway Path and owned by Florence Callihan's brother Bert Grubb. Bert and Florence lived on the same street in Garfield Heights during the school year, but summer brought the families to Chippewa, where their children and nieces and nephews were free to swim, fish, and play from sunrise to sunset. Spending some fishing time on a nearby dock in 1958 below are, from left to right, friends David Lias, Barb Jamieson, and Alex Jamieson, all of whom were connected to the Callihan/Grubb clan in one way or another. (Both, Gayle Baxter Foster.)

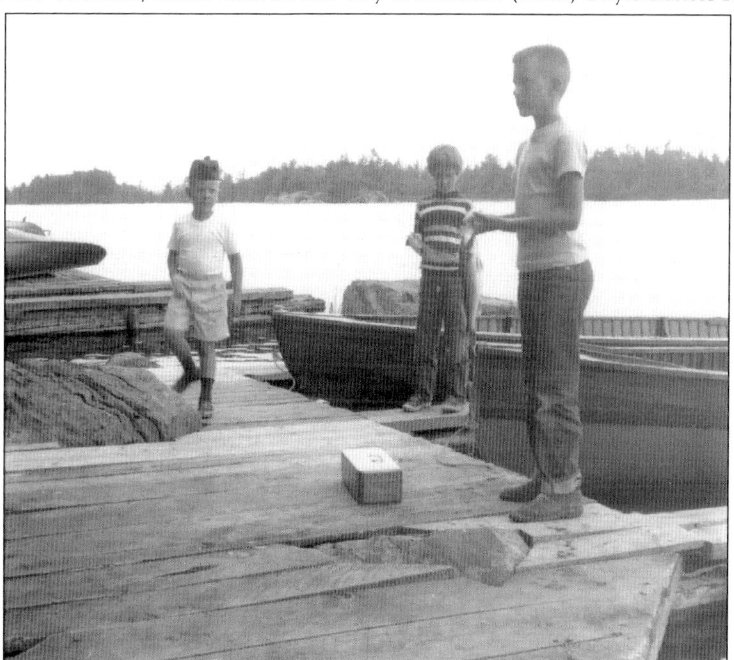

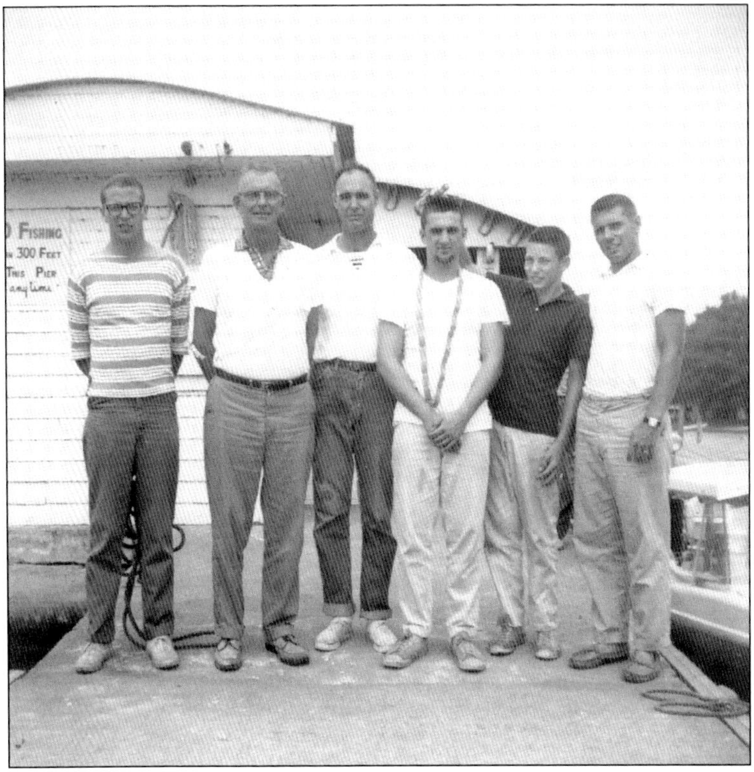

Chippewa Lake Park brought the communities of the area together. Whether it was through work or play or only during the summer year after year, all were part of the Chippewa family. The "Pier Crew" is pictured here in 1960; they are, from left to right, Buzz Van Pelt, Corl "Ed" Edwards, Al Tanner, Tim Emerick, Bobby ?, and Chad Grubb. (Chad Grubb.)

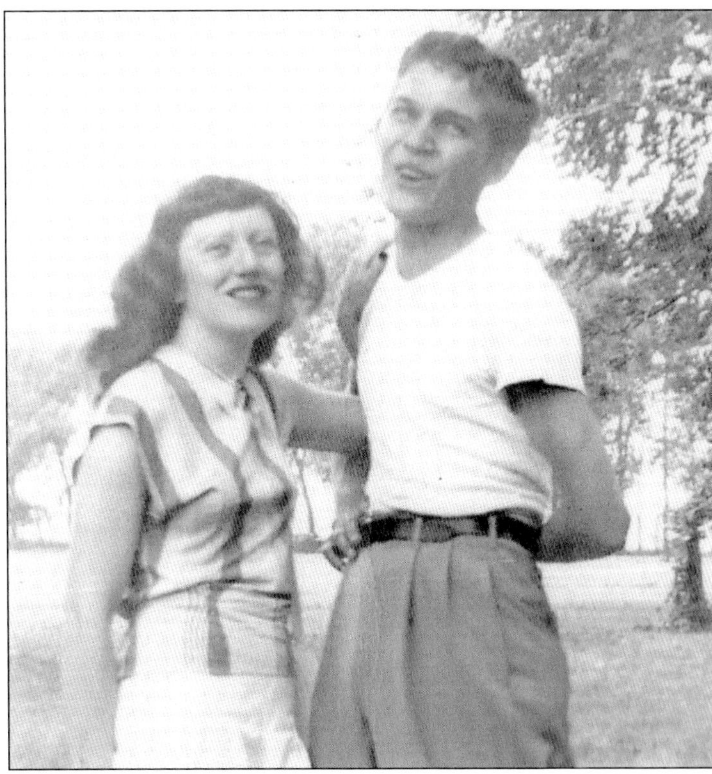

Roberta McDonald Humbel and her husband, Bert, built a home at 368 Craggy Creek Drive where they raised their family. Roberta and her three brothers were born in the McDonald home on Chippewa Road, and all were descendants of John Morton, a signer of the Declaration of Independence. One of Bert's three jobs was deputy sheriff. Roberta was a member of the Briarwood Beach Garden Club and played the organ at the Chippewa Church at the Lake United Methodist. If there was a wedding or funeral, Roberta was there. (McDonald family.)

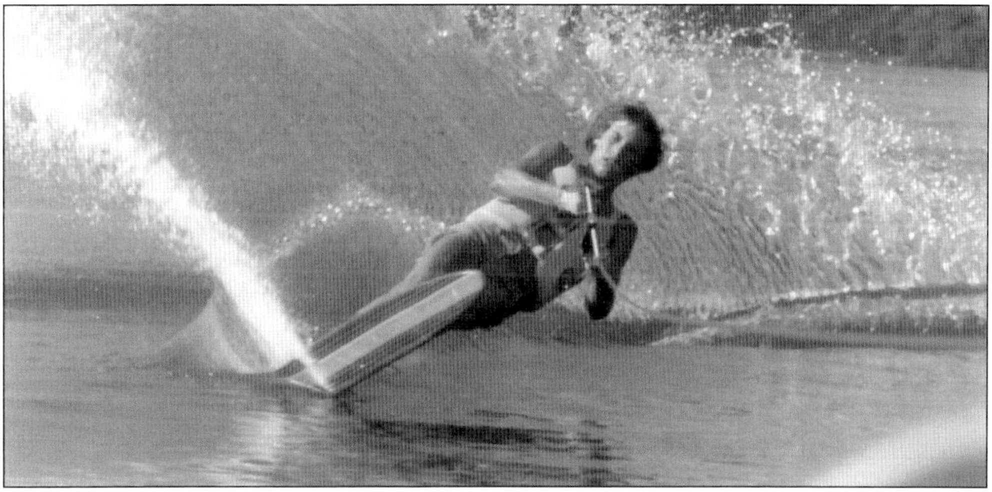

During the 1960s and 1970s, there was a flurry of waterskiing activity on the lake. Boys would get up early and ski on a lake of glass before skiing all day—or whenever they could. Scott Dunn, age 16, is shown on a Cypress Gardens slalom ski in 1971. Dunn's family has enjoyed the lake and the park dating back to the historic years of big bands performing in the once-popular dance hall. To this day, in the very early hours of the morning, barefoot skiers take advantage of the still water of the lake. (Jill Heck.)

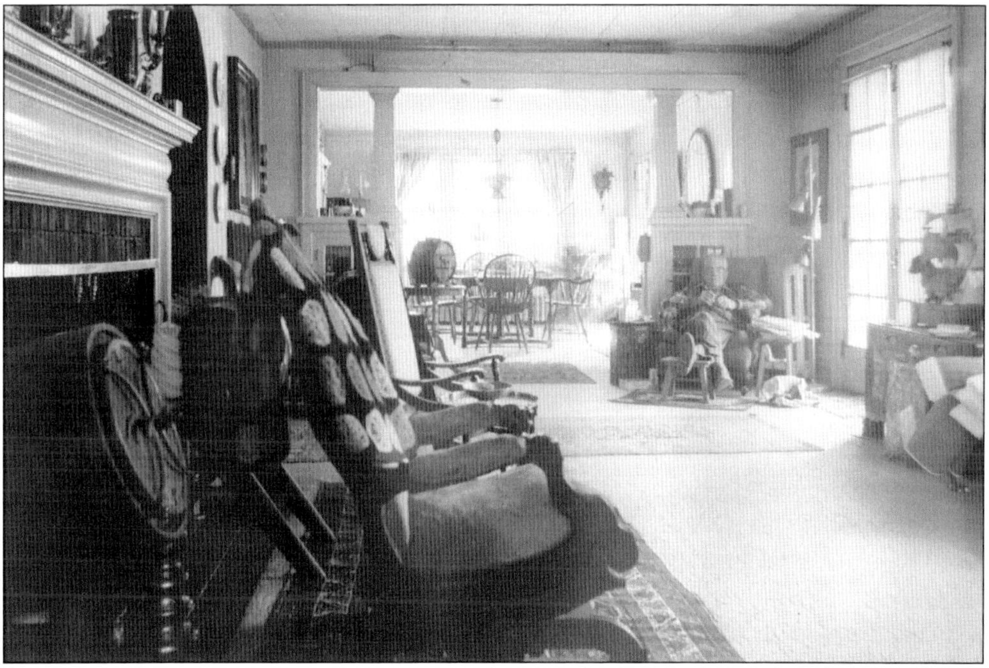

Milt Ruder grew up on a farm on Chippewa Road and farmed for most of his life, but he also worked for Medina County Sanitary Engineers, served as superintendent of the Chippewa Lake waterworks, and drove a school bus for Cloverleaf schools. He became active in local politics in the 1960s, serving as councilperson for the Village of Chippewa-on-the-Lake for two terms. He married Bernice Bostwick in 1950, and they enjoyed 20 years together before her passing in 1970. He lived to be 96 years old and passed away in May 1995. Although he was not one to be idle for long, Milt is shown here in a rare moment of relaxation at home. (Jeffrey Schmitt.)

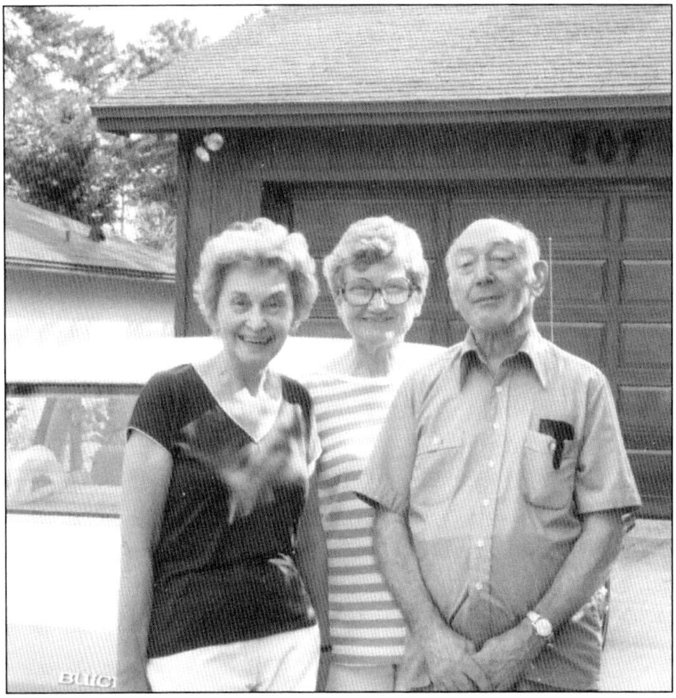

Over the years, these good friends spent many hours together at Chippewa-on-the-Lake; their cottages were located next to one another on Cottage Cove Drive. From left to right are Eleanor Trausch, Hilda Melter, and Bill Trausch. (Melter family.)

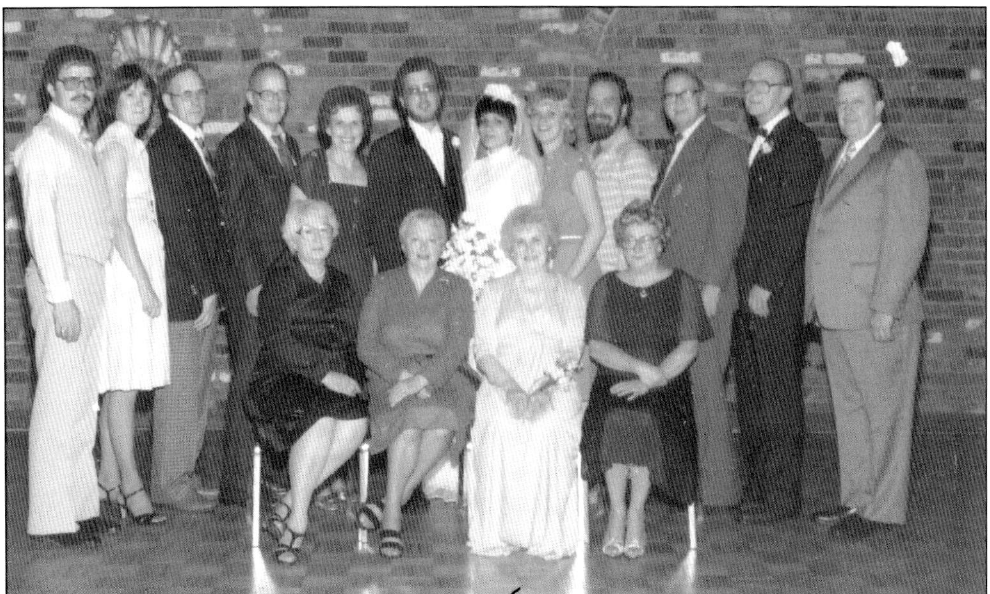

The 1940s, 1950s, and 1960s held many memories for property owners, summer residents, and their families. As the years progressed, many of their children got married, and many residents would attend these weddings. It is amazing to see even to this day how many of those children have kept property in the family and have remodeled or rebuilt cottages and homes. This group of summer residents from the Bungalow Bay circle area are attending a wedding. From left to right are (first row) Elsie Nixon, Hilda Marring, LaVerne Sefl, and Ruth Rogers; (second row) Herb and Ruth Napier, Lawrence Nixon, George and Rita Shepard, Ken and Sandra Sefl, Mary Beth Schleter, Michael Stanko, Jack Rogers, Ralph Sefl, and Howard Marring. (Sharon Sefl Karhan.)

Five

FUN AT THE LAKE

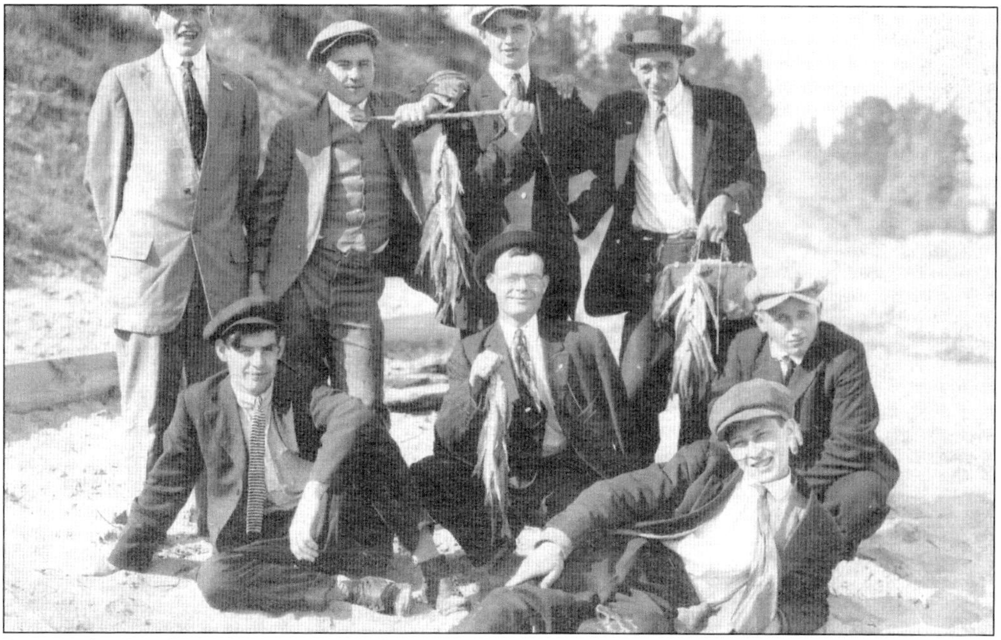

During the Butcher's Picnic in 1915, these young men had a productive day of fishing at Chippewa Lake. A butchering contest provided the most excitement of the day, though, as two expert butchers competed to see who could finish the job first. (Cyndy Naragon.)

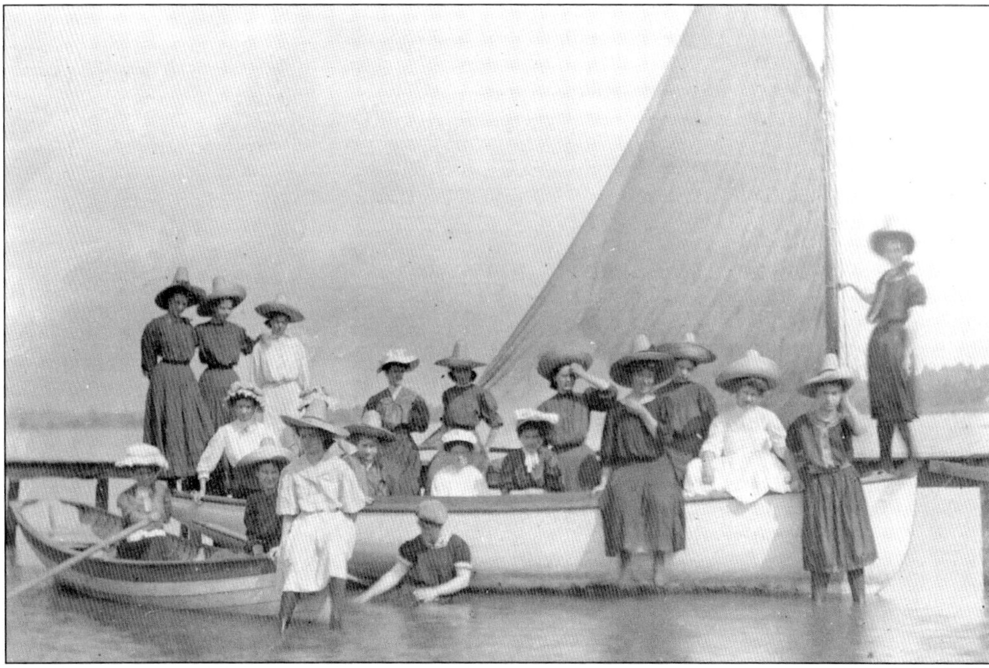

The waters of Chippewa seem to have a relaxing effect on those who love being on the water. Even the gals shown here are out to enjoy a peaceful afternoon sailing on the lake. Whether it is in a sailboat, rowboat, motorboat, or today's ski boats, it is always fun to travel around the lake enjoying the wildlife and scenery. (Beach family.)

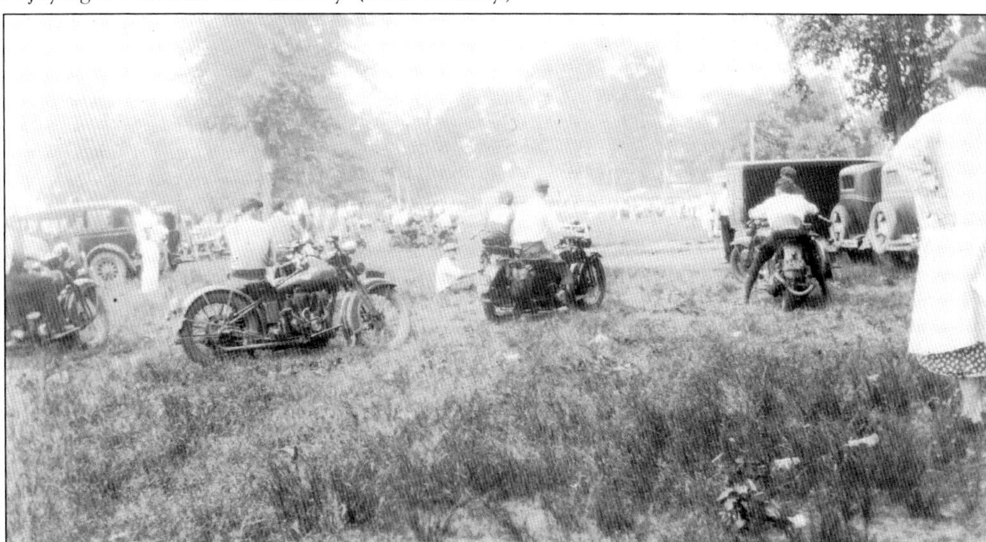

Indian is recognized as the first major American motorcycle manufacturer, with production established in Springfield, Massachusetts, in 1901—two years before Harley-Davidson. Competition between the two manufacturers was fierce, and in the early days, Indian gave Harley-Davidson a run for the money with many innovations, including the first V-twin engine. Out of the dozens of motorcycle manufacturers in the United States, including Yale, Henderson, and Cleveland, these two are probably the most well known. The locals of Chippewa Lake are shown gathered for a motorcycle race in 1932. (Sandra Bushi.)

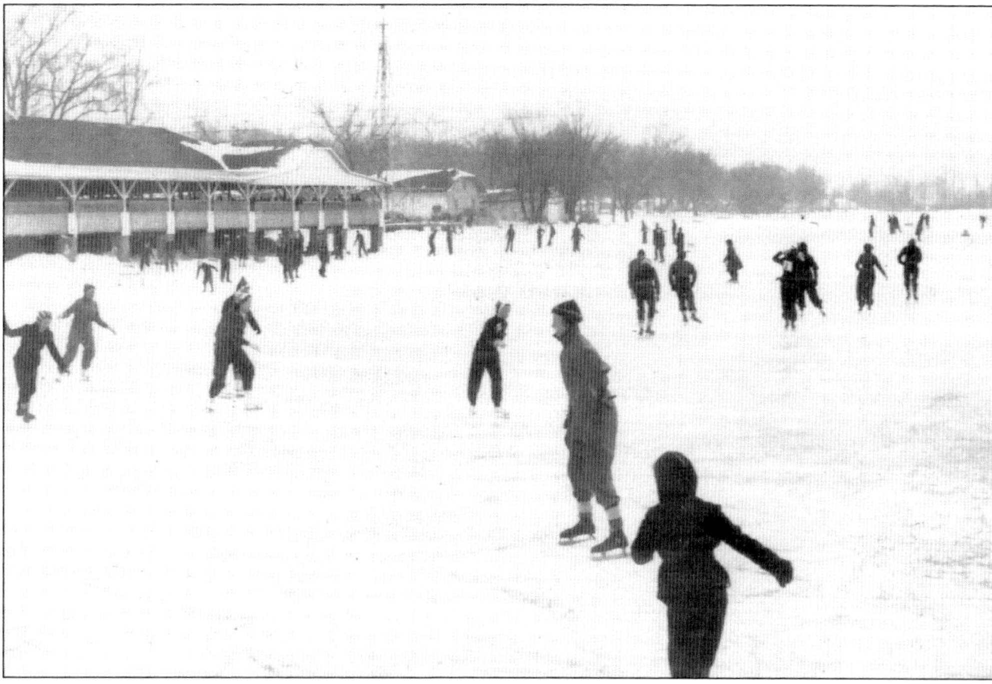

Having fun on the ice is an ageless pastime! Above is the pavilion at Chippewa Lake Park with skaters enjoying the frozen lake. Below, on a sunny and cold Chippewa day, people are skating, walking dogs, sledding, ice-boating, and visiting in and around the park pier and beyond. These images show the surprising amount of winter activity on the lake considering how few people made Chippewa Lake their wintertime home. Before refrigeration, iceboxes were used to keep food fresh and cool. The iceboxes had a compartment for a block of ice that would melt and drip into a pan that needed to be emptied lest it overflow. Chippewa Lake was noted for ice harvesting in the winter months. Large blocks of ice were cut from the lake and stored in an icehouse that had easy access to a rail spur. Some of the larger icehouses in Chippewa were Oscar Townsend's, Knickerbocker, Forest City, Standard Ice, and Independent Ice. (Above, Stephenson collection; below, Beach family.)

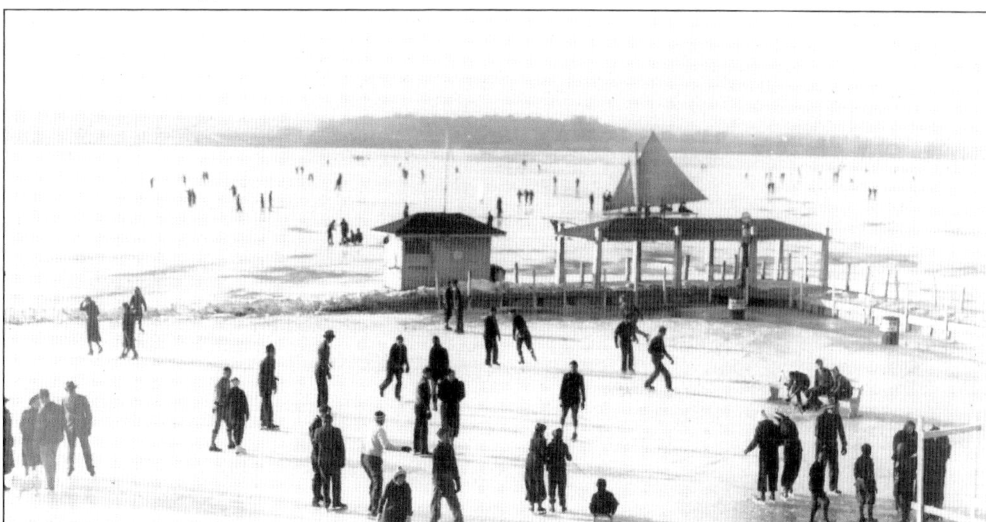

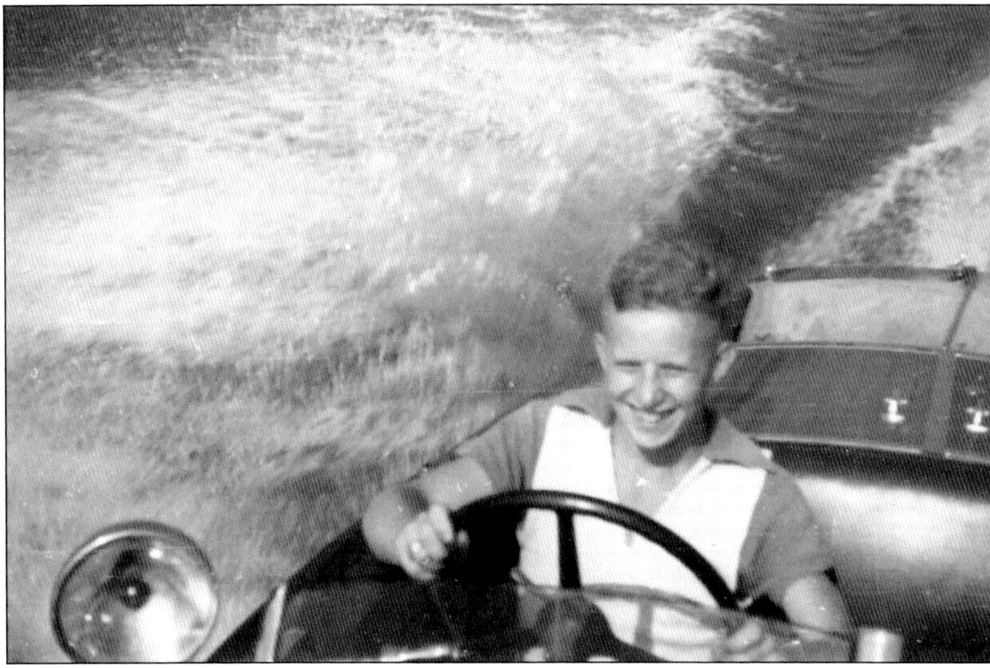

Bob Rutledge is shown in 1935 racing around Chippewa Lake. It appears that he does not have a care in the world and is having the time of his life. The photographer must have had nerves of steel. (Stephenson collection.)

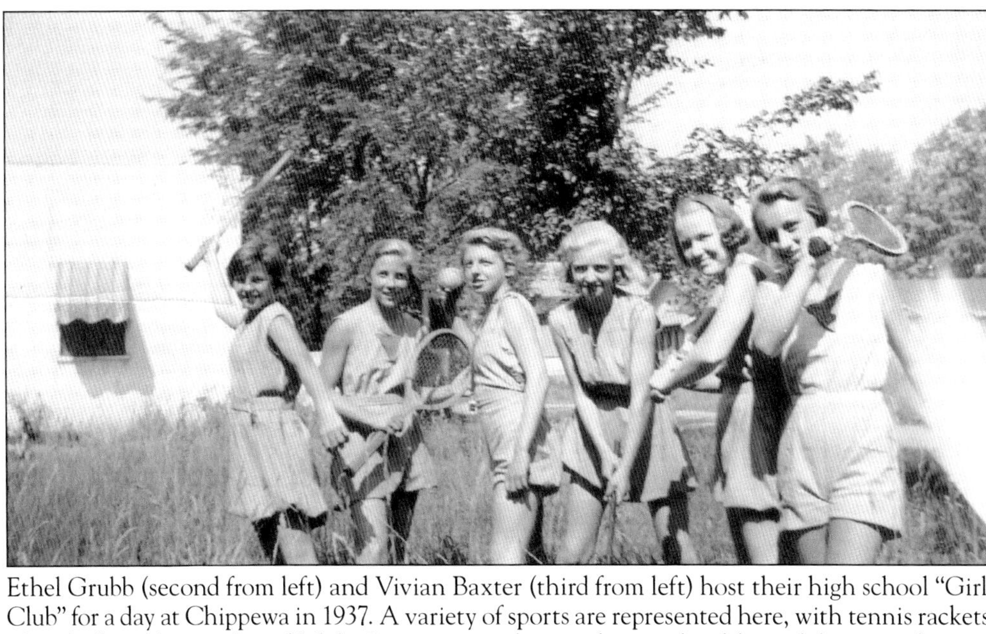

Ethel Grubb (second from left) and Vivian Baxter (third from left) host their high school "Girls Club" for a day at Chippewa in 1937. A variety of sports are represented here, with tennis rackets, a baseball and bat, and a golf club. One may wonder—is this a girls athletic club, or are they just being silly for the camera? (Gayle Baxter Foster.)

Horseback riding was also a popular leisure activity around Chippewa. Parker Beach had horses on his farm and could often be seen riding down his path; it was lined with beautiful full-grown trees that led to the road by the Oaks Lodge and entrance to the park. How beautiful it was watching him strut his horse down that path. From left to right, Lynn, Fred, and Parker Beach are pictured here in 1940 in front of the ballroom. (Beach family.)

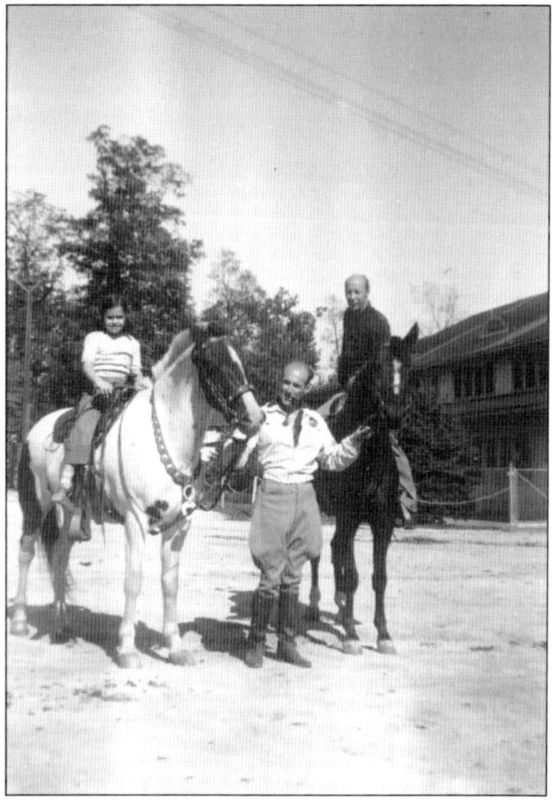

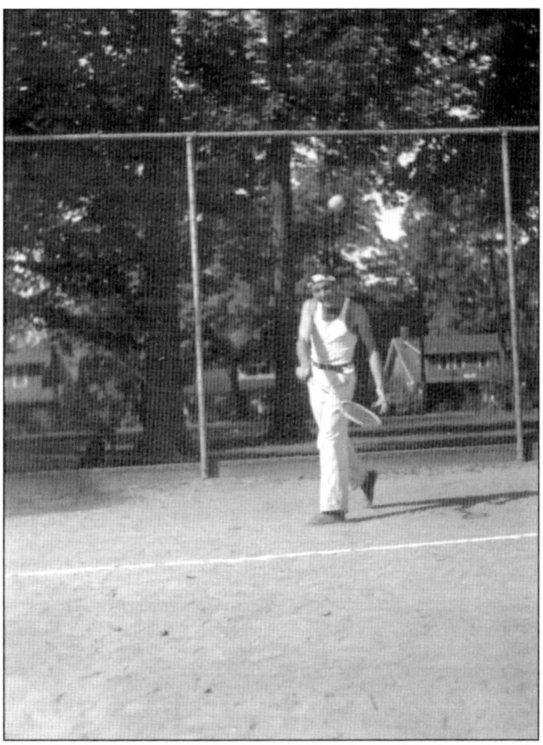

A sunny afternoon in Chippewa Lake in 1934 seemed like a good time for a game of tennis. Milt Ruder is shown laying one down on the Bungalow Bay circle. (Stephenson collection.)

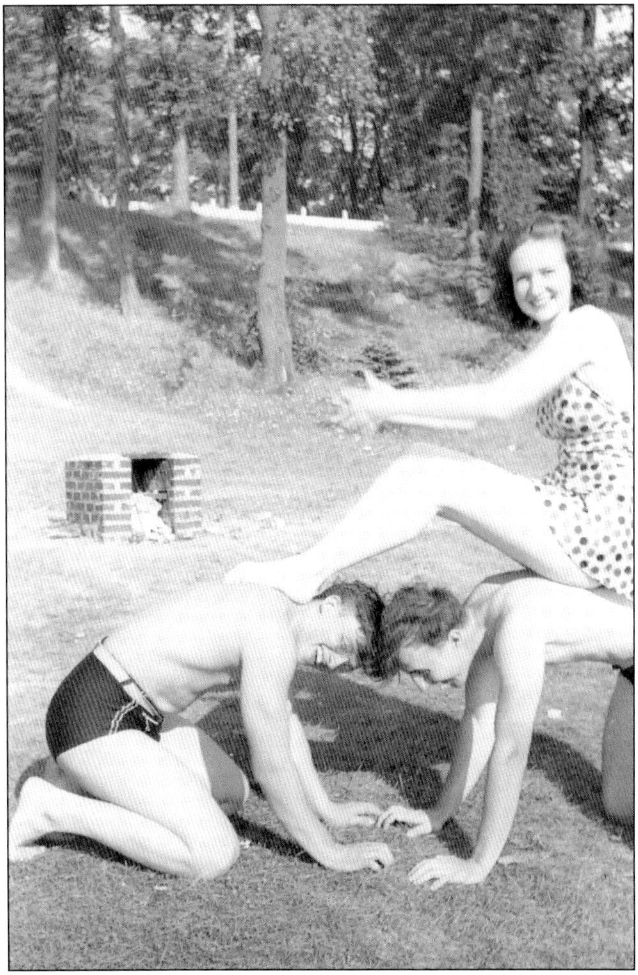

Bill Baxter (left) had some fun on the beach with his friends in 1941. Young people have always gravitated to the beach for fun in the sun and the water, finding it a good place to socialize. Note the grill in the background. Grills were provided by the village for the use of residents. They were removed in the 1950s. (Gayle Baxter Foster.)

DeeDee Schmitt Duecker (left) is heading to the Gloria Glens beach with her great-aunt Lilian "Lil" Kick and an unidentified friend in 1948. At this time, there were benches along the beach; it would be several years before the fence was erected. (DeeDee Duecker.)

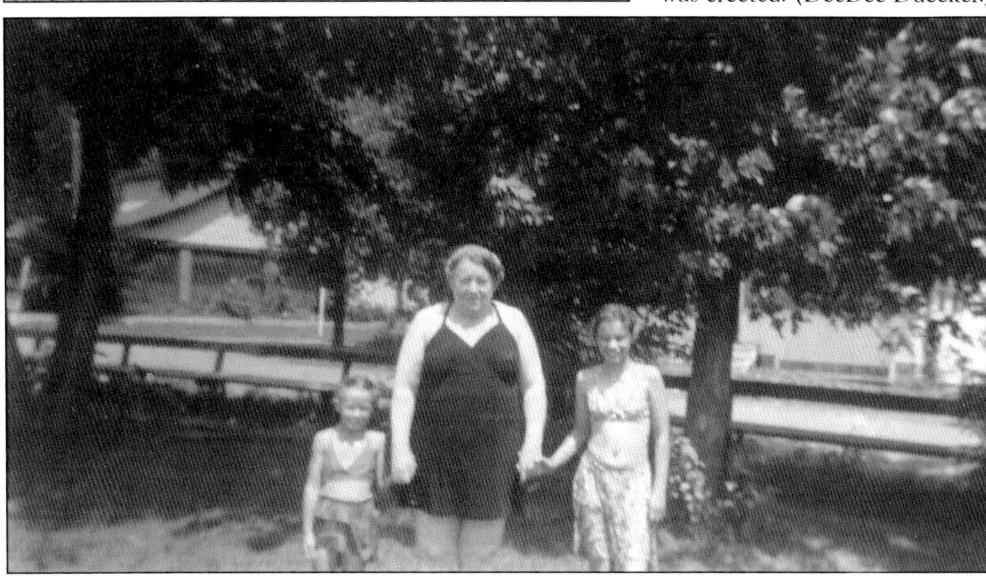

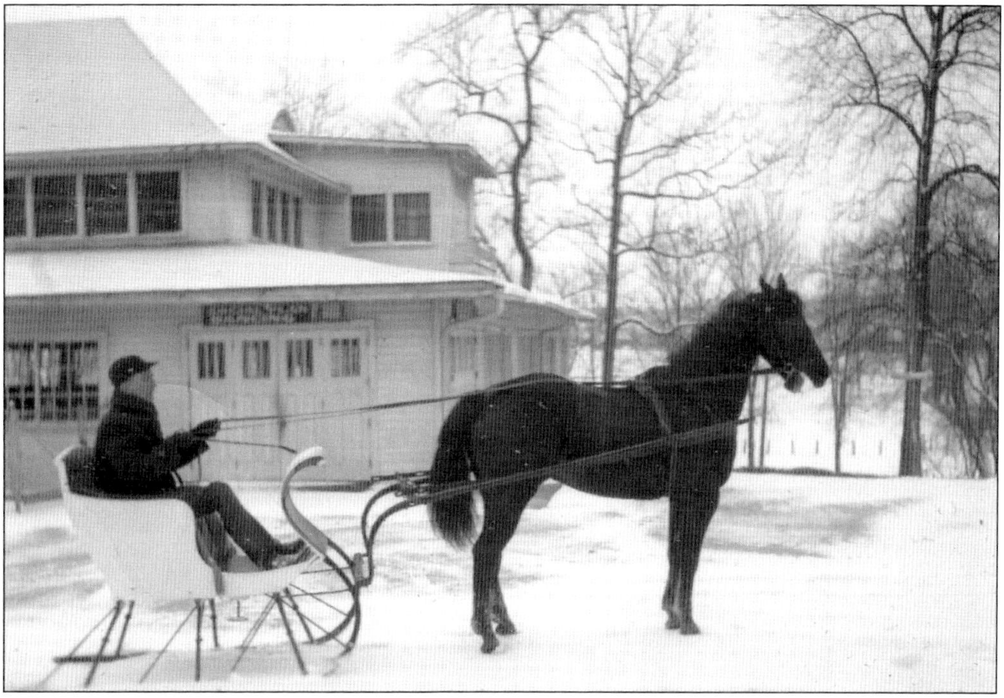

While wintertime at Chippewa Lake is certainly quieter than the summer months, those who do make their home at the lake in winter always find a way to enjoy the snowy, cold weather. The dance hall is in the background in this 1940s photograph. (Stephenson collection.)

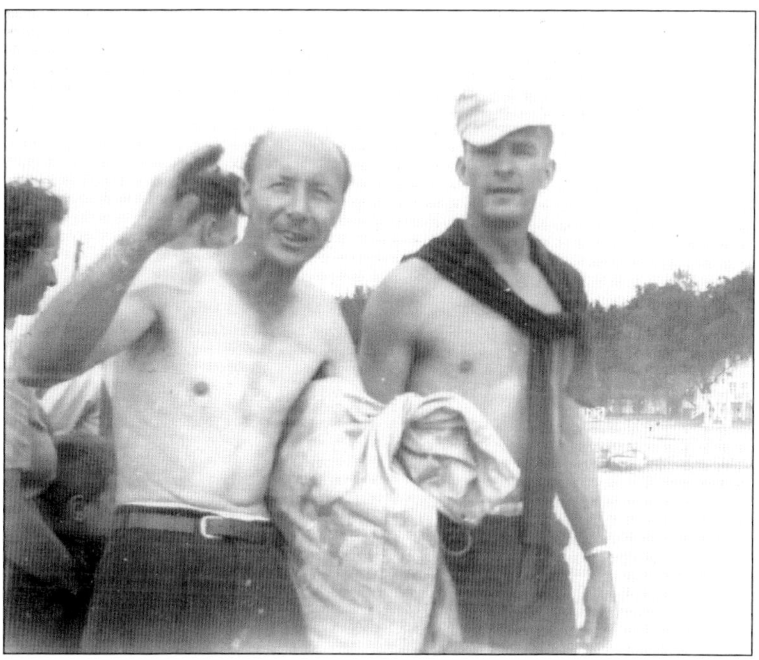

Although this was considered an activity reserved for children, Parker Beach (left) and Willard "Steve" Stephenson decided to join in the fun during this 1946 duffle bag race. While it is a simple game, winning is anything but easy. (Beach family.)

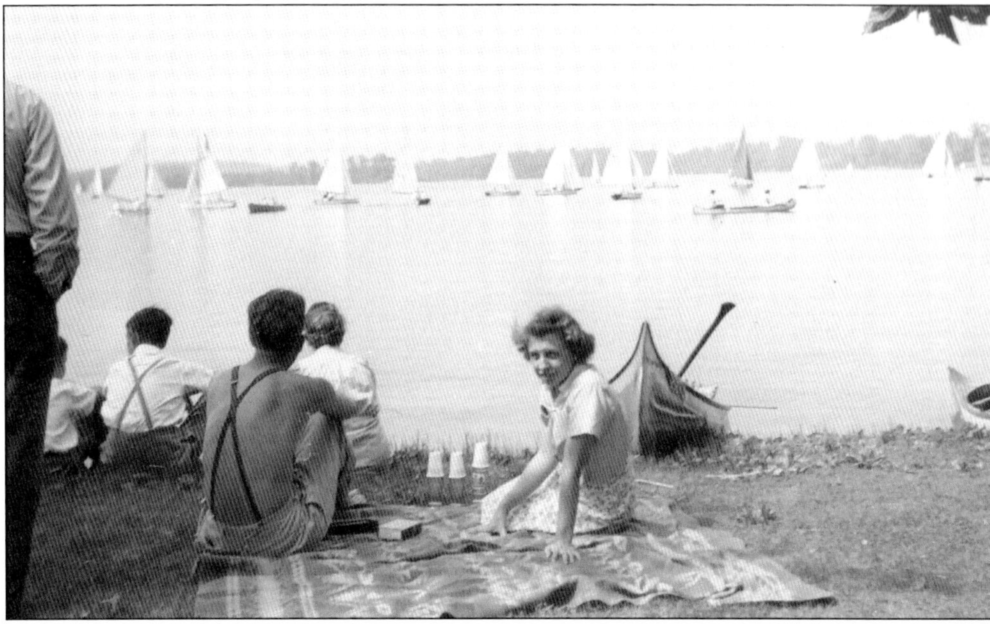

Sailboats have been popular on Chippewa Lake since the formation of the Chippewa Yacht Club. Sailing regattas have been held every summer since, drawing sailors from as far away as Canada to join the competition. Preferred sailboats were the Y-Flyer and the Snipe. (Gayle Baxter Foster.)

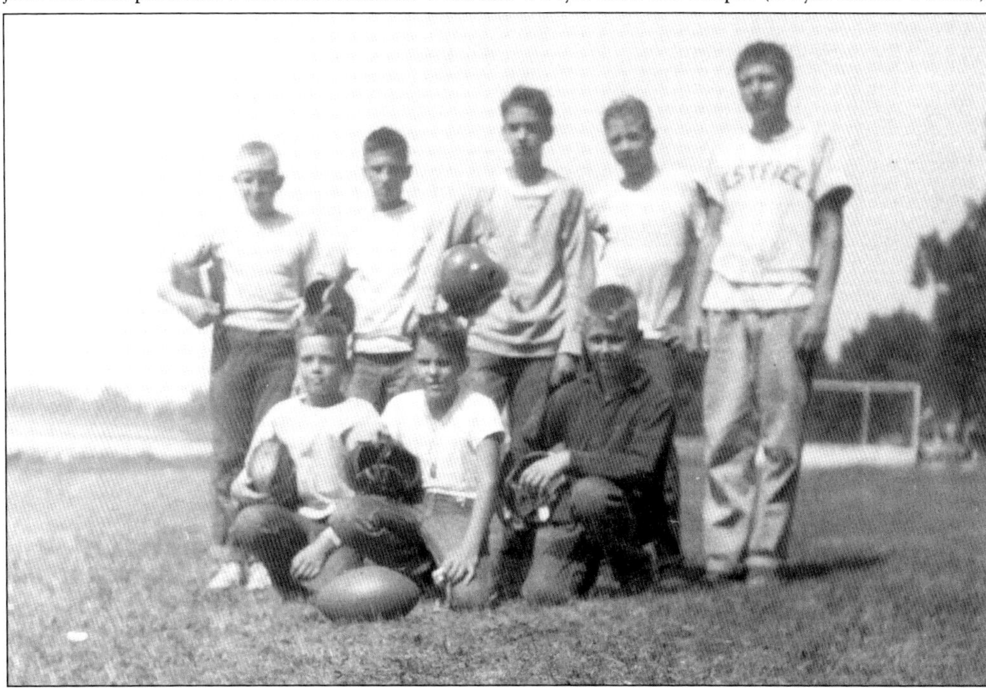

Fred Wiedenman generously donated odds and ends of football uniforms to start the first Chippewa-on-the Lake–Briarwood Beach football team. Games were played on the lakefront south of the beach. Chippewa-on-the-Lake's first football team is pictured here in 1956. They are, from left to right, (first row) Dick DeLuna, Jack DeLuna, and unidentified; (second row) Davey Stephenson, Tim Emerick, Donny Smith, "Buzz" Van Pelt, and Chad Grubb. (Chad Grubb.)

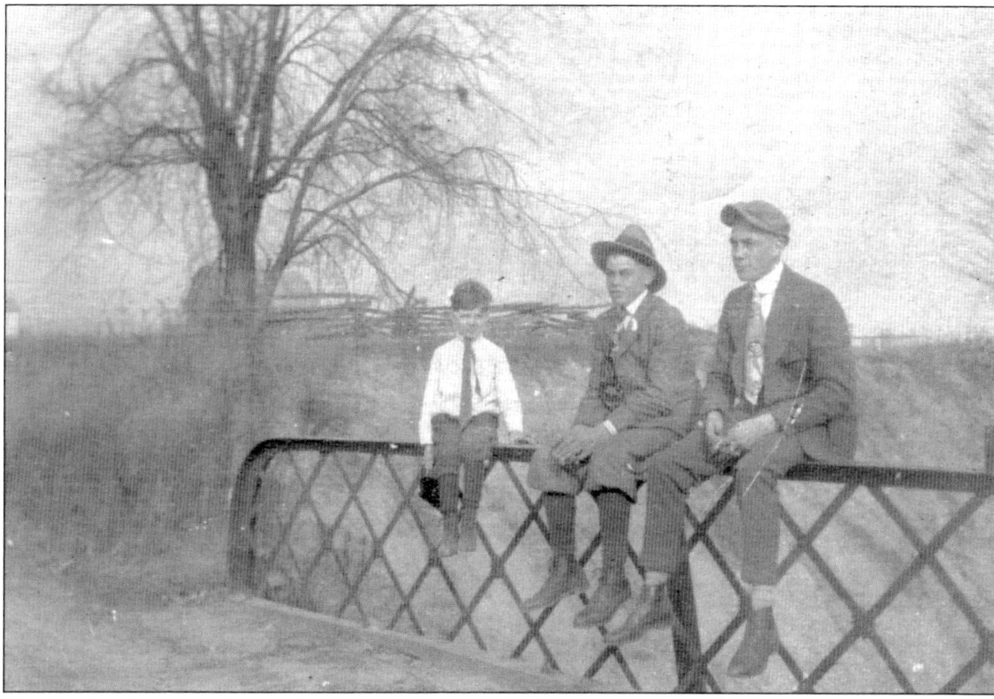

The Ruder farm was located on the west side of the Chippewa inlet. From left to right, brothers Martin, "Flick," and Milt are perched on the rail of the bridge over the inlet on Chippewa Road. Perhaps the chores were done and church awaited. (Jeffrey Schmitt.)

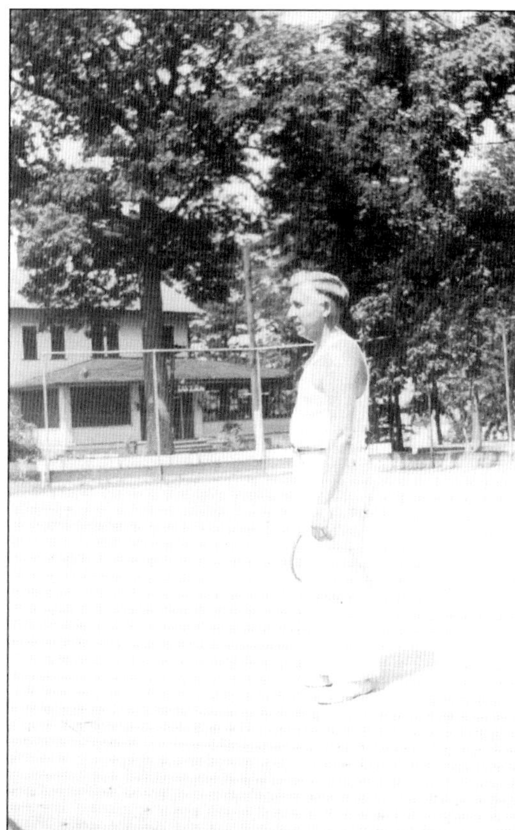

Bert Grubb, owner of a cottage on Parkway Path, was a pretty good tennis player in his day. He was still able to swing a racket and hit a tennis ball when he was 80 years old—some 40 years after this picture was taken at the tennis courts on Bungalow Bay Boulevard in 1936. Tarry Tavern is in the background. The tennis courts were installed by 1929. (Gayle Baxter Foster.)

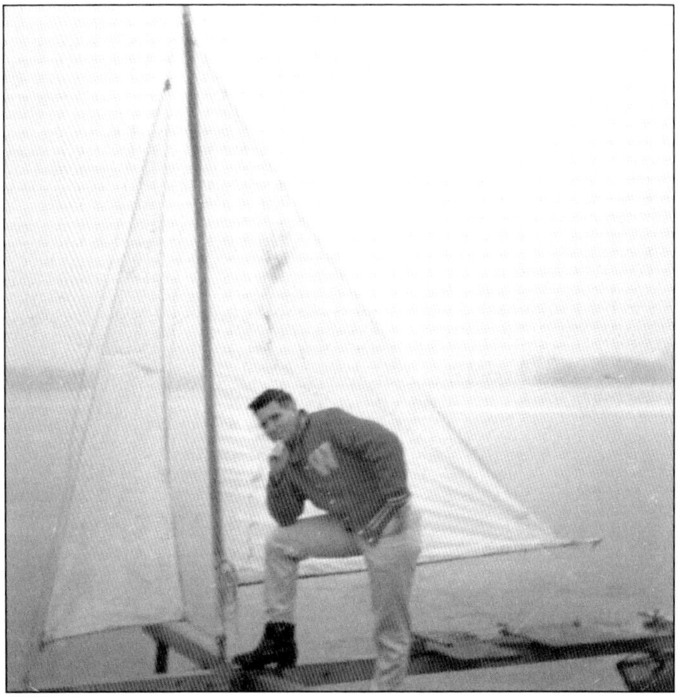

Throughout the years, the frozen lake has provided opportunities for ice fishing, skating, snowmobiling, and iceboating. Creative and daring young people were known to build their own iceboats from scraps of wood and fabric to catch the wind and sail the length of the lake. At left, Chad Grubb proudly shows off his iceboat in 1959. Below, an iceboat excursion in 1937 did not end well. (Left, Chad Grubb; below, Stephenson collection.)

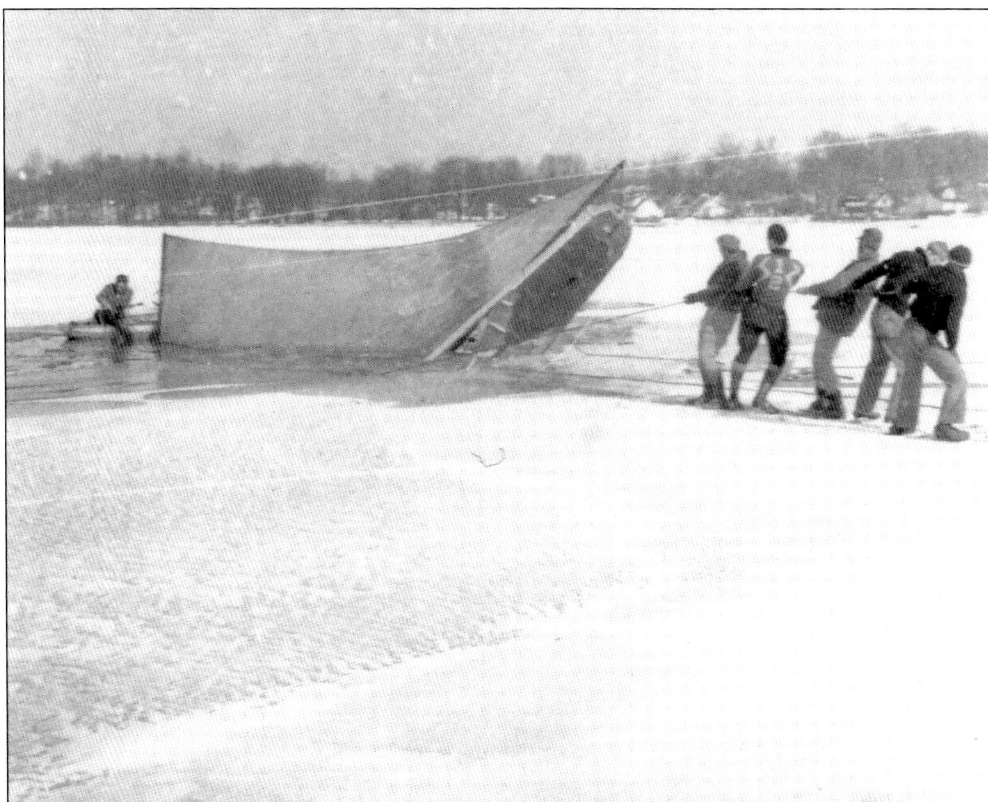

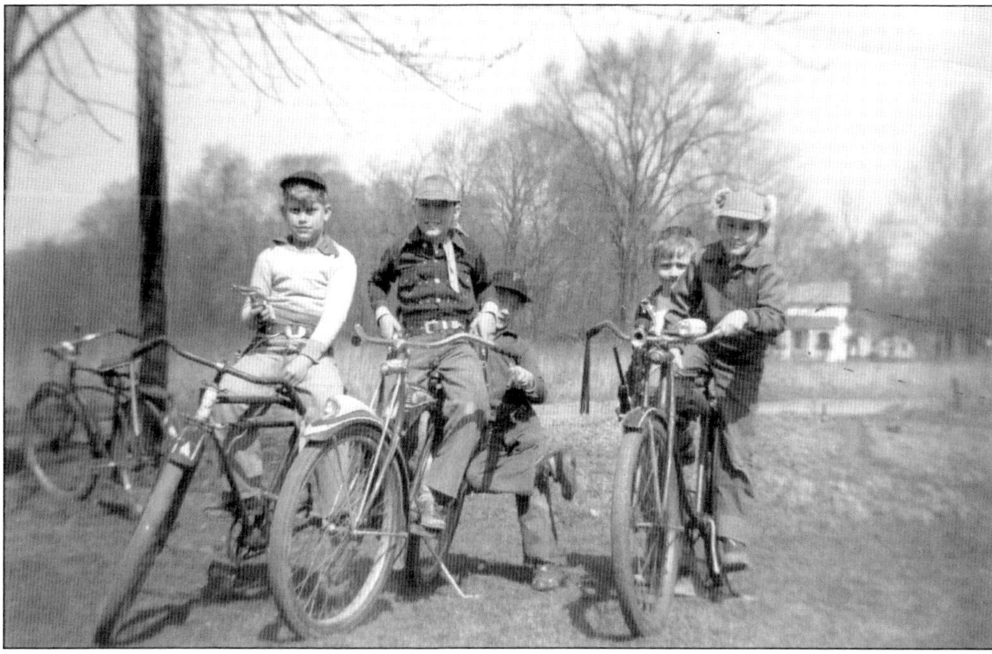

This 1950s photograph shows, from left to right, brothers Bob and Jack Rozell, brothers Jerry and Jim Favri, and Dave Lowry as they pause for a break at the Lowry residence at 374 Craggy Creek Drive. (Jim Favri.)

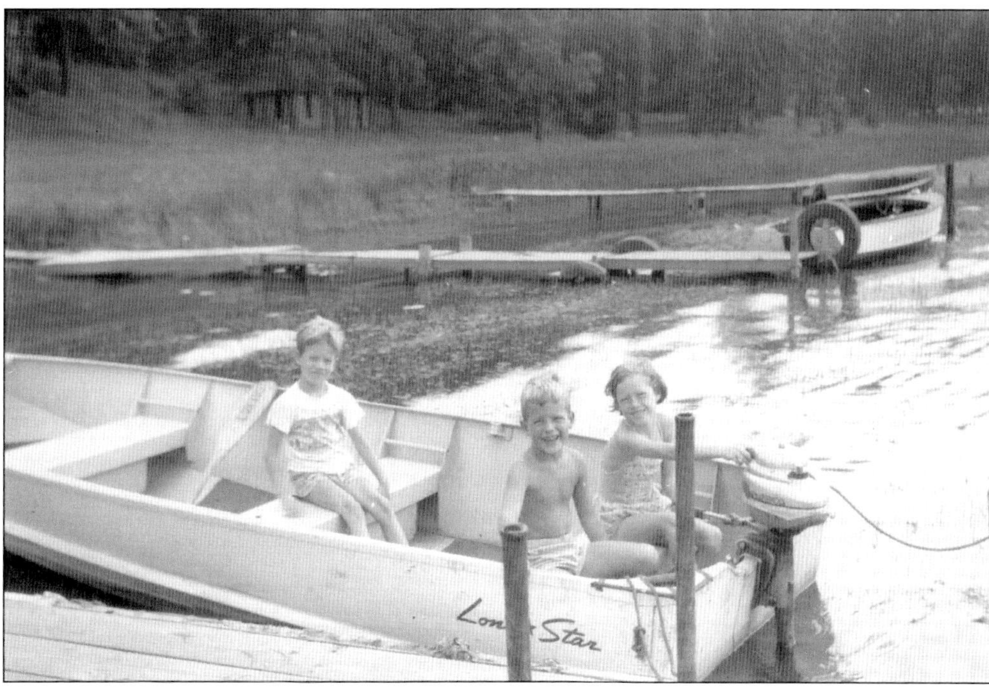

Pictured on the Chippewa-on-the-Lake lakefront in the summer of 1955 are, from left to right, Fred Van Pelt, Bruce Baxter, and Mary Van Pelt as they tie off on the pier down the hill from the former Tarry Tavern. The pump house is visible in the background. Farther up the hill on the right was the home of Bernice and Milt Ruder. (Gayle Baxter Foster.)

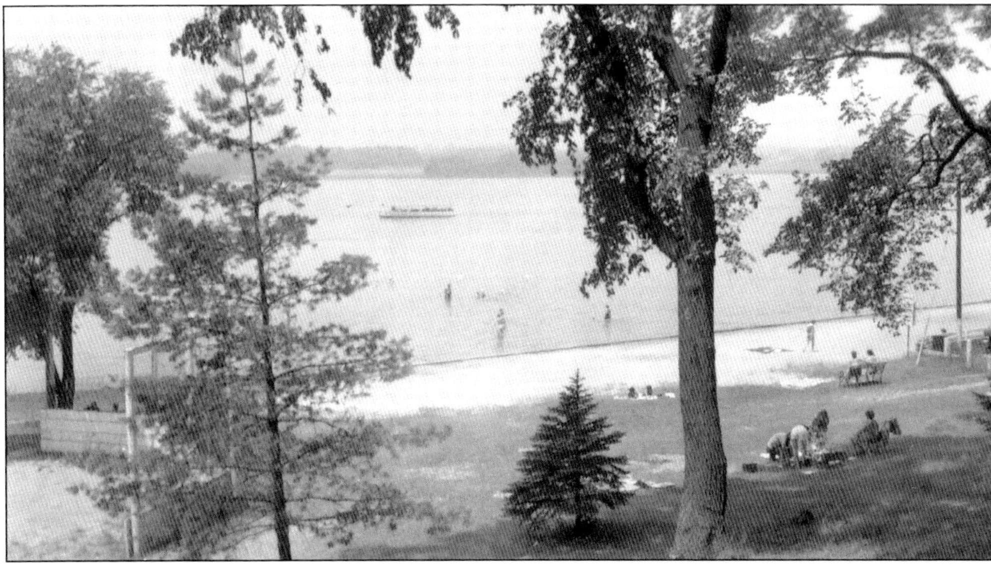

Above is a typical summer day overlooking the beach at Chippewa-on-the-Lake from the top of the hill and the walkway to the beach. At left is a backstop to a baseball diamond at the water's edge, where many a baseball was lost. Shown plying the water in the distance is the launch *Miss Chippewa* from Chippewa Lake Park. The boat took passengers on a leisurely trip around the lake with the pilot of the boat narrating along the way, often citing places such as "Lilypad Heights" to the north. Tim Emerick, a former teenage boat pilot from the park pier, noted the number of passengers the launch could carry: "Per Parker Beach, 48 was the max. He told me that many times!" (Above, Melter Family; below, Gayle Baxter Foster.)

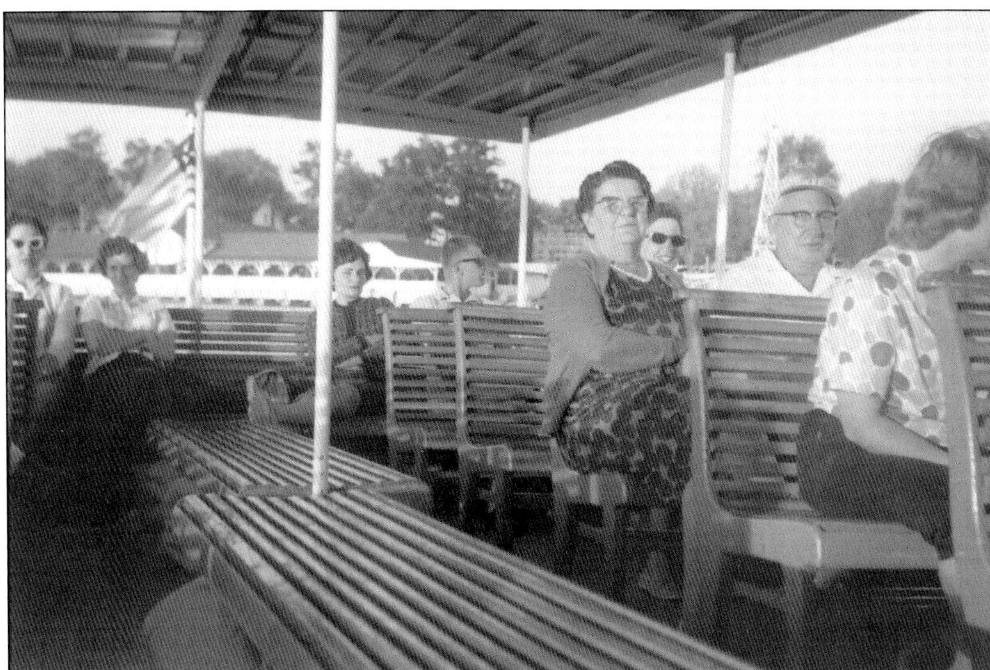

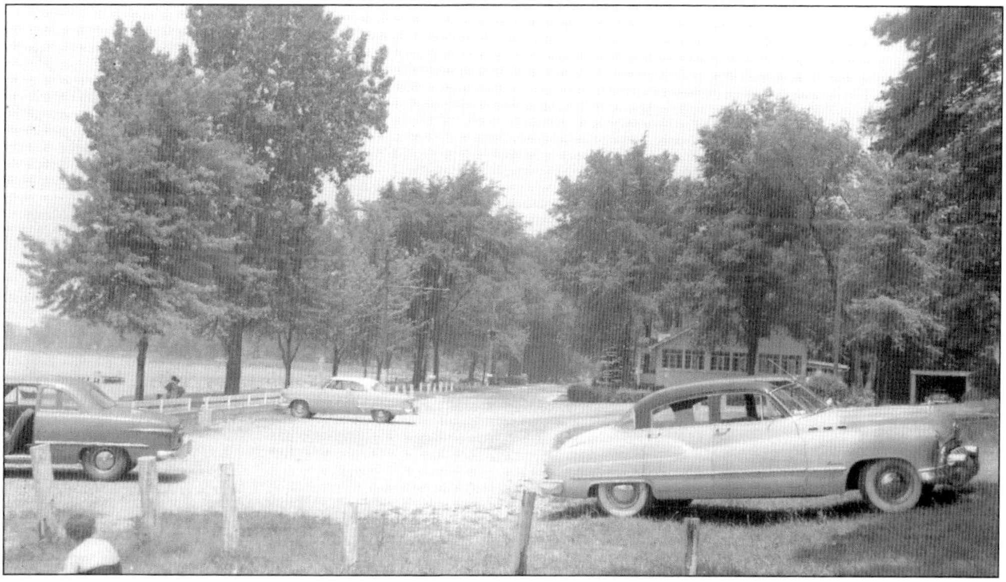

This photograph looks north toward the shorelines of Chippewa-on-the-Lake and the Village of Briarwood Beach. The benches were already in place, but the village had not yet erected the fence around the beach area. Docks were not nearly as plentiful in 1953 as they are today. (Melter family.)

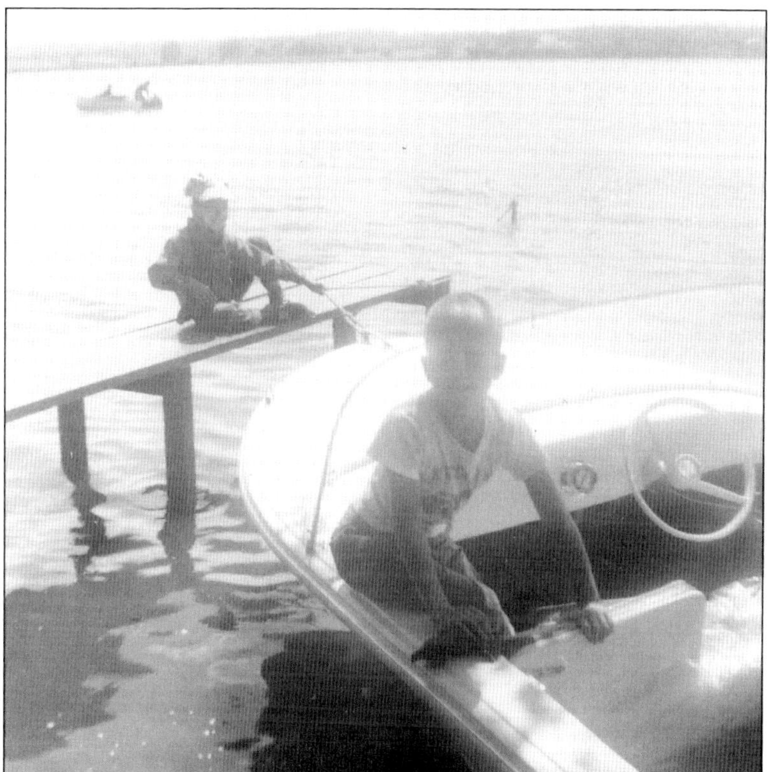

Spending summers at Chippewa Lake fulfilled many children's dreams. Tom Melter is shown enjoying time on the lake in his family's boat on July 19, 1960. (Melter family.)

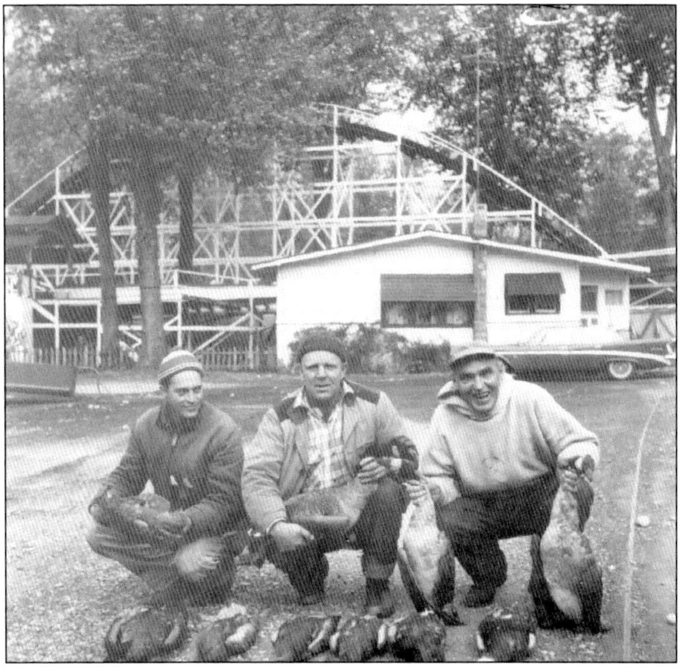

It was not all work for Chippewa Lake Park employees. From left to right, brothers Virgil, Nelson, and Bob Foster are pictured in 1963 after a successful day of hunting geese. Bob lived in the park year-round preparing the rides for the busy summer ahead, putting them to rest in the fall, and acting as caretaker through the winter. Phil Harper, also a year-round resident of the park, ran the roller coaster, and his cottage is visible in the background. (Gayle Baxter Foster.)

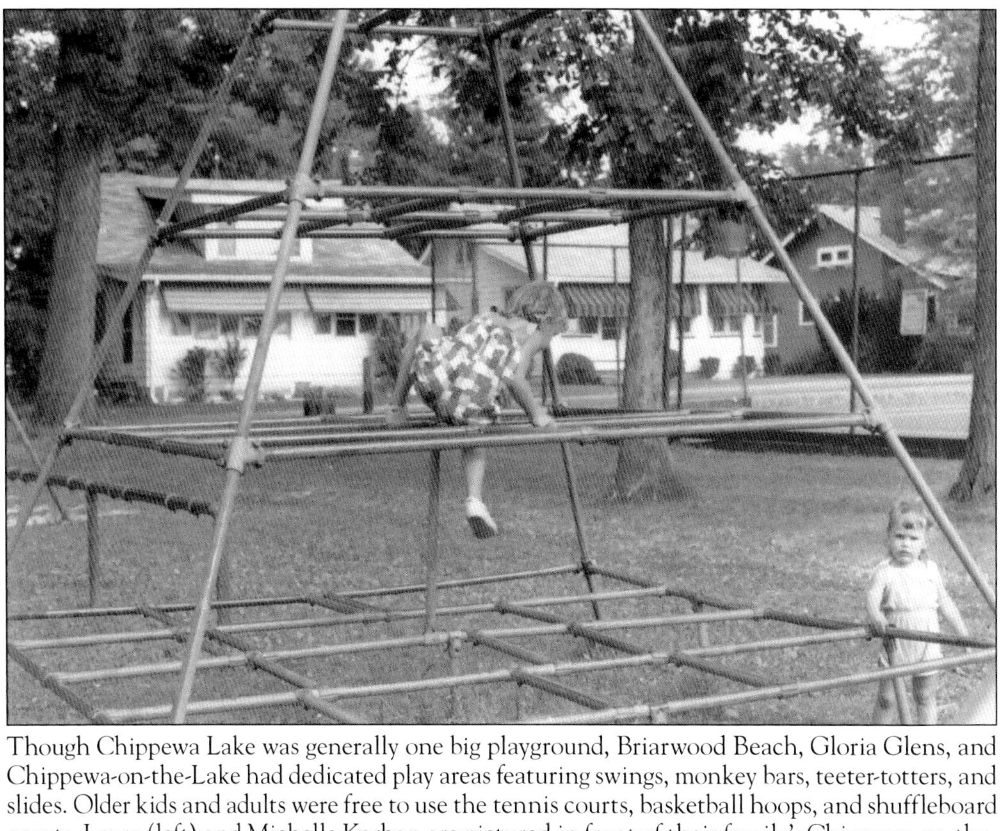

Though Chippewa Lake was generally one big playground, Briarwood Beach, Gloria Glens, and Chippewa-on-the-Lake had dedicated play areas featuring swings, monkey bars, teeter-totters, and slides. Older kids and adults were free to use the tennis courts, basketball hoops, and shuffleboard courts. Laura (left) and Michelle Karhan are pictured in front of their family's Chippewa-on-the-Lake cottage in 1982. (Sharon Sefl Karhan.)

Six

Businesses

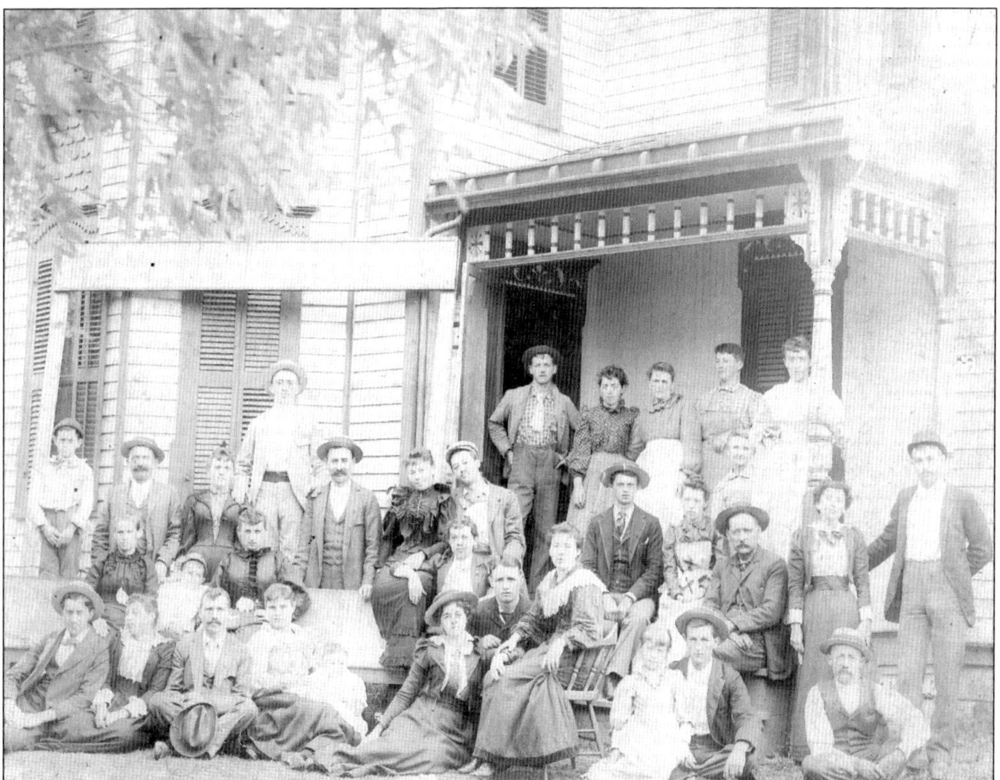

The Interurban arrived in Chippewa Lake in 1903. Visitors needing a place to stay found rooms at the Hotel Markle, which was in operation from 1904 through 1917. It was owned by Gideon and Clara Palmer Markle, who were united in a second marriage for both of them. Gideon died in 1907, and Clara continued to run the Markle until 1917, when she sold it to Peter Moore. There were dances at Moore's Hotel, which served chicken dinners for 50¢ on Sundays and was a popular place for boarders. It was known by various names through the years and is currently the Village Inn. Hotel Markle is pictured here in 1904 during its first year of operation. (Helen Riehm.)

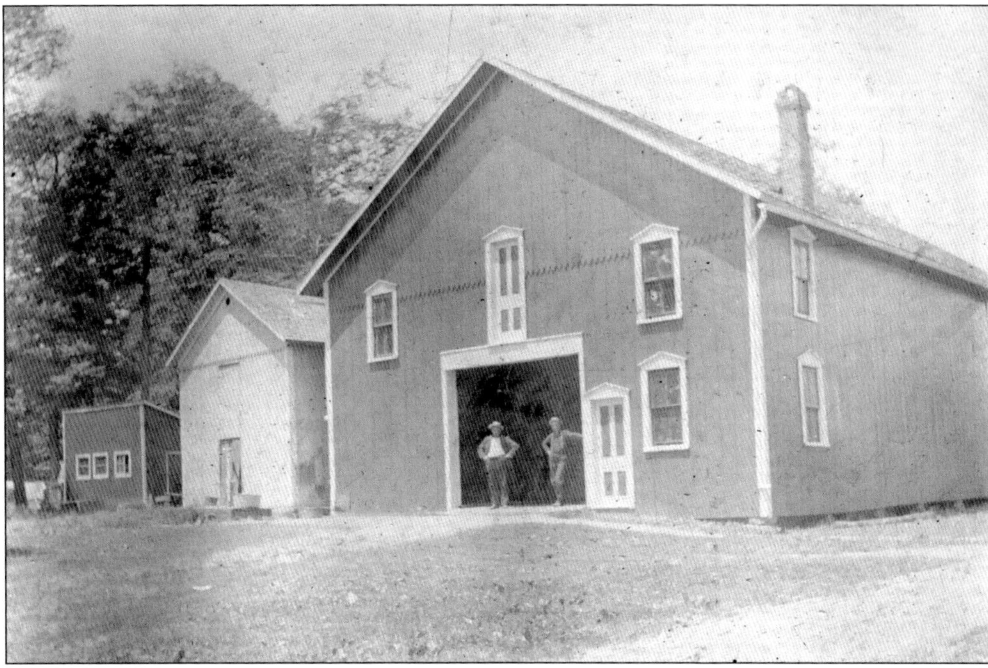

The Chippewa Livery was located on the west side of Lake Road just south of Chippewa Road, affording folks visiting the area an opportunity to enjoy a horseback ride along the many paths and roads. It has been renovated and is currently an apartment building. (Helen Riehm.)

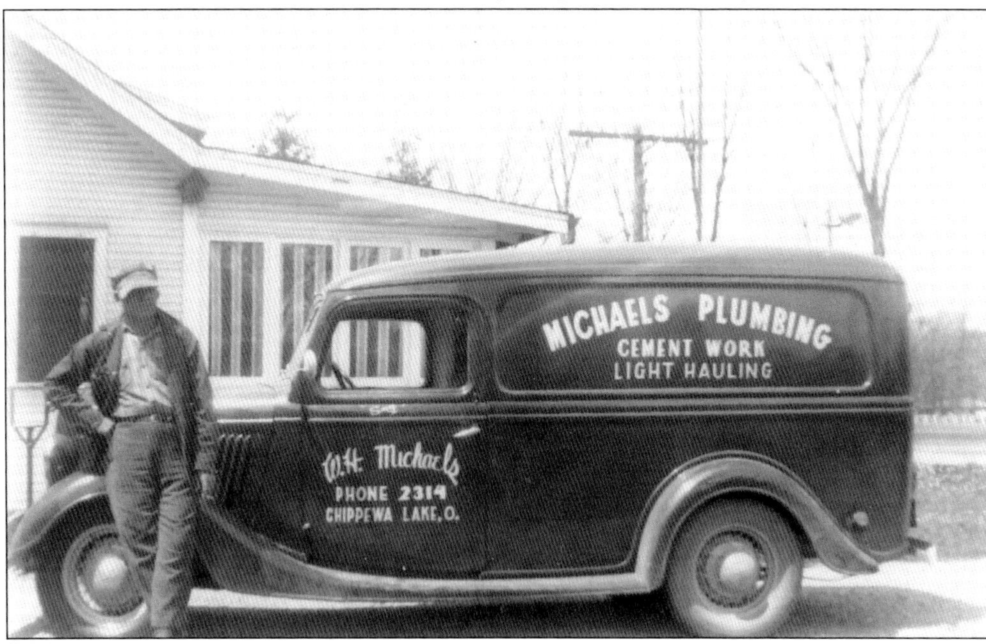

W.H. "Smokey" Michaels was a local Chippewa Lake plumber. Note the four-digit phone number on his panel truck. Eventually, the Chippewa area was assigned the MO 8 (MO for Morris) prefix, which ultimately became 769. Phones had party lines in the early 1950s, with families sharing a line with one or two others. Calls were limited to three minutes, often forcing a quick redial to complete conversations. (DeeDee Duecker.)

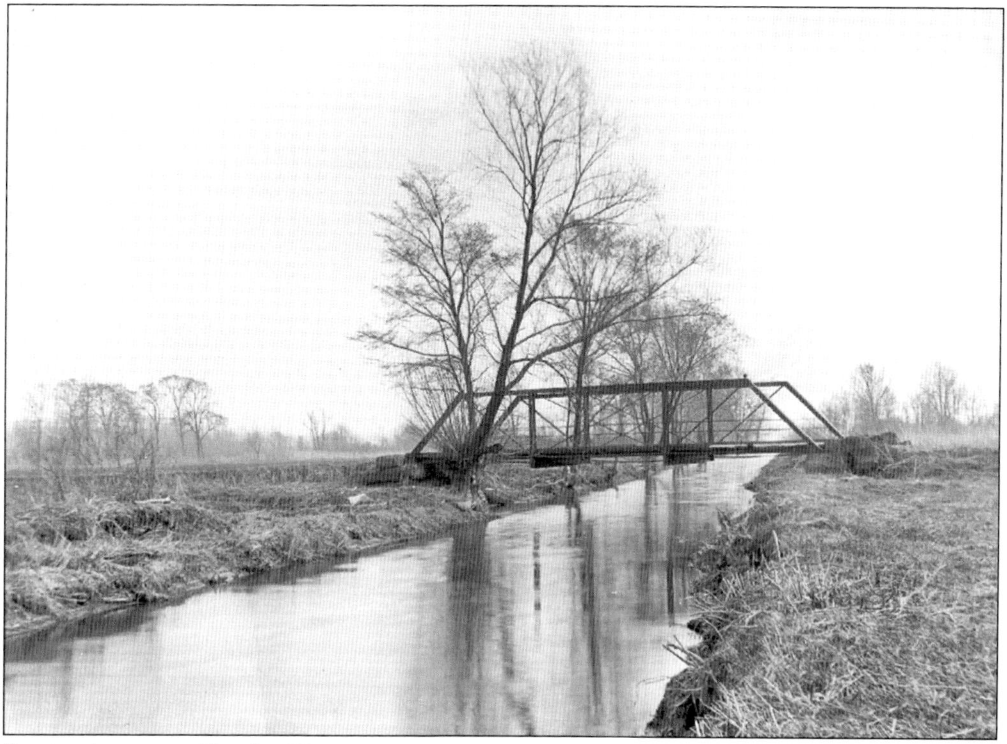

Previously operated by the Chippewa Shale Brick Company, Medina Clay Products took over in 1921, building three new kilns that summer. They manufactured drain tile, building blocks, and building and paving bricks. It was located east of the Chippewa Lake Rail Trail north of Chippewa Road. The 1880 map at right shows the spur that ran west off the Cleveland, Lorain & Wheeling rail line to the clay beds. Above is the inlet and the Chippewa Road bridge. The land to the north was swamp. In 1868, the county commissioners had a ditch dug with lateral channels to drain the land, lower the lake level, and make the land usable. Assessed to affected landowners, the project cost $15,000. (Above, Liverpool Historical Society; right, Medina County Historical Society.)

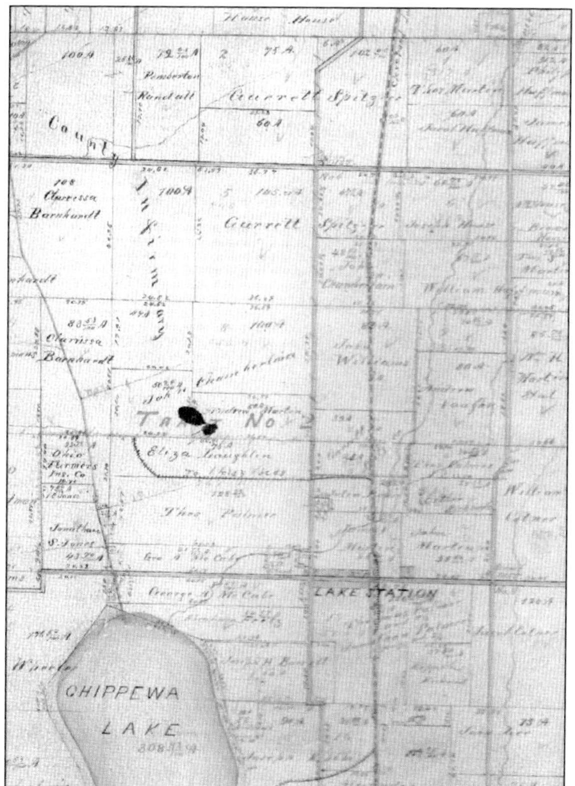

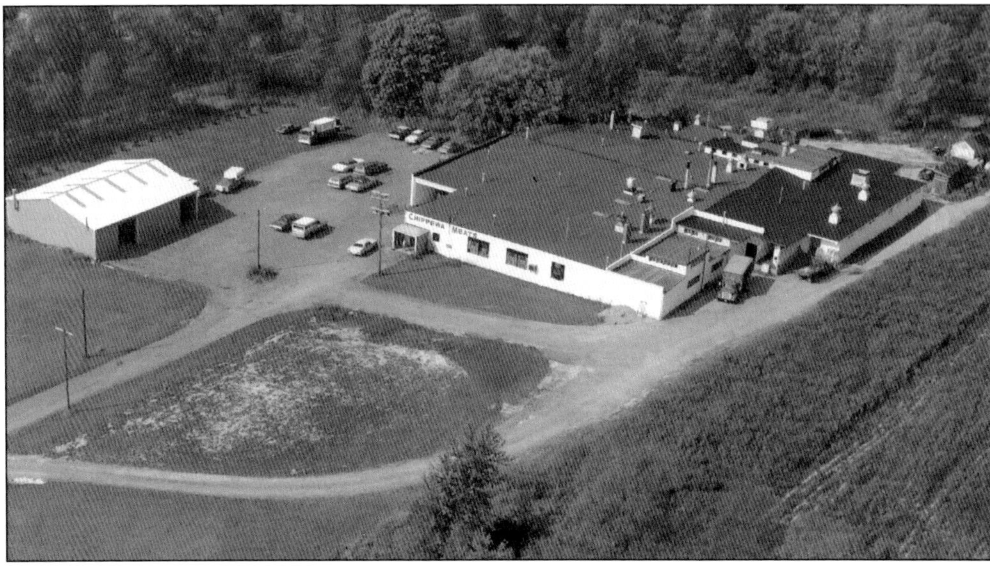

Reinhard Latzke began his career in the meat business in his native Germany before immigrating to America as a young married father in 1936. Following his dream, Latzke and his junior investor, William Riske, began Chippewa Meats Inc. in 1946 on the north side of Chippewa Road near the Chippewa Elevator. Butchering was done onsite, and the company furnished meats to family-owned grocery stores and restaurants throughout a wide area, including the Jungle Larry Wild Animal Show at Chippewa Lake Park. Customer favorites included country sausage, smoked hams, and their famous hot dogs. Following Riske's retirement, Latzke continued to work until his death in 1979. The company continued until 1984, when it was sold. Latzke was a loyal supporter of Medina County 4-H and FFA clubs, buying many grand champion steers at the Medina County Fair for 33 years. The Medina County Fair Board recognized him in 1980 for his promotion of agribusiness in the county vocational school, as he believed agriculture feeds the nation, and youth should be supported since they will be the suppliers of agricultural products in the future. Latzke is pictured below at left at the fair in August 1976. (Both, Marliese Latzke Leggett.)

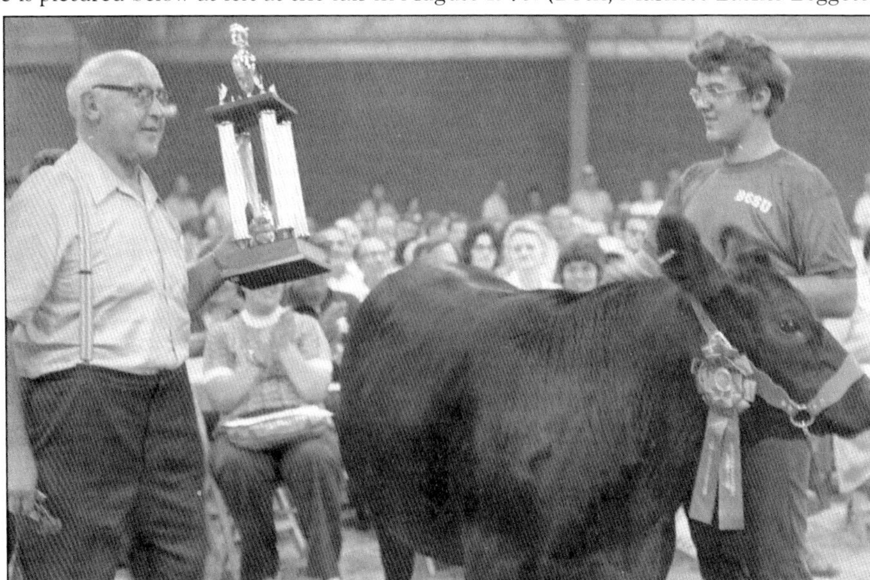

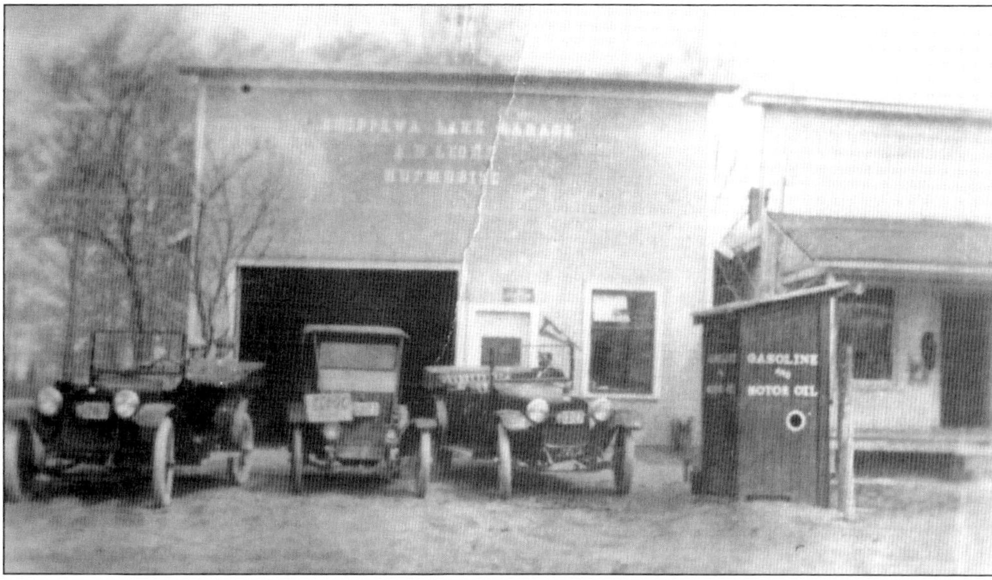

"Alf" Leohr (pictured below), the founder of Leohr Motors Inc., was born in 1881 on a farm south of Chippewa Lake. He looked into the future and saw that the automobile was going to put horses back on the farm. In 1911, he began selling Hupmobiles, often taking a horse and buggy in trade and teaching the new owner how to drive the car. The business moved from its original location (above) on Chippewa Road to its permanent home on Lake Road in 1928. Alf's son William joined the company in 1925, when it became a Chrysler dealer. Alf's grandson William Jr. joined the family business and remained until he sold the business and retired in 1996 after 85 continuous years, remaining open through both world wars and the Great Depression. (Both, William Leohr Jr.)

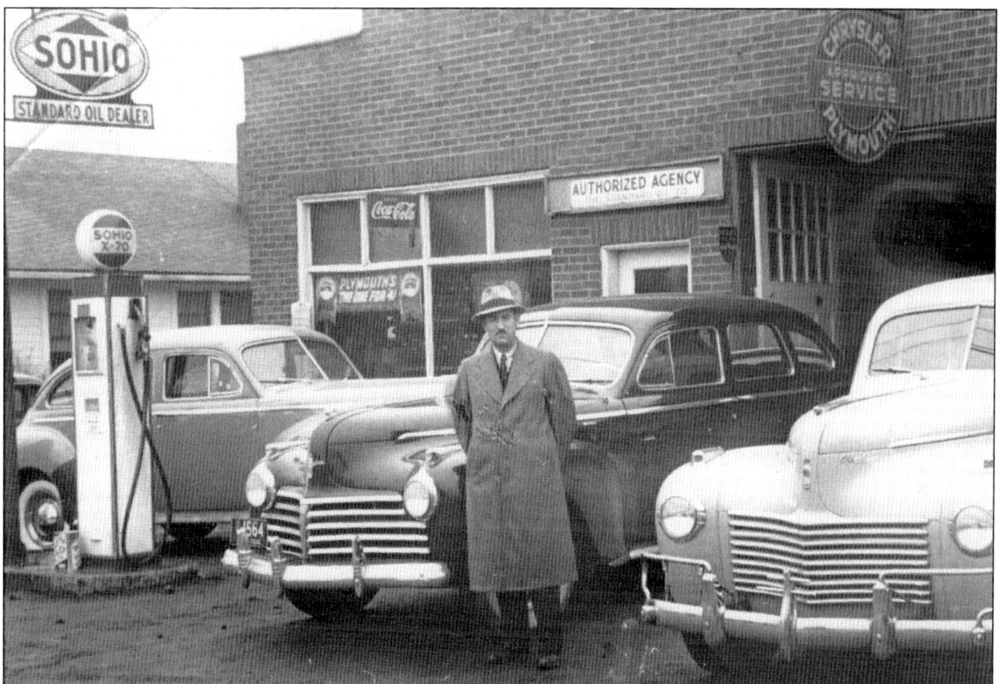

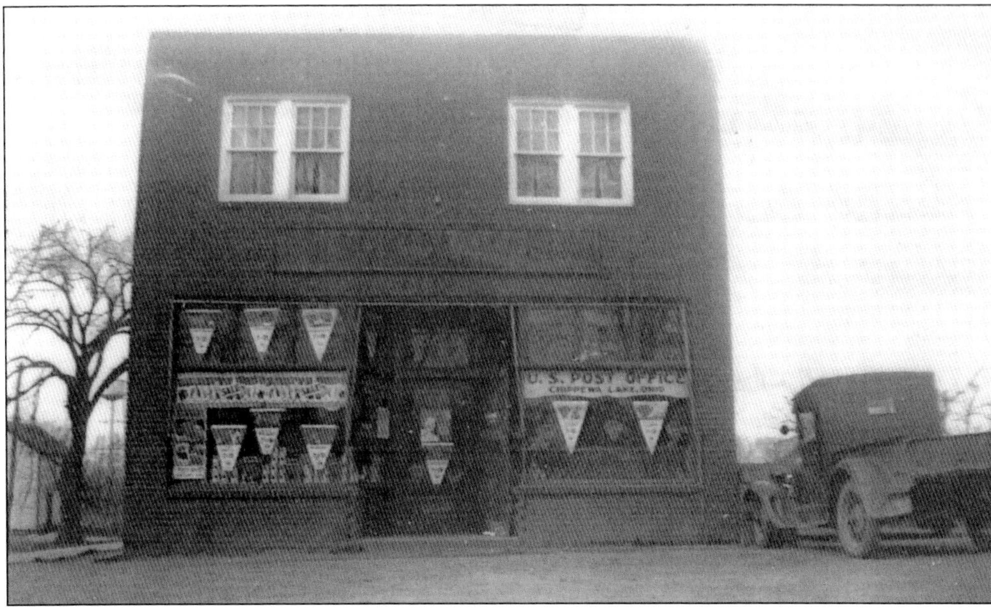

Bay Taylor built the store at the corner of Heather Hedge Drive and Lake Road in 1925. He was also the postmaster. Taylor would shut down the store in the wintertime and allow children to roller-skate through it. After operating the store for many years, he sold it to Bob Duecker in the early 1960s. Duecker ran it until his retirement. He also operated the store under the ballroom at Chippewa Lake Park during the summer. Barb and Lindsey Goodman currently own and operate Goodman's Corner Cupboard, which opened in 2003. (McDonald family.)

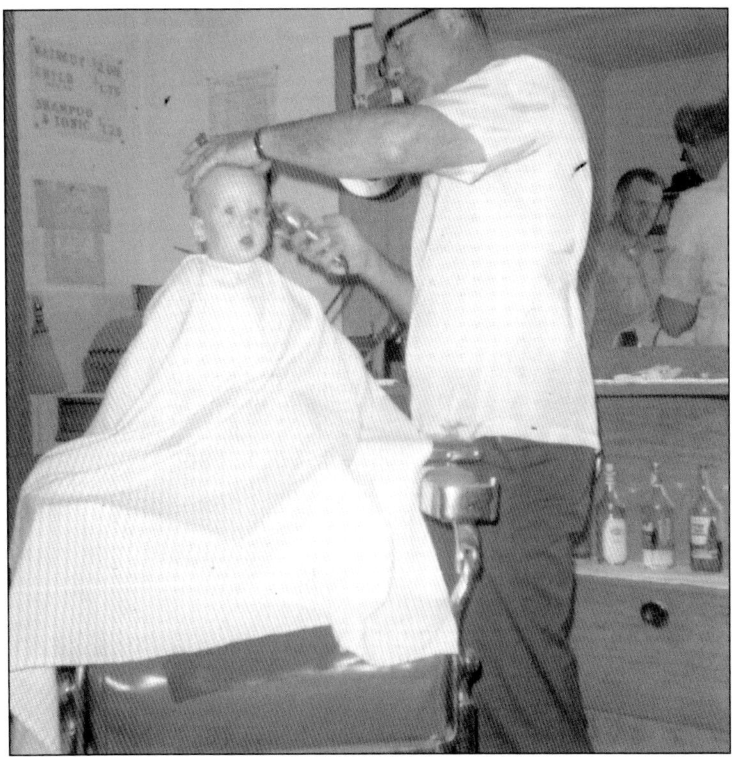

Dick Lett ran a barbershop on Lake Road for a number of years. Here, one-year-old David Foster sits patient and unafraid as Lett gives him his first haircut in 1969. The small cinderblock shop still stands, although it has been unused since the end of the 1970s. (Gayle Baxter Foster.)

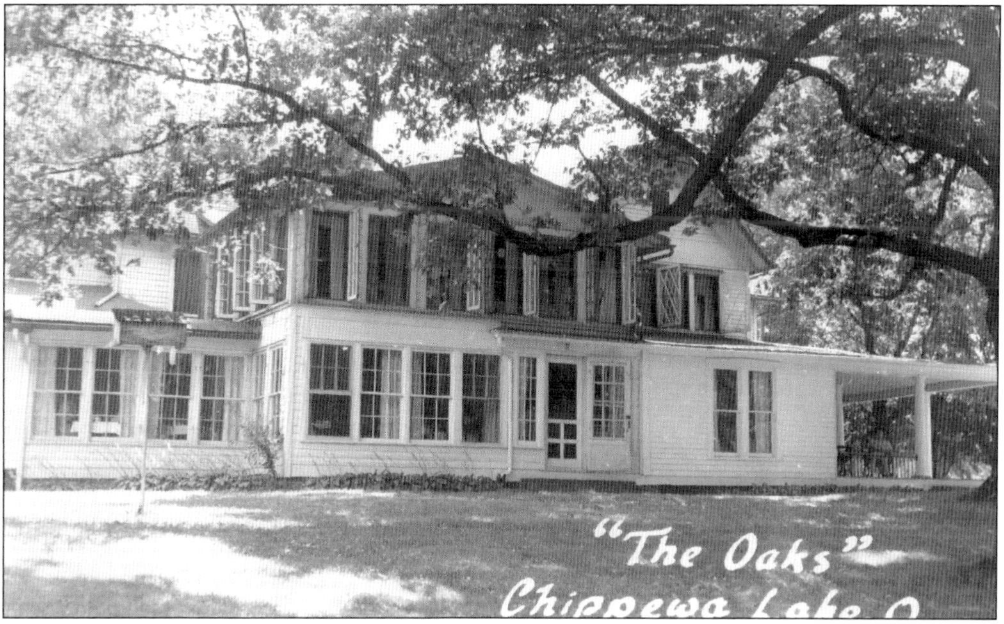

Fred Townsend created this estate, which he named Five Oaks for the five trees that stood on the property facing the lake. He added a barn, a carriage house, a boathouse, and a formal garden. Townsend raised a flag bearing the name Five Oaks on a 125-foot flagpole that could reportedly be seen from Wooster Pike (Route 3). The estate was completed in 1914 at a cost of $110,000, and played host to the rich and famous of the day. It was a private residence until the late 1950s. Today, the Oaks Lakeside Restaurant and Event Center offers fine dining and is a popular site for weddings and receptions. (Beach family.)

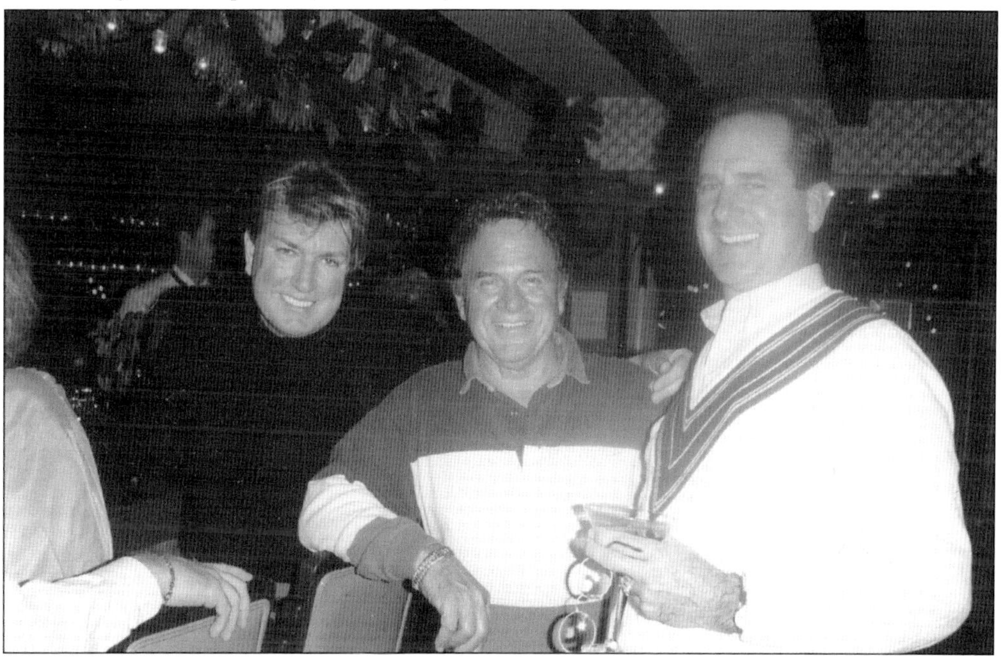

Don Casper (center), owner of the Oaks Lakeside Restaurant from 1961 until his death in 2003, is pictured here with Bob Boran (left) and Dr. Bill Evanko. (Johnny and Audrey Pollizi.)

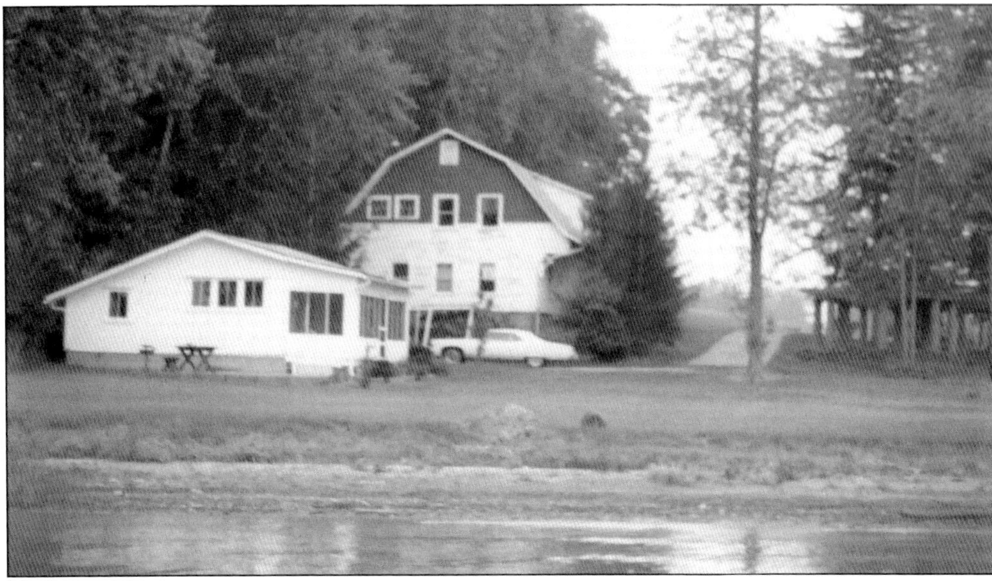

J.F. Townsend, owner of the original 200 acres that encompassed Five Oaks (now home to the Oaks Lakeside Restaurant), built the Coop to house his prized roosters; it still stands at the water's edge. The estate dates back to the late 1800s. The Coop, as well as the famed colonnade (at right) was completed in 1918. The large building behind the Coop was called the Annex and offered overnight accommodations to overflow guests from the Oaks Lodge when it was a hotel. The annex was moved up the hill in the mid-1970s and contains three apartments today. The current owners of The Oaks keep the Coop for personal use, occasionally renting it out on weekends during the summer season. (Beach family.)

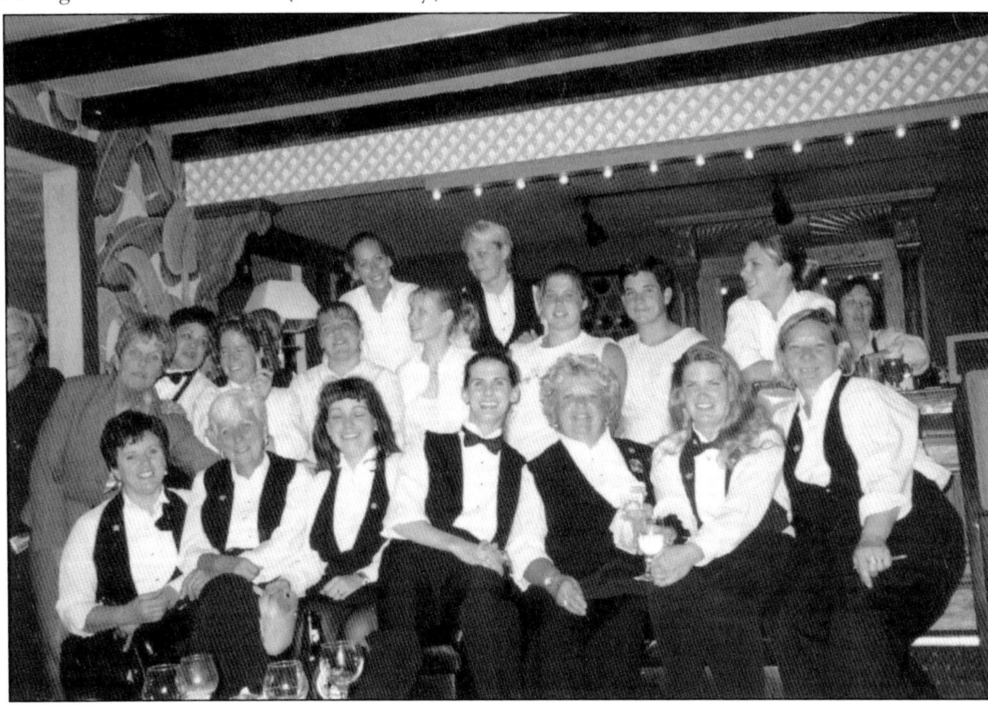

The Oaks Lakeside Restaurant staff is pictured here in 1985. (Johnny and Audrey Pollizi.)

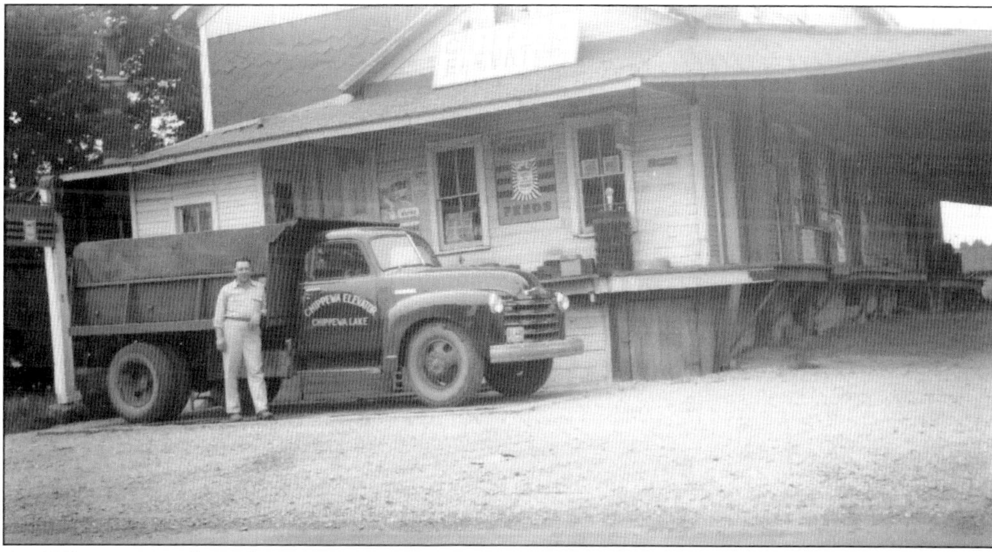

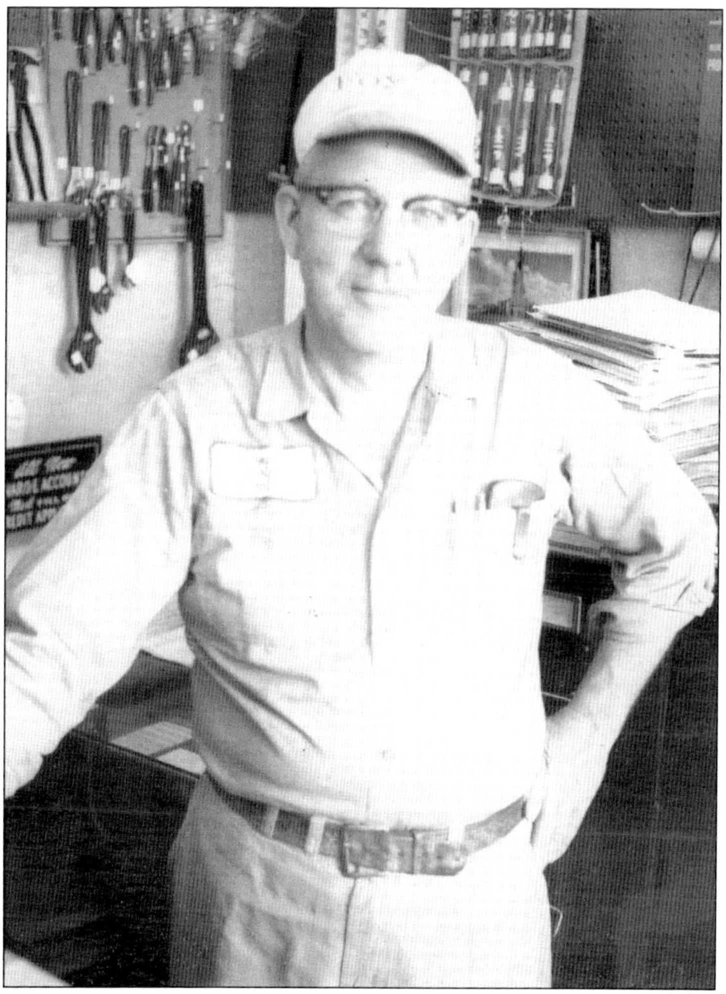

Carl Thomas purchased Chippewa Elevator in 1946 and was the sixth owner of the building, which dates to 1900. Grain, livestock, potatoes, hay, and straw were shipped from the elevator via rail before it was purchased in 1946. Thomas sold gravel, stone, coal, cement block, and brick out of the building. In addition to being a Chippewa Lake business owner, Carl Thomas was a spotter for the National Weather Service and was paid 50¢ each time he reported more than a half-inch of rain. In the photograph at right, he is behind the counter of Chippewa Elevator in the early 1960s. (Both, Carla Thomas.)

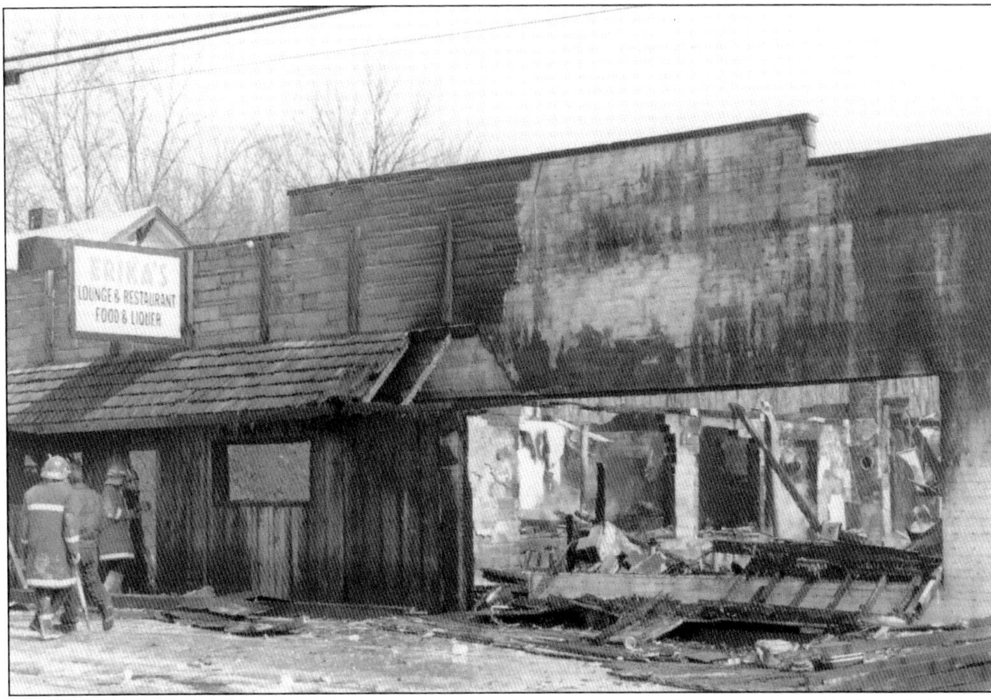

The cement block building across the street from the entrance to Chippewa Lake Park at 7695 Lake Road was a popular watering hole that went by many names during its lifetime: the Gay Nineties, Spanish Gardens, Steve's, the Bloody Bucket, and, most recently, Erika's. It was frequented by park employees at the end of the evening during the summer months, and locals during the remainder of the year. The front room held a wraparound bar, while the back room had tables, a jukebox, and a dance floor, with live music on occasion. During its heyday, it had a questionable reputation mostly due to a clientele whose prime concern was the arrival of the beer truck. The building was destroyed by fire on February 26, 1987, and never rebuilt. (Brad and April Winter.)

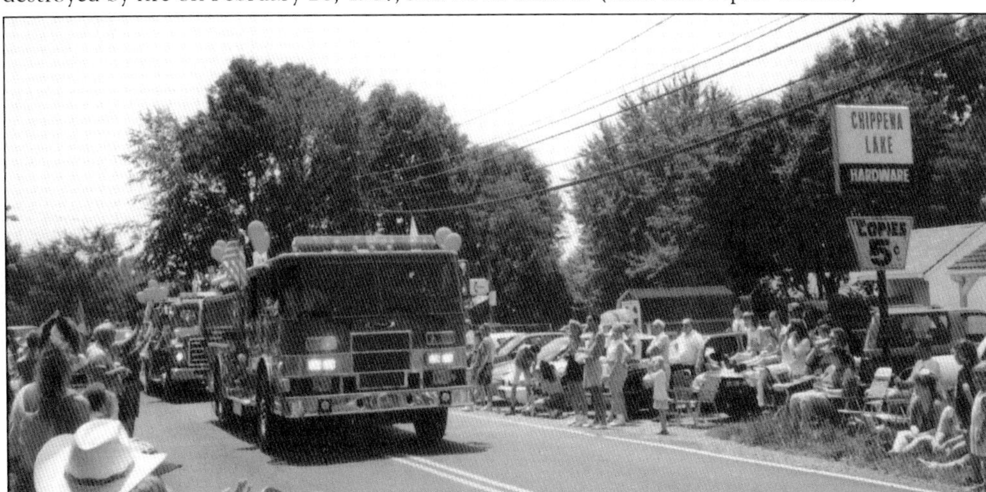

Chippewa Lake Hardware was located on the corner of Heather Hedge Drive and Lake Road. Over the years, this building has held gas stations, a produce stand, a baseball card shop, two thrift stores, Habitat for Humanity, and, most recently, a service business. (Brad and April Winter.)

Seven

CHURCHES, SCHOOLS, GOVERNMENT, AND CIVIC LIFE

The Methodist church was built in 1905 on the northeast corner of Lake and Chippewa Roads. The Methodists merged with the Evangelical United Brethren in the early 1960s and formed the United Methodist Church. The original Methodist church was torn down in the early 1970s to make room for Chippewa Valley Bank. The bells from both churches stand in front of the United Methodist Church, built in 1968. (Gayle Baxter Foster.)

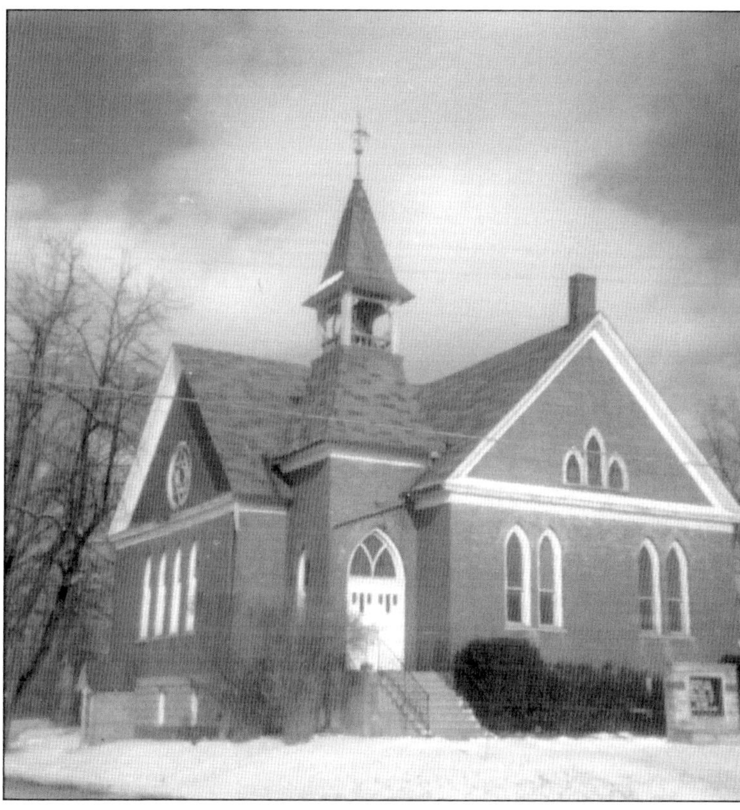

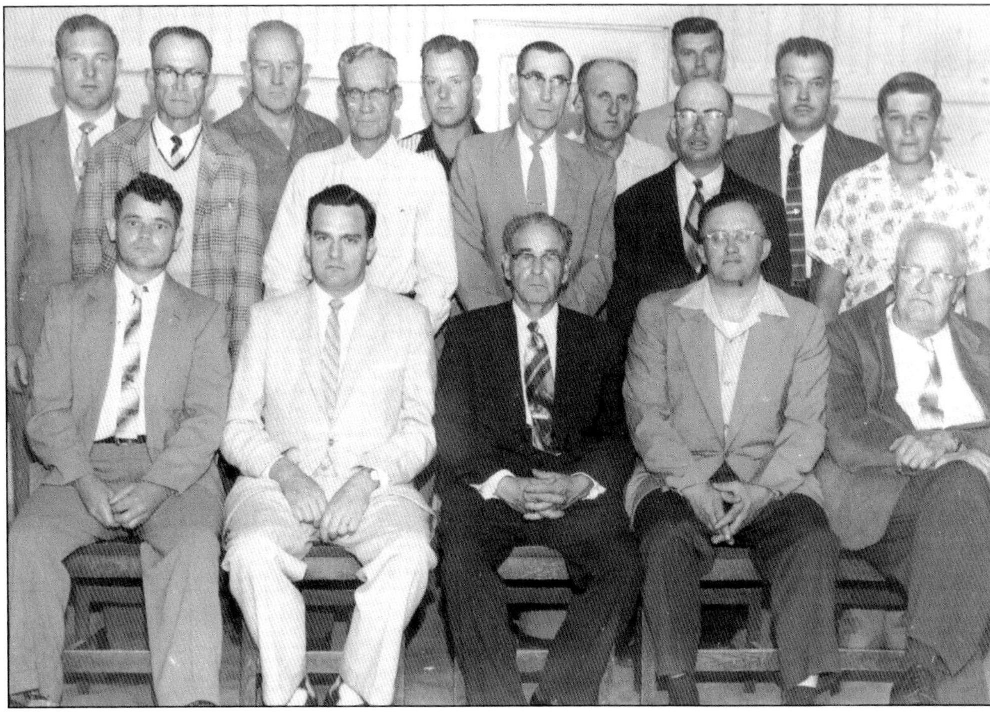

The Methodist men pictured here in 1957 are, from left to right, (first row) Harold Vest, unidentified, Don Kindig, Bill Baxter, and Robert McCullogh; (second row) Forest Lees, Eb Callihan, two unidentified, and Bert Humbel; (third row) Phil Shook, Harold Stephenson, Harold Jenny, Frank Hamilton, and unidentified; (fourth row) Don Eads. (Gayle Baxter Foster.)

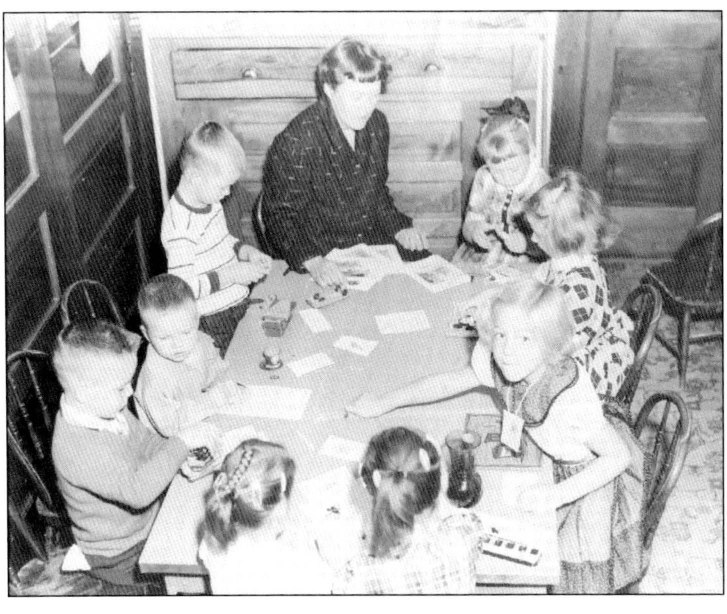

Evangelical United Brethren Church Sunday school teacher Leona Gregory explains a craft to her young students. Clockwise from Gregory's right are her daughter Donna Gregory, unidentified, and Nancy Grubb. The rest are unidentified. (Nancy Greve Jarvis.)

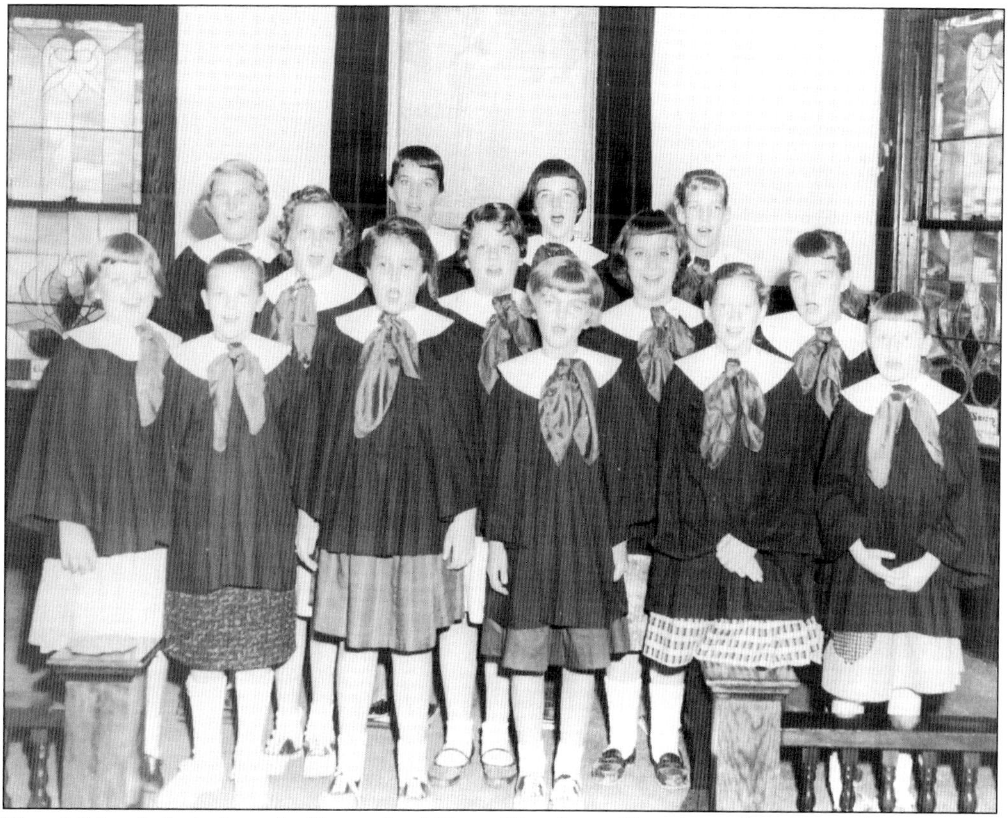

The children's choir from the Evangelical United Brethren Church at Chippewa Lake is pictured here in the mid-1950s. From left to right are (first row) Judy Hall, Sandy Cotner, Cathy Harnden, Sandy Smith, Mary Van Pelt, and Nancy Greve; (second row) unidentified, Carla Thomas, and Nancy Bender; (third row) Jeanette Gregory, Margie Corp, Joyce Barnum, Barbara Brown, and Beth Baird. Stained-glass windows are currently part of the decor at the Oaks Lakeside Restaurant. (Nancy Greve Jarvis.)

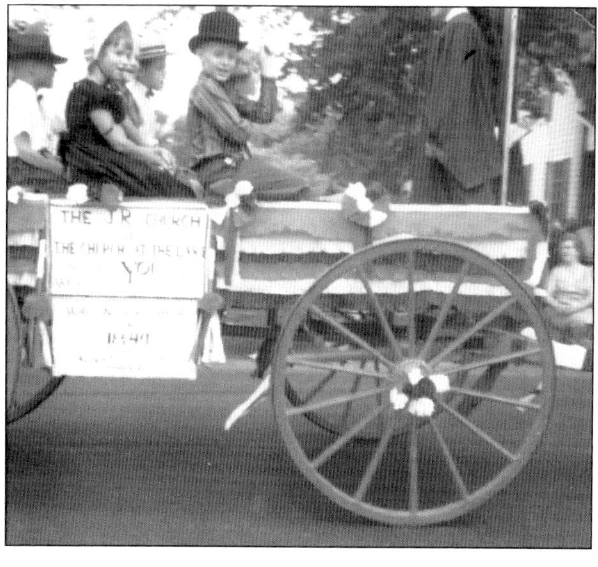

The Lions Club–sponsored Fourth of July parade is one of the most popular events in Chippewa, drawing thousands of spectators along the mile-long route. Here, children from Chippewa Church at the Lake United Methodist Junior Church have the privilege of riding on a float and waving to their friends and families along the way. Carol Mowrey is the little girl with the hat in the back. (Dee Dee Duecker.)

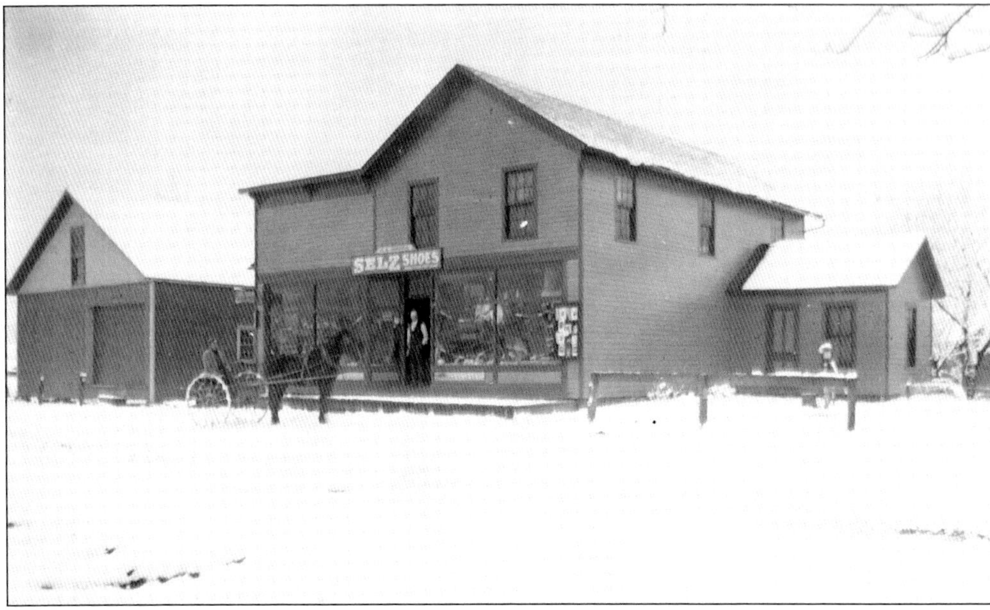

Early residents of Chippewa Lake found their mail at the Whittlesey post office established in 1850 in Lafayette Township. This photograph shows an early Chippewa Lake post office on Chippewa Road. The Chippewa Lake post office was established in 1878. Early post offices were often located in existing businesses—usually a local store, as the Selz Shoes sign indicates. Mail at Chippewa was later handled in the grocery store that now stands at the corner of Heather Hedge and Lake Road, with the post office finally moving into its own separate building on Heather Hedge Drive. (Cyndy Naragon.)

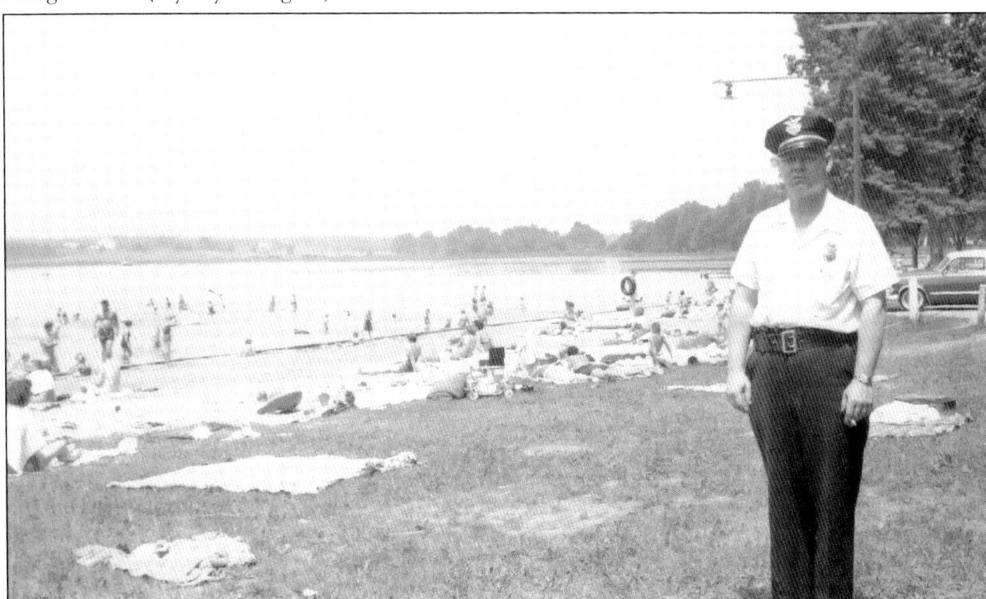

Henry Gween was the local policeman at Chippewa-on-the-Lake in 1955. Here, he maintains law and order at the beach. Once Tarry Tavern was put out of business for suspected illegal activities, crime in the neighborhood consisted of parking violations, barking dogs, loud music, and an occasional act of minor vandalism. (Gayle Baxter Foster.)

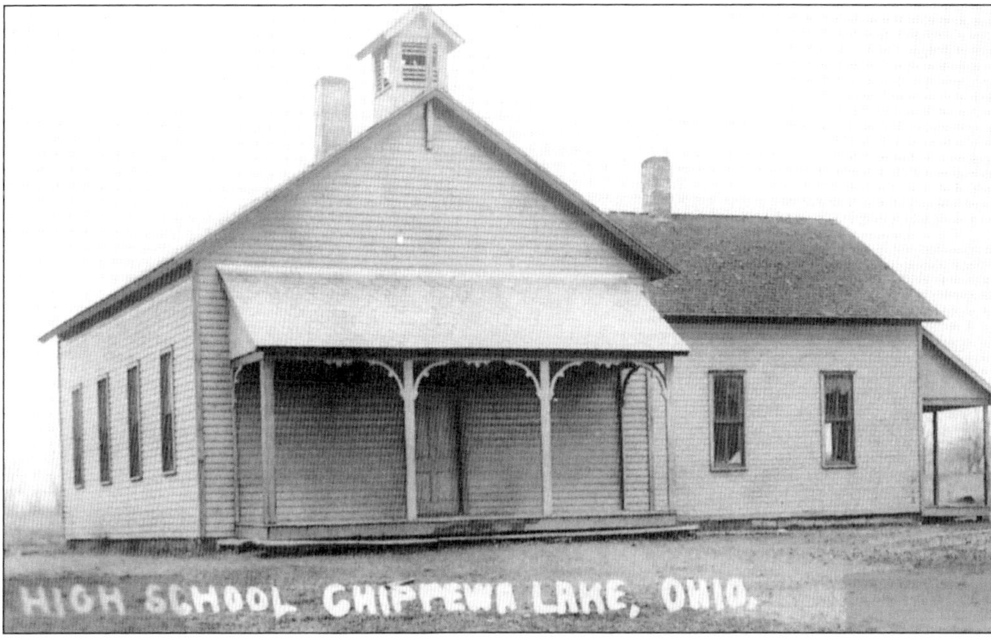

Chippewa Lake High School is pictured here in 1910. The school was east of the depot on Chippewa Road. It was a replacement for a school that was destroyed by fire and was one of 12 high schools in Medina County at the start of the 20th century. As people wanted better education for their children, the high school movement began in the last quarter of the 19th century. Eventually, a second room was added, with one room serving first through fourth grades and the other serving fifth through eighth grades. During the 1930s, residents decided to consolidate their school districts, and this school was abandoned. The building sat empty for a number of years but was eventually moved to Briarwood Boulevard in the Village of Briarwood Beach. Clyde Moore, a local carpenter, used both sections of the school to build two houses that still stand on Briarwood Boulevard just east of the old Interurban track. The photograph below was taken on April 18, 1894. Roy Palmer is second from left in the third row. (Above, Jackie Wills family; below, Helen Riehm.)

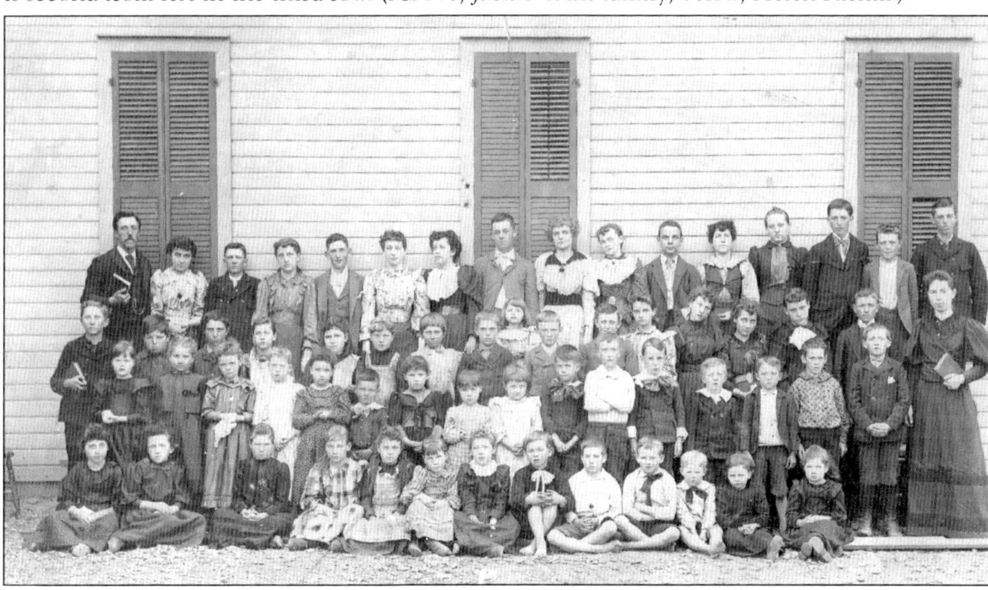

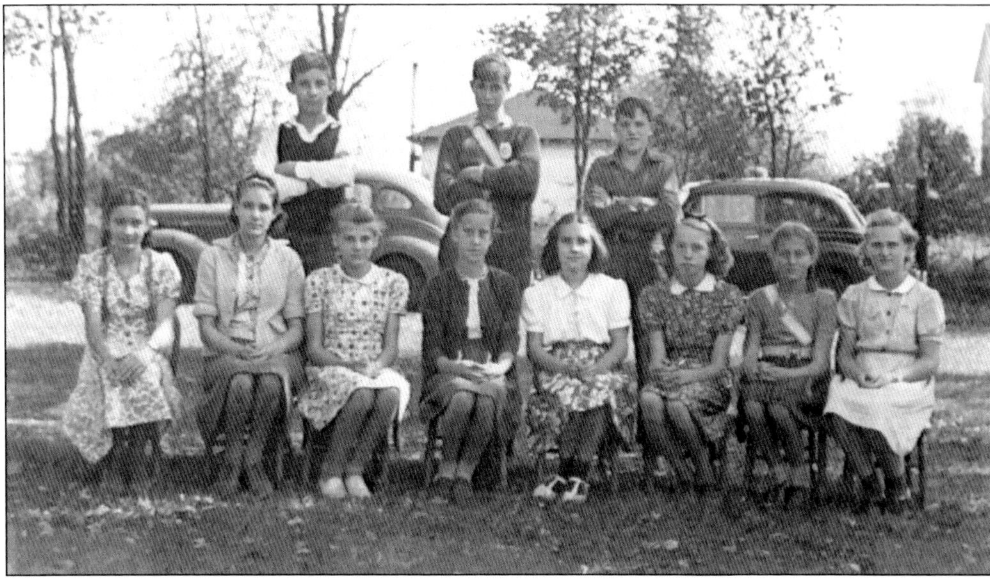

Students from the Chippewa Lake Local School are pictured around 1936. From left to right are (first row) Alma Buehler, Ruth Gift, Donna McFadden, Joan Eickenberg, Phyllis Tompkins, Betty Hartman, Betty Lou Lee Harpe, and Helen Harvey; (second row) Marvin Gift, Harold Davis, and Nate McDonald. (Jackie Wills family.)

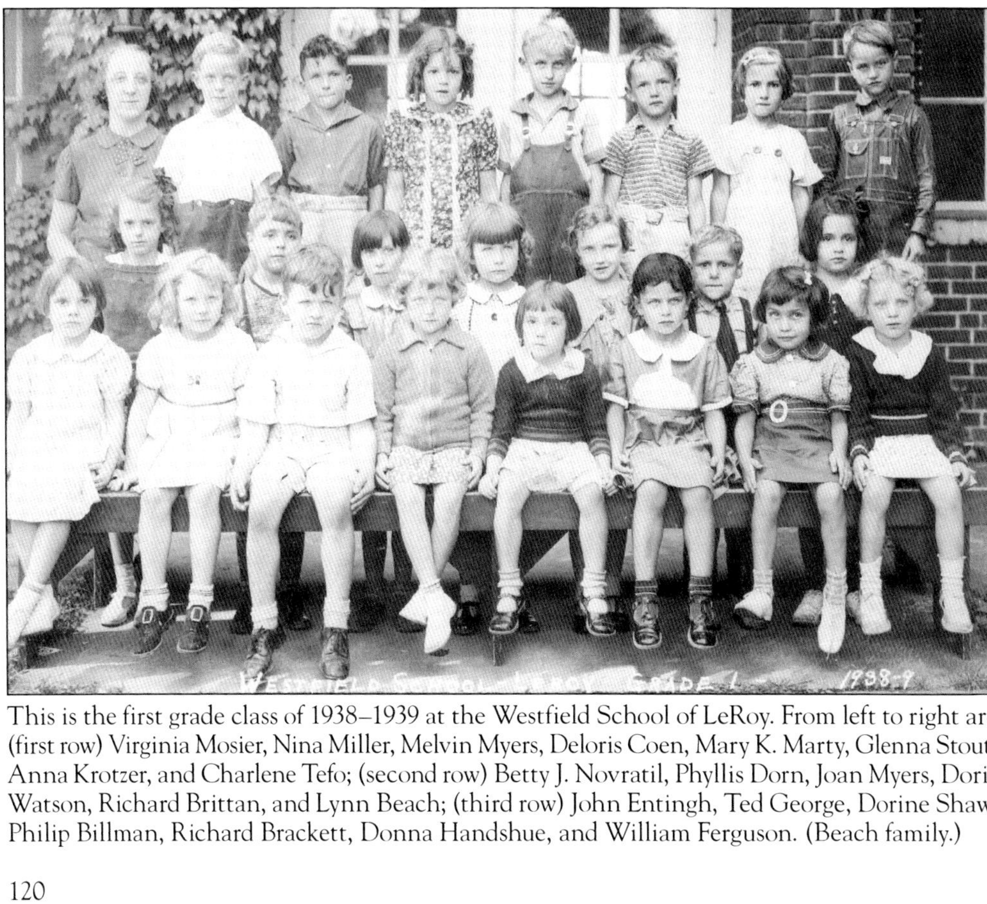

This is the first grade class of 1938–1939 at the Westfield School of LeRoy. From left to right are (first row) Virginia Mosier, Nina Miller, Melvin Myers, Deloris Coen, Mary K. Marty, Glenna Stout, Anna Krotzer, and Charlene Tefo; (second row) Betty J. Novratil, Phyllis Dorn, Joan Myers, Doris Watson, Richard Brittan, and Lynn Beach; (third row) John Entingh, Ted George, Dorine Shaw, Philip Billman, Richard Brackett, Donna Handshue, and William Ferguson. (Beach family.)

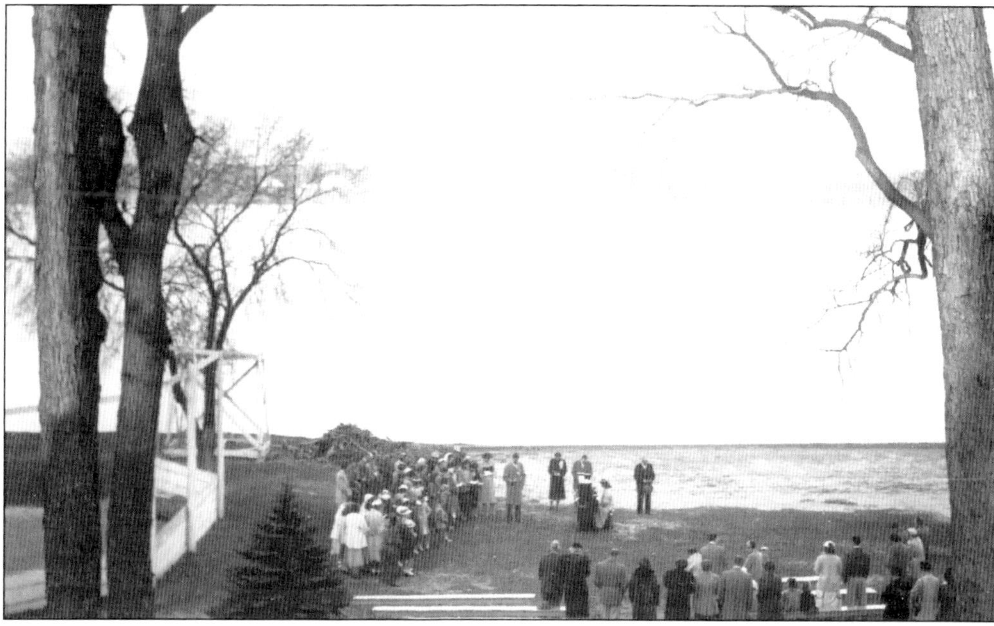

Local churches came together to celebrate Easter sunrise services on the beach at Chippewa-on-the-Lake for many years. Roberta Humbel is shown playing the piano that was loaned from the Methodist church in April 1955. She was church organist from the age of 12 until she died 70 years later, never missing a Sunday. (Gayle Baxter Foster.)

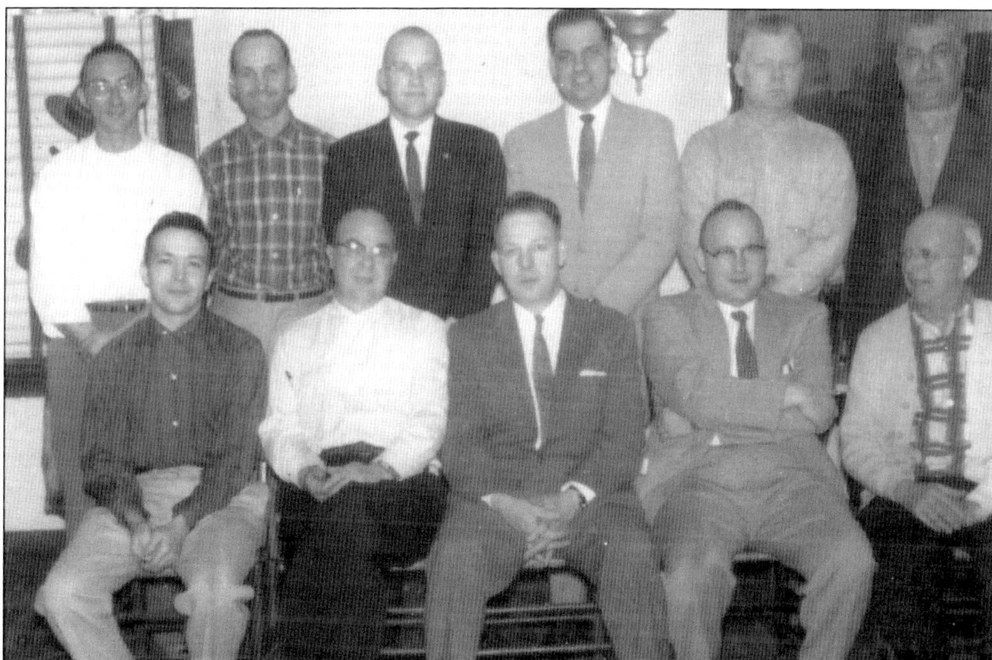

The Chippewa-on-the-Lake Village Council is pictured here in January 1958. From left to right are (first row) unidentified, James Gunder, mayor Carl Thomas, and two unidentified; (second row) Ken Walter (whose father Otto was the former mayor), unidentified, John Dye, Herb Grubb, Henry Gween, and Fred Wiedenman. (Carla Thomas.)

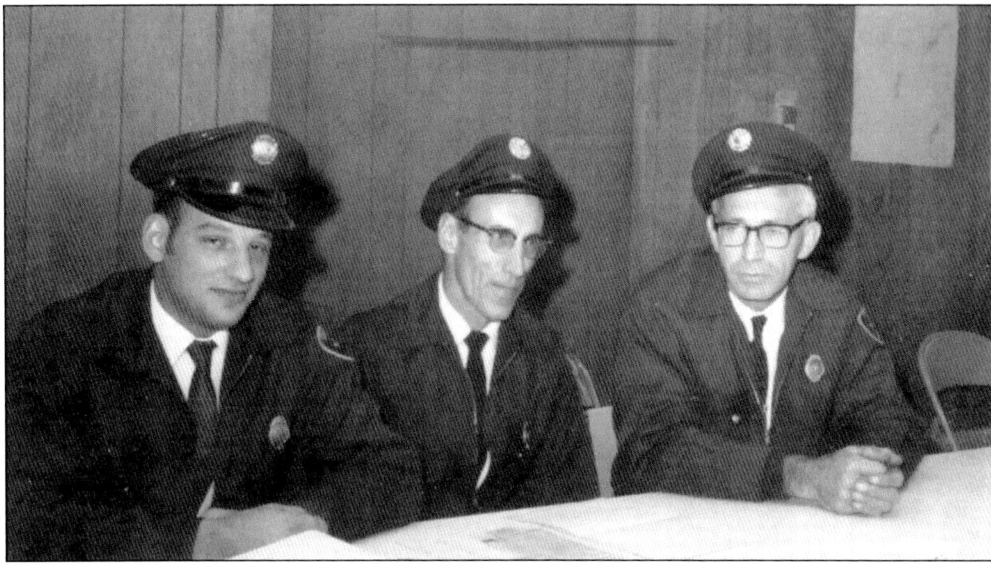

The Chippewa Lake Fire Department was first organized in January 1919. Members of the department pictured here on November 3, 1970, are, from left to right, Keith Riedel (first assistant), James Baker (chief), and Don Roshon (second assistant). The first meeting in their newly built fire station on Heather Hedge Drive was held in January 1931. This building was at the location of the current Chippewa Lake Post Office. (Brad and April Winter.)

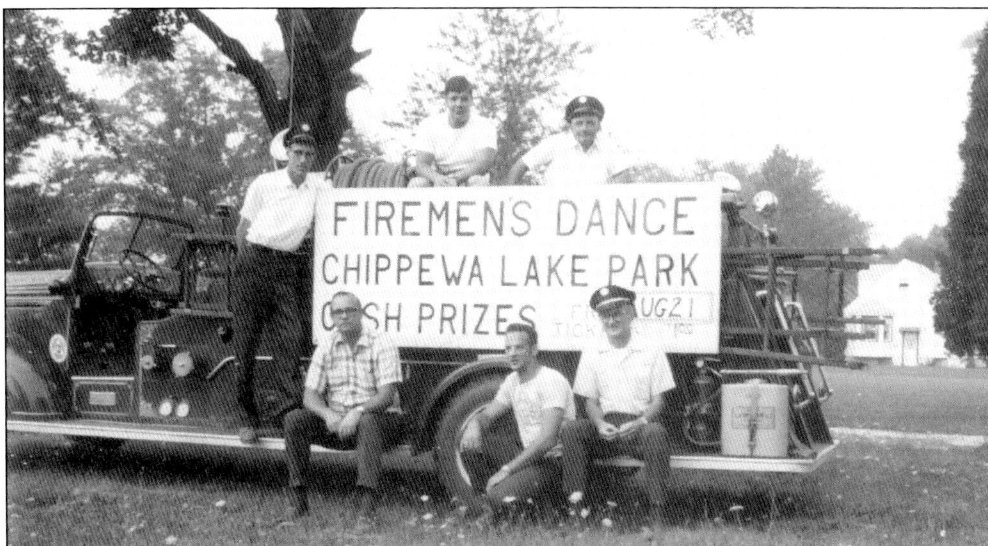

The annual fireman's dance took place at Chippewa Lake Park from the late 1950s until the park closed in 1978. Pictured on August 15, 1970, are, from left to right, (first row) unidentified, Keith Riedel, and Chief Mike Wilder; (second row) Jim Baker, Jerry Hall, and Gray Moore. The reel hose cart was stored at the Medina County Water and Sewer Building at Chippewa Lake Park. The fireman's ball was a fundraiser to benefit the Chippewa Lake Fire Department, and Parker Beach always made a contribution. To help defray costs, fire department personnel also walked through the village collecting $1 from each household. For a number of years, it was truly a volunteer fire department. The firemen were issued checks in December for time worked during the past year; they endorsed their checks and handed them back to the chief. (Brad and April Winter.)

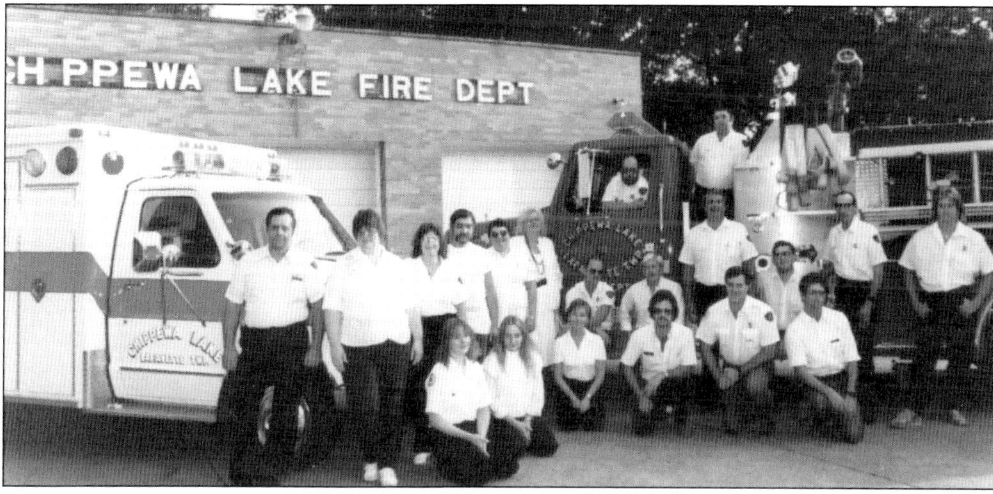

Chippewa Lake Fire Department personnel are pictured here in the late 1980s. They are, from left to right, (first row) Tami Howard, Candy Webster, Jackie Lardie, Gary D'Angelo, Tadd Davis, and Doug Brantner; (second row) Tom Lazar, Jan Brantner, Pat Halasey, Doug Webster, Maggie Hilton, Mary Walter, Ken Walter, Tom Lardie, Bill Leohr, Bob Stewart, Jim Baker, and Lee Walter; (third row) Bill Hilton and Dave Varisco. (Brad and April Winter.)

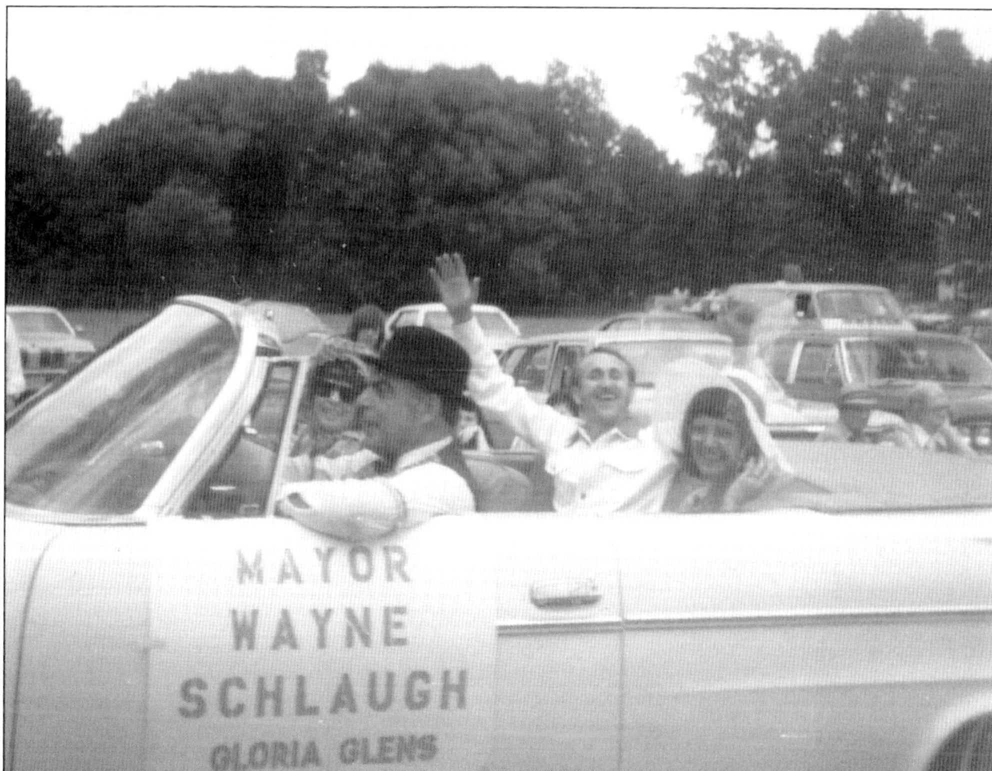

Gloria Glens mayor Wayne Schlauch is accompanied by his wife, Carol, as they greet neighbors and friends as they pass by during the bicentennial Fourth of July parade at Chippewa in 1976. They are driven by Walter and Joyce Henshal. The creator of this poster misspelled the mayor's name. (Wayne Schlauch.)

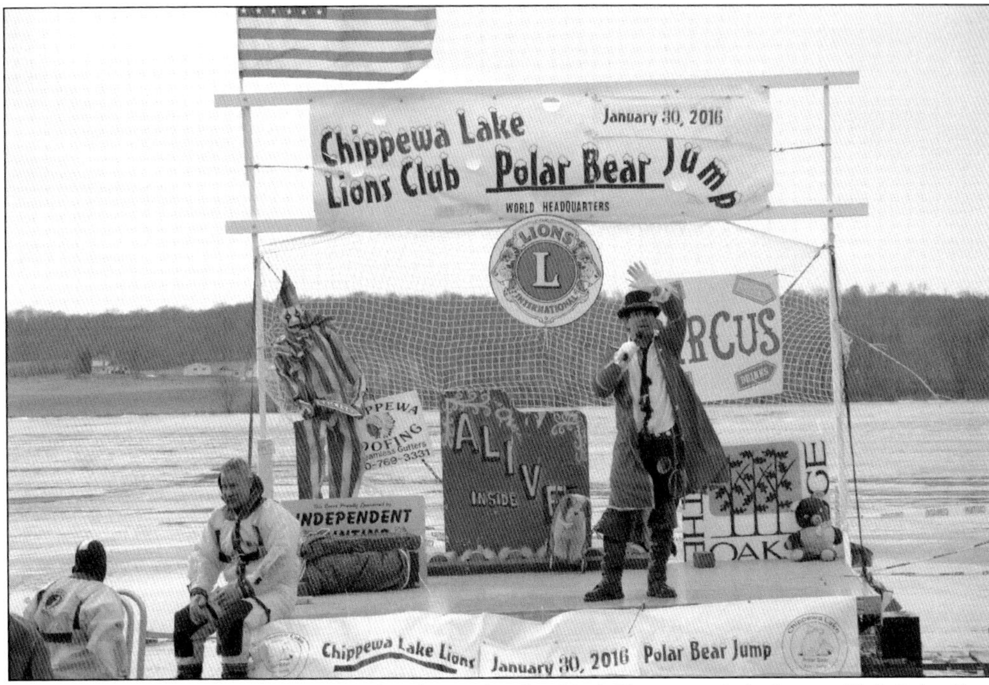

"The Greatest Show on Earth" was the theme for the 2016 Chippewa Lake Lions Club Polar Bear Jump, complete with a working merry-go-round on the ice. Emcee/ringmaster Eric Neiger does a fine job of ushering each participant into the icy waters of Chippewa Lake on the last Saturday each January. This 2016 jump was a race to the finish before the ice melted and dumped everyone into the chilly lake water. In 2016, the Lions Club raised $20,000—the highest amount to date. The Lions are a service organization that provides support to their community through monetary and food donations. (Sharon Sefl Karhan.)

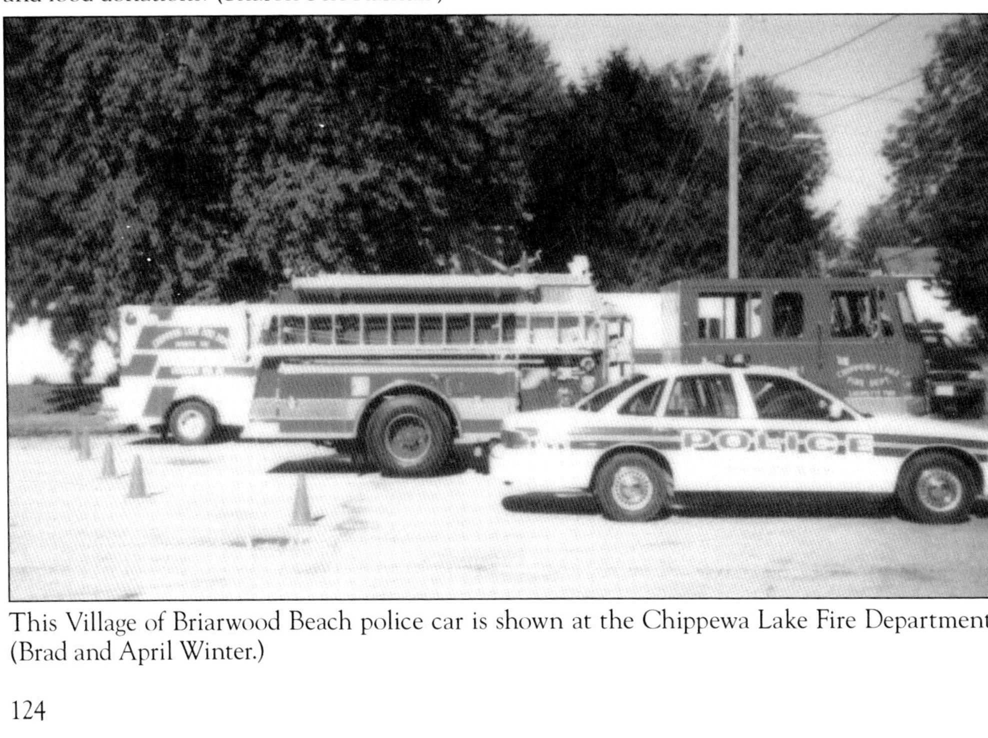

This Village of Briarwood Beach police car is shown at the Chippewa Lake Fire Department. (Brad and April Winter.)

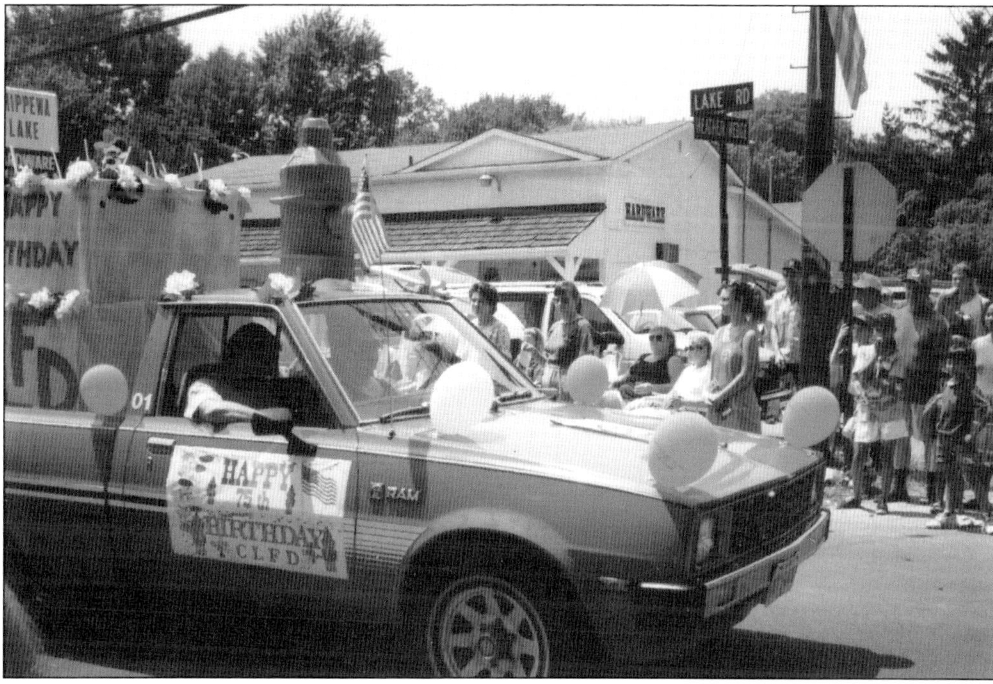

Celebrating the 75th birthday of the Chippewa Lake Fire Department in 1995 is Briarwood Beach service truck No. 1. The village's service garage was located on Circle Crest where the Village of Chippewa Lake's town hall is now located. Chuck (left) and Peggy Plues are in the truck. The villages of Chippewa-on-the-Lake and Briarwood Beach merged in 1998 to form the Village of Chippewa Lake. (Brad and April Winter.)

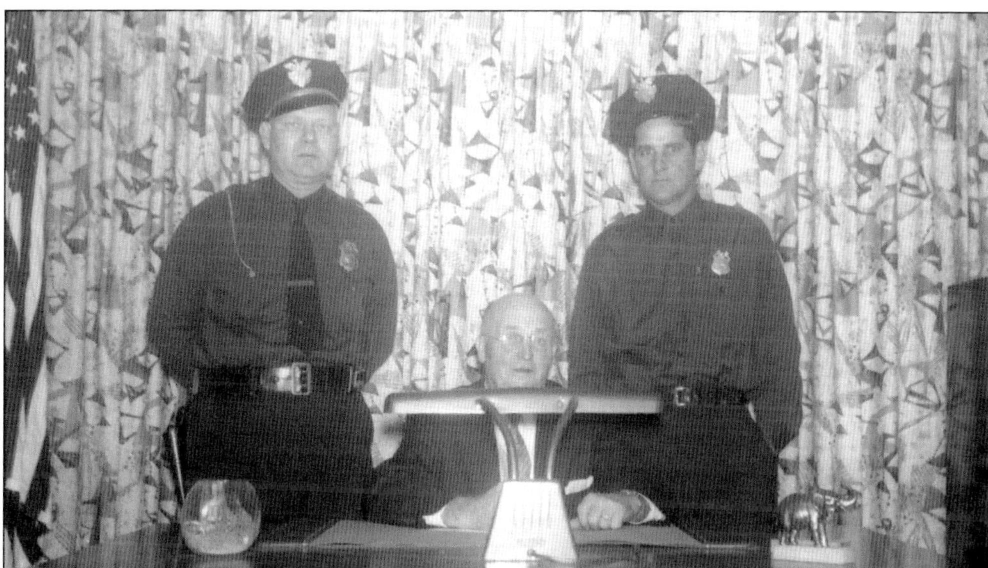

Pictured here in 1957 are, from left to right, Chippewa-on-the-Lake police chief Henry Gween, mayor Walter Lampe (who served as mayor of the village from 1956 through June 1, 1957), and police officer Herb Emerick. (Carla Thomas.)

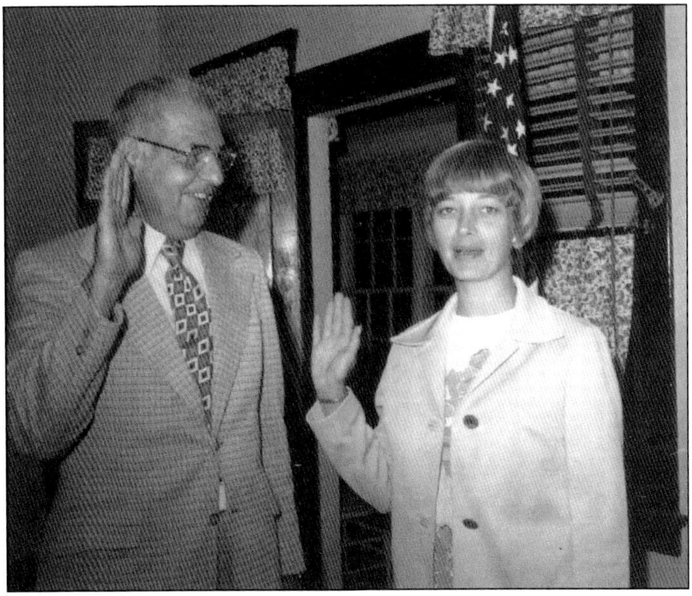

Herb Grubb (left), mayor of Chippewa-on-the-Lake from 1972 through 1979, swears in councilwoman Betty Kepler. At this time, council meetings were held at the Women's Club on the circle where the Friends of the Circle pavilion stands. Kepler lived on Shadywood Drive across from the Hunt Club with her husband, Ross, who was chief of the Lafayette Township Police Department, which provided police service for Chippewa-on-the-Lake. (Barbara Grubb Whitlam.)

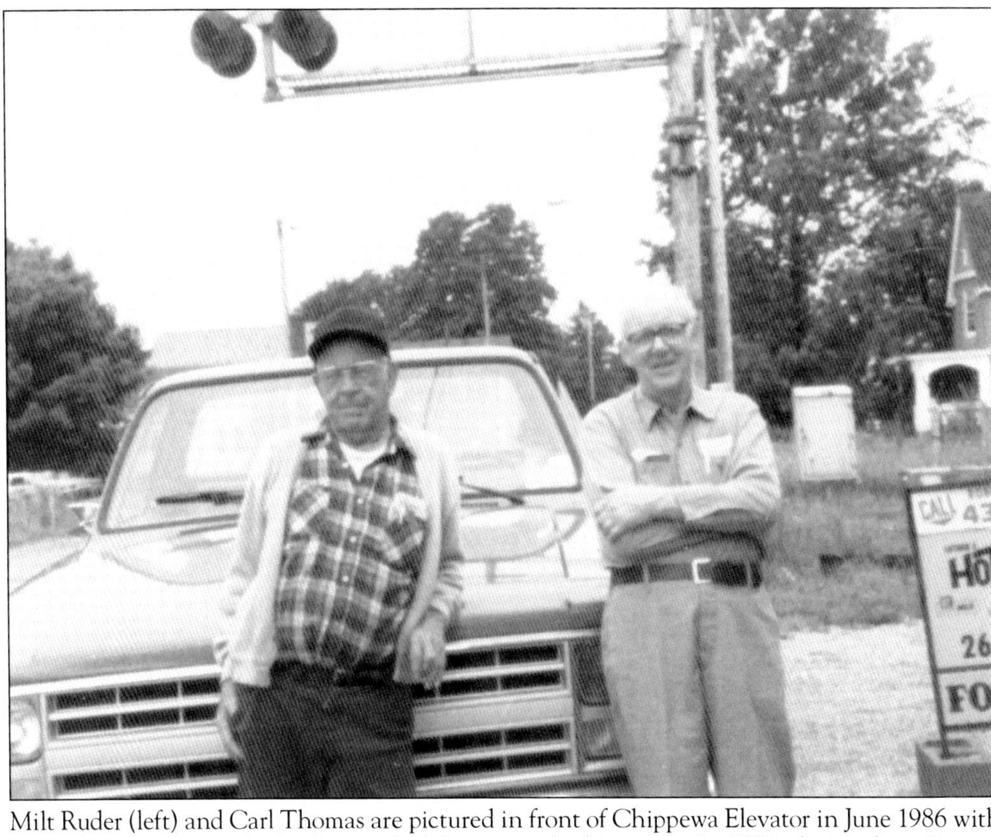

Milt Ruder (left) and Carl Thomas are pictured in front of Chippewa Elevator in June 1986 with the railroad tracks in the background of this image looking west. In 1991, the Medina County Park District purchased a portion of the abandoned CSX railway stretching from Chippewa Road to Wycliffe Drive from CSX Railroad Corporation with money received from a grant from the Ohio Department of Transportation. (Carla Thomas.)

In Memoriam: Chad H. Grubb

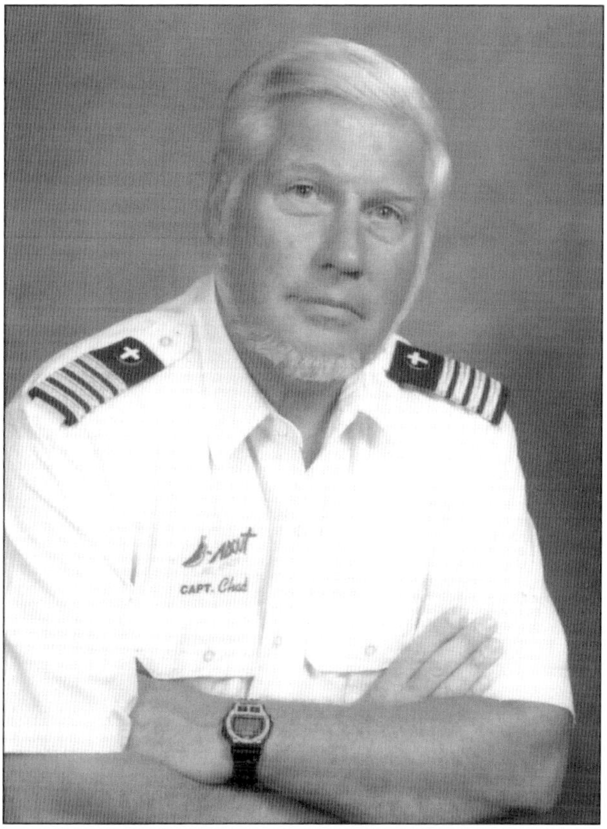

In memory of Chad H. Grubb (1941–2016), who had a vision of creating a small booklet of memories held dear by people who knew and loved Chippewa Lake Park before those memories were lost to the passage of time. That booklet quickly grew into the establishment of the Chippewa Lake Ohio Historical Society (with Chad as president!) and this book, which contains a photographic history of the entire Chippewa area—not just the amusement park the lake was famed for.

Chad grew up in Chippewa, where he developed a fondness for the water, piloting rowboats, speedboats, and iceboats on Chippewa Lake. He left to join the Navy, serving during the Vietnam War years. He was ultimately licensed to sail Lake Erie, where he captained the tall ship *Journey*, a 65-foot schooner, as part of a Christian ministry that offered experiences for troubled teens and special-needs groups that they might never have had.

Captain Chad never forgot his deep roots at Chippewa Lake. A bench dedicated to him overlooks the lake he loved, steps away from the home he grew up in on Shadywood Drive. (Ellie Grubb.)